PERSUASION
IN GREEK TRAGEDY

A Study of *Peitho*

PERSUASION IN GREEK TRAGEDY

A Study of *Peitho*

BY

R.G.A. BUXTON

Lecturer in Classics in the University of Bristol

CAMBRIDGE UNIVERSITY PRESS

CAMBRIDGE

LONDON   NEW YORK   NEW ROCHELLE

MELBOURNE   SYDNEY

Published by the Press Syndicate of the University of Cambridge
The Pitt Building, Trumpington Street, Cambridge CB2 1RP
32 East 57th Street, New York, NY 10022, USA
296 Beaconsfield Parade, Middle Park, Melbourne 3206, Australia

© Cambridge University Press 1982

First published 1982

Printed in Great Britain at the University Press
Cambridge

Library of Congress catalogue card number: 81 — 17073

British Library Cataloguing in Publication Data
Buxton, R.G.A.
Persuasion in Greek tragedy.
1. Greek drama (Tragedy)—History and criticism
I. Title
882'.0109   PA3131
ISBN 0 521 24180 4

CONTENTS

Contents

PLATES

(Between pages 50 and 51)

1   Attic 'onos' from Eretria (Athens, National Museum 1629) (refs. at ch. 2, n. 56). Peitho with Aphrodite, Eros, Harmonia, Kore, Hebe and Himeros. Reproduced from E. Pfuhl, *Malerei und Zeichnung der Griechen* (Munich, 1923) III, pl. 562.

2   (a) Boston skyphos of 490-480 (Museum of Fine Arts, Boston, 13186) (refs. at ch. 2, n. 60). Peitho, holding a flower, present at the abduction of Helen. Reproduced by courtesy of the Museum of Fine Arts, Boston; Francis Bartlett Collection.

    (b) Berlin amphora from later fifth century (Berlin Museum 30036) (refs. at ch. 2, nn. 62, 63). Helen on the knees of Aphrodite, with Peitho to the left. Reproduced from L. B. Ghali-Kahil, *Les Enlèvements et le retour d'Hélène* (Paris, 1955) pl. VIII.

3   Vatican oinochoe of 430-425 (Vatican H. 525) (refs. at ch. 2, n. 65). Menelaos, in pursuit of Helen, is subject to the power of Peitho. Reproduced by courtesy of the Archivio Fotografico, Musei Vaticani.

4   London hydria by late-fifth-century Meidias painter (British Museum E 224) (refs. at ch. 2, n. 114). The abduction of the daughters of Leukippos, with Peitho rushing from the scene. Reproduced from Pfuhl *Malerei* III, pl. 593.

TO MY MOTHER
AND FATHER

PREFACE

At the risk of discouraging the reader at the outset, I must begin with the admission that this book has its roots in a Cambridge Ph.D. dissertation, completed in 1976. The work then consisted of a rather perfunctory account of *peitho* in Greek culture, followed by detailed analysis of *peitho* in Aischylos and Sophokles. Since that time I have wholly rewritten and greatly expanded the cultural introduction, which forms chapters 1 and 2 of the present book; and I have added a chapter on Euripides. The sections in the thesis devoted to Aischylos and Sophokles have been revised and slightly abbreviated, but there is in this case considerable continuity between thesis and book.

Having by implication belittled the genre of the Ph.D. dissertation I must redress the balance a little by expressing my gratitude to the two scholars who successively supervised my research: Professor Sir Moses Finley and Mrs P.E. Easterling. The one set me a monumental example of intellectual rigour; the other, with inexhaustible patience and tact, sharpened at very many points my awareness of what is at stake in the tragedies.

In recalling my other academic debts I think first of King's College, Cambridge, where I was an undergraduate. In particular, Patrick Wilkinson and Geoffrey Lloyd showed me in their different ways what a university may ideally be like. While a research student in Paris I had the pleasure of learning from Pierre Vidal-Naquet, whose brilliant seminars always avoided τὸ δεσποτούμενον yet never quite touched τὸ ἄναρχον. I also owe thanks to my Ph.D. examiners, Professor G.S. Kirk and Professor R.P. Winnington-Ingram; to Theo Korteweg and Christopher Rowe, who have commented on part of my manuscript; and above all to Jan Bremmer and Michael Ewans, who read and criticized all of it with skill and precision. My hope is that none of these scholars will be offended if, very occasionally, I have been stubborn enough to risk rejecting their advice.

Some of the work associated with this book was done while I was enjoying the delightful hospitality of the Fondation Hardt near Geneva. I am most grateful to the selection committee of that institution, who made my stay possible. I am also happy to acknowledge the help given me by my own university at Bristol in respect of travelling and typing expenses.

Finally, it is a pleasure to thank Janet Gliddon and Caroline Latif for their impeccable typing, Elizabeth Ovenden for the assistance she has given me with proof-reading, and Pauline Hire, of Cambridge University Press, for the care with which she has guided this book through to publication.

Bristol 1981   R.G.A.B.

ABBREVIATIONS

The following abbreviations for standard works are employed:

ARV[2]	J.D. Beazley, *Attic Red-Figure Vase-Painters*[2], Oxford, 1963.
CAF	*Comicorum Atticorum Fragmenta*, ed. T. Kock, Leipzig, 1880-.
CVA	*Corpus Vasorum Antiquorum.*
Daremberg/Saglio	C. Daremberg and E. Saglio, *Dictionnaire des antiquités grecques et romaines d'après les textes et les monuments*, Paris, 1877-.
DK	*Die Fragmente der Vorsokratiker*[6], ed. H. Diels/W. Kranz, Berlin, 1951-2.
EAA	*Enciclopedia dell' arte antica classica e orientale*, ed. R. Bianchi Bandinelli and G. Becatti, Rome, 1958-.
FGrH (Jacoby)	*Die Fragmente der griechischen Historiker*, ed. F. Jacoby, Berlin, 1923-.
FPG	*Fragmenta Philosophorum Graecorum*, ed. F.W.A. Mullach, Paris, 1860-.
IG	*Inscriptiones Graecae.*
LSJ	*Greek-English Lexicon*[9], compiled by H.G. Liddell and R. Scott, revised by H.S. Jones, Oxford, 1940.
OCT	Oxford Classical Text.
PLF	*Poetarum Lesbiorum Fragmenta*, ed. E. Lobel and D.L. Page, Oxford, 1955.
PMG	*Poetae Melici Graeci*, ed. D.L. Page, Oxford, 1962.
P. Oxy.	*The Oxyrhynchus Papyri.*
RE	Pauly/Wissowa, *Real-Encyclopädie der classischen Altertumswissenschaft*, Stuttgart, 1894-.
Roscher	W.H. Roscher, *Ausführliches Lexikon der griechischen und römischen Mythologie*, Leipzig, 1884-.
TGL	*Thesaurus Graecae Linguae*, ed. Hase, Paris, 1831-.
TrGF	*Tragicorum Graecorum Fragmenta*, vol. I, ed. B. Snell, Göttingen, 1971.

For quotations from Aischylos I have normally used the OCT by D.L. Page; fragments are numbered as in H.J. Mette, *Die Fragmente der Tragödien des Aischylos*, Berlin, 1959. Sophokles is normally cited as in the

OCT by Pearson. Quotations from Euripides' *Medea* are based on Page's edition (Oxford, 1938), those from *Hekabe* on Murray's OCT, those from *Suppliants* on Collard's edition (Groningen, 1975). Tyrtaios and Semonides are cited as in M.L. West's *Iambi et Elegi Graeci* (Oxford, 1971).

Names of ancient authors and their works are for the most part abbreviated according to the practice of LSJ and the *Oxford Latin Dictionary*. Where I diverge from their practice the aim is usually to remove Latinization (e.g. *Hkld.* for *Hcld.*, *Her.* for *H.F.*). However, I have occasionally preferred familiarity to consistency: so *Aj.*, not *Ai.*; *P.V.*, not *P.D.* (See also *Note* on transliteration, below.)

Names of periodicals are abbreviated as in *L'Année philologique*.

All scholarly works which are referred to more than once are cited in full on their first occurrence, and thereafter by author's name and abbreviated title only; the key to the abbreviated titles can be found in the bibliography, pp. 228-31. Works referred to once only are cited in full at the point where they occur, and are not included in the bibliography.

NOTE ON TRANSLATIONS AND TRANSLITERATION

In order to make this book accessible to non-Hellenists I have included translations of virtually all quotations from Greek. Translations from the three tragedians are normally my own. Where I have borrowed from versions by others I have tried in all cases to acknowledge the fact.

In transliterating I have preferred 'Aischylos' to 'Aeschylus', 'Sophokles' to 'Sophocles', 'Dioskouroi' to 'Dioscuri', and so forth, except in a very small number of instances where avoidance of the Latinized form seemed to me unnatural. (For example, I use not 'Iokaste' but 'Jocasta'.) When citing the words of a scholar who transliterates in a different manner from myself, I alter the quotation to correspond with my own practice; but in referring to *titles* of books or articles I retain the original transliteration.

INTRODUCTION

In this book I offer an account of an aspect of Greek behaviour, *peitho* ('persuasion'), together with an analysis of how the implications of that behaviour are explored in the tragedies of Aischylos, Sophokles and Euripides. Now *peitho* is a notion which bears on several areas of experience which nowadays we should regard as distinct: politics, rhetoric, love, morality, philosophy. It can refer to a goddess with her own cult and spheres of activity, or it can have as 'secular' a sense (again in our terms) as the English word 'persuasion' normally does. *Peitho*'s connotations vary considerably between contexts, and in at least one respect—the importance of rhetoric—its associations alter over time in parallel with a development in Greek political life. The aim of the first part of this study, chapters 1 and 2, will be to build up a picture of the various modes of and contexts for persuasive behaviour as it was practised and reflected upon in ancient Greece. The evidence, of course, is affected by the familiar geographical imbalance, so our account can hardly fail to be more or less Athenocentric. Yet the fact that Athens bulks large in the following pages is not simply a reflection of a distortion in the sources: it is partly also a function of the importance which *peitho*, particularly 'public' or 'political' *peitho*, had, in both practice and ideology, at Athens as compared with other states.

Given this role in Athenian life, it is not surprising that *peitho*, along with countless other facets of experience, was explored in that preeminent arena for Athenian self-examination, tragedy. Sometimes in the plays it is *peitho*'s erotic side which is prominent, sometimes its political or moral implications as a mode of behaviour contrasted with, say, violence or deceit. In the second part of this book I shall analyse the treatment of these issues in tragic drama, and shall attempt to describe what is individual in Aischylos', Sophokles' and Euripides' handling of them.

Since this study will deal both with an aspect of social behaviour and with plays, it will span two areas which might be called 'cultural history' on the one hand and 'literary criticism' on the other. Now, depending on one's standpoint, one may approach the relationship between social life and literature in various ways; and it will be as well for me to spell out the assumptions which underlie my own method.

Every play worth the name is a unique imaginative creation, a complex of words, silence, gestures, movement and (sometimes) dance and song: all of which, taken together, constitute the work's total effect or 'meaning'. If the play comes from one's own culture, most of the effects produced by (say) the associations and interactions of words will be accessible without too much work on the part of the audience beyond the act of concentrated attending which characterizes any serious concern with literature. However, in regard to the tragedy—or any other literature—of the Greeks, an aesthetic response has to be prefaced by a great deal of intellectual, social and moral archaeology:* the meanings of words have to be recovered, the implications of types of social behaviour brought to light, and so forth. Putting it bluntly, we might say that an awareness of the experiential *banalities* of Greek culture is an essential precondition for a perception of the way in which that culture's artists transcended those banalities. To take a specific example, one of the central issues in Sophokles' *Antigone* is the nature of *nomos* (usage, custom, convention, law) and the sorts of claim it can make upon individuals. In order fully to appreciate the uniqueness of *Antigone* as a dramatic statement we must first recover the significance which the common word *nomos* might have had at the time when Sophokles used it. *Mutatis mutandis* the same applies to social behaviour as to words: criticism of *Agamemnon,* a play which explores the moral resonances of a specific act of sacrificing, depends on a prior awareness of the ordinary place of sacrifice in Greek culture.

The kind of intellectual archaeology just mentioned is precisely the type of enterprise which the first part of the book is intended to be. I aim to provide an extended definition of *peitho* and the sorts of behaviour associated with it. Because our eventual interest will be in *peitho* in tragedy, the period down to the end of the fifth century is

---

* The notion of 'intellectual archaeology' has been developed extensively by M. Foucault, but his analysis of *l'archéologie du savoir* is far removed from anything I am doing. For instance, the opposition originality/banality is explicitly excluded by Foucault from the 'territory' of his archaeology (cf. *The Archaeology of Knowledge,* Eng. tr. 1972, Tavistock Publications, 141ff).

clearly of prime importance; but fourth-century (and, occasionally, later) material will be included too if it enables us either to fill out *peitho*'s mythological connotations or to locate more accurately the significance which the concept had in the Athenian democracy.

Once this semantic and behavioural excavation is complete we shall turn to see how the social and personal issues raised by *peitho* are examined in certain imaginative works. I want to emphasize at the outset that I shall not be treating the plays of Aischylos, Sophokles and Euripides as documents, as sources of evidence for what the Athenians in general, or Aischylos, Sophokles and Euripides in particular, might have *thought* about *peitho*. These dramatists were not in the business of producing a discursive 'philosophical' argument about *peitho*, or about anything else; they were writing plays, in which statements were made through performed action and through language. The aim of my analysis will be to reveal how a particular facet of human experience is realized in precise dramatic terms.

The distinction between the so-called 'thought' of a literary artist, on the one hand, and the exact sequence of words (and, in the case of a dramatist, movements) which he creates, on the other, is a vital one. Just as we ought not to separate 'what' a poet or novelist says from the exact words in which he says it, so the analysis of any theme in a play should be conducted in terms of the full range of circumstances —tone, imagery, movement, and so forth—through which the theme is presented to the audience. This being the case, each of my studies of *peitho* in particular plays will locate the theme, as fully as space allows, in the dense texture of its context, so as to be as faithful as possible to the stature of the plays as works of art.

In order to avoid covering too much ground too thinly I have restricted myself to a detailed consideration of only six plays, together with an extremely cursory look at the *Oresteia*. My choice of plays is not intended to be 'representative' of the whole of Greek tragedy, or even of the whole of extant Greek tragedy. It is simply that each of the works selected illustrates aspects of the material introduced in chapters 1 and 2 and, it is hoped, will make fuller sense in the light of that material. Such selective treatment inevitably means passing over works which deserve analysis at greater length. The most difficult decision was that which led me to give only a brief account of *peitho* in the *Oresteia*. In some ways this subject would merit a book in itself, and to have dealt with it comprehensively would have upset the balance between the three dramatists. I would ask any reader who wants a less summary version of my views on this topic to consult the section on the *Oresteia* in my thesis.*

Finally, why *peitho*? As I have already suggested, its interest lies partly in its many-sidedness, in the way it forms a link between areas of experience which we tend to mark off as distinct. But it also offers insights into how three great artists dealt with an important feature of their experience. It would evidently be foolish to exaggerate the significance of *peitho*—to imply, for instance, that the goddess Peitho had anything like the stature of Dionysos, or Athene, or Zeus. But it would be equally wrong to underrate the role of *peitho;* particularly in Athens. For Athens was a city dominated by the power of the word. Her literature of the classical period is almost as full of argument, discussion and debate as real Athenian life must have been. But the power of the word was not taken for granted: philosophers reflected on it, orators exalted it, dramatists presented its strengths and inadequacies in the theatre. If the failures and triumphs of human communication, and the meaning of different strategies for getting one's way—persuasion, violence, deceit—do not rank in dramatic importance with issues such as man's relation to the gods or the place of justice in the universe, nevertheless they do in certain works achieve sufficient prominence to justify a special analysis; and, more importantly, they raise and explore questions which, albeit in different guise, still urgently concern us as moral agents.

* '*Peitho:* its place in Greek culture and its exploration in some plays of Aeschylus and Sophocles', Cambridge Ph. D. diss., 1977.

1

THE PERSUASIVE WORD IN GREECE

One of the distinguishing features of classical Greek civilization was the value which it placed upon public argument, debate and disputation. This generalization is truer of some periods in Greek history than others, and truer of some places in Greece than others; but, by and large, it faithfully reflects a difference between Greece and the other major cultures of the ancient Near East. Not only did Greeks implicitly and often explicitly stress the value of persuasive argumentation; they also extended the range of issues which might be publicly argued about to include an unprecedentedly wide area: politics, morality, law, ontology, theology, medicine—and the list is not exhaustive. The aim of the present chapter will be to look more closely at this preeminence accorded by Greeks to the use of persuasive argument.

1.1 Early Greece

As our enquiry depends on access to at least some written evidence, we can begin no earlier than the stage of Mycenaean civilization recorded on the Linear B tablets. Unfortunately these tell us next to nothing that is relevant to the role of discourse in everyday social life in Mycenaean Greece. Nevertheless, two points are perhaps worth making, since they mark significant political differences between the civilization of Mycenae and that of the classical Greek polis—a matter which is of considerable importance for the theme of this book in view of the fundamental connection between *peitho* and the polis.

First, the political system was centred on the palace, and at its head was the *wanax*, ruler. This marks not only a point of similarity with other Near Eastern cultures (cf. sect. 1.4) but also a crucial point of difference from the later Greek polis, in which government moved into the hands of the citizen group. Second, the administrative machinery could not have operated without the use of writing. The intimate connection between Mycenaean culture and the script employed to run it is suggested by the fact that, when the former collapsed, the latter disappeared too. Knowledge of this syllabic script will have been largely restricted to those involved in palace administration, who were obliged to master the script in order to fulfil their duties. In fact the use of writing in Mycenaean times had the effect (it may be argued) not of publicizing information, but of confining it.[1] Knowledge of the details of government was stored and owned by the ruler in the palace.[2]

The fall of Mycenae was an end; the borrowing and adaptation by Greeks of the Phoenician alphabetic script symbolizes a new beginning. Linear B had never been well adapted to express Greek since, to take one instance, it did not discriminate between such significant oppositions in Greek as *k/kh, t/th, p/ph*.[3] The new script made it at last possible to transcribe the great narrative poems of Greece, hitherto transmitted orally. And it is with these poems that we begin to have solid ground to go on.

Both the *Iliad* and the *Odyssey* are rich in the spoken word: messages, prayers, oaths, abuse, reminiscence, deception, exhortation. What about persuasive argumentation? The answer to this is inseparable from a consideration of the way in which Homer presents the reaching of public decisions. In a brief but characteristically incisive study of freedom of speech in antiquity[4] A. Momigliano has set out what he takes to be the main features of the Homeric assemblies. Four of these features may be recalled here: (i) assemblies are irregular, being convened only in special circumstances; (ii) assemblies are summoned not by nonentities but by 'important' individuals; (iii) the assembly gives its approval or disapproval of the views expressed by 'important' people, but no vote is taken; (iv) intervention from the floor is frowned on, although (Thersites) it does happen. We cannot miss the main point about Homeric assemblies: their working depends on the authority of those who convene and run them. The power of persuasion is the prerogative of the 'kings', the nobility, the 'heroes'.[5] Hesiod gives divine sanction to this association between kings and oratory in the following passage from the *Theogony* (79–90):

... Καλλιόπη θ᾽· ἡ δὲ προφερεστάτη ἐστὶν ἁπασέων.
ἡ γὰρ καὶ βασιλεῦσιν ἅμ᾽ αἰδοίοισιν ὀπηδεῖ.
ὅντινα τιμήσουσι Διὸς κοῦραι μεγάλοιο
γεινόμενόν τε ἴδωσι διοτρεφέων βασιλήων,
τῷ μὲν ἐπὶ γλώσσῃ γλυκερὴν χείουσιν ἐέρσην,

τοῦ δ’ ἔπε’ ἐκ στόματος ῥεῖ μείλιχα· οἱ δέ νυ λαοὶ
πάντες ἐς αὐτὸν ὁρῶσι διακρίνοντα θέμιστας
ἰθείῃσι δίκῃσιν· ὁ δ’ ἀσφαλέως ἀγορεύων
αἶψά τι καὶ μέγα νεῖκος ἐπισταμένως κατέπαυσε·
τούνεκα γὰρ βασιλῆες ἐχέφρονες, οὕνεκα λαοῖς
βλαπτομένοις ἀγορῆφι μετάτροπα ἔργα τελεῦσι
ῥηιδίως, μαλακοῖσι παραιφάμενοι ἐπέεσσιν·

... and Kalliope, the first of all [sc. the Muses]; for she accompanies august kings. Whenever the daughters of great Zeus honour one of the god-nurtured kings and look on him at his birth, they pour sweet dew upon his tongue, and from his mouth there flow gentle words. The people all look to him as he decides judgements with straight justice; and he speaks unerringly, quickly and wisely stopping a great dispute. For herein lies the wisdom of kings *[interpretation dubious]*, that they easily reverse any harm done to men in the agora, by soothing with soft words.

The picture of persuasive speech offered by the epics[6] was, then, that of a faculty belonging by divine grace to a limited group of the population. Also, the range of issues submitted to debate even amongst that limited group was quite restricted. Nor is this surprising:

after all, the basic values of the society were given, predetermined, and so were a man's place in the society and the privileges and duties that followed from his status. They were not subject to analysis or debate, and other issues left only the narrowest margin for the exercise of what we should call judgement (as distinct from work skills, including knowledge of the tactics of armed combat).[7]

This last quotation, with its implication that the society depicted in the Homeric poems can be analysed in the same way as an 'actual' society, brings us face to face with one of the most contentious problems in Homeric scholarship: to what extent do the social and political conditions evoked in these poems correspond to life as it was actually lived in Greece at some point in her past? Fortunately, for present purposes we do not, I think, have to find an answer. Whatever relationship the 'world of Odysseus' bore to some real past, it remains undeniable that the epics contain paradigms of behaviour (including verbal behaviour) which were accepted as vital and authoritative—though not as unchallengeable—by Greeks of the classical period, thanks to the central educative role which the two poems fulfilled. The *Iliad* and the *Odyssey* offered patterns for speech and action which might be followed or deviated from, but which, because of the status the poems had acquired, could not be ignored.

In respect of the two questions, 'Who had the right to persuade?' and, 'What issues were available for debate?', the picture which we find in Homer contrasts very strongly with the historical situation obtaining in the city whose theory and practice of arguing we know best—democratic Athens. Before turning to Athens, though, it is necessary to see whether we can point to anything in archaic Greece which represents an intermediate stage between the Homeric and Athenian valuations of persuasive argument.

In the sixth century B.C. Ionia saw the origins of what has come retrospectively to be called 'Presocratic' philosophy. The detailed speculations of Thales, Anaximander, Anaximenes and their successors are of no concern to us. But what is relevant is the pluralistic character of this intellectual development. We have the impression of men who are, certainly, highly individualistic, but who are at the same time recognizably engaged in a debate[8] in which each tries to improve on the speculations of his predecessors or rivals. Many of the problems they deal with (is the world one or many? can there be such a thing as change?) recur over and over again in different forms; but the process of posing and answering them is conducted by means of a continual urging of thesis and counter-thesis.

How is this growth of argumentative speculation to be explained? One important factor was surely the rise of literacy, which facilitated the comparison and criticism of rival views when these were available for simultaneous inspection 'on paper'.[9] Another plausible line of explanatory approach has been to link the growth of argument with 'the rise of the polis'.[10] Part of what is meant by this phrase is the development of communities in which, whatever the particular political complexion of their city-state, citizens felt they had a 'like' share in their city, a share denied to non-members such as women, slaves and foreigners. This increased sense of group solidarity on the part of the citizenry had important implications for the location and character of power and authority within the city. In a number of different spheres of activity in archaic Greece we can detect a similar pattern: namely, an extension of privileges from a restricted section of the population to a wider one, and above all a tendency to make public that which used before to be restricted to a select group. We observe this pattern in warfare, where hoplite tactics led to the involvement of the whole citizen group in fighting instead of just the horse-owning aristocratic élite.[11] We observe it in law, where judgements which used to depend on authoritatively powerful utterances by men like Hesiod's 'bribe-devouring kings' (*W.D.* 38-9, 220-1, 263-4) had to be related in future to the publicly accessible provisions of written law-codes.[12] And we observe it in relation to a certain change in the way in which value was represented: alongside the view—clearly seen in Homer—that worth was an intrinsic property of certain sorts of objects which circulated between nobles in certain social situations (prizes at contests, ransoms, marriage gifts), there developed a more 'objective' and quantitatively measurable standard for ascribing value, the standard provided by coined money.[13]

Given these and other comparable features of the social life of archaic Greece it is intelligible that in the field of intellectual speculation, too, debates and disputes between 'like' citizens should come to be resolved, not by reference to an authority, but through the application of a more abstract and (loaded though the word is) rational standard.[14] Hence the notion of a 'reasoned debate' might make headway.

That the making public of argumentation received its impetus from Ionian Greece is not something which we can fully explain. To put it down to the circumstance that in the archaic period the eastern Aegean was culturally the most advanced part of the Greek world, and might hence be expected to be the first to experience social changes which only later spread westwards, is really only to restate the very thing that needs explaining. We should be in a better position if we knew more about early Ionian assemblies,[15] but in fact it is not easy to say how democratic they were.[16] Of course, we must not be simplistic about the connections between argumentation and democracy: for one thing, Anaximenes of Miletos, Xenophanes of Kolophon, Herakleitos of Ephesos, and later Anaxagoras of Klazomenai, all wrote under the domination of the autocratic Persian Empire. Yet this must in turn be qualified by the relative leniency with which Persians imposed uniformity upon their subjects,[17] as compared with other imperial powers of the Near East like Assyria and Babylonia; and by the consideration that, even if they lived under Persian domination, early Greek thinkers seem to have been pretty well informed about one another's speculations. At all events it would be misleading to deny a link between democracy and the growth of debate. Greeks themselves were certainly aware of the possibility of such a connection. The 'invention' of rhetoric was located in Sicily during a brief democratic respite between tyrannies (see below, p.24). Again, when in Herodotos' famous and intriguing 'debate on constitutions' the Persian noble Otanes advocates the establishment of democracy in his country, he says:

Under a government of the people a magistrate is appointed by lot and is held responsible for his conduct in office, and all questions are put up for open debate (βουλεύματα δὲ πάντα ἐς τὸ κοινὸν ἀναφέρει).[18]

But the main reason for positing a link between persuasion and democracy lies in Athens. For it was Athens—which had, thanks to its unique political development towards democracy, produced a set of arenas for debate such as no other city could match—that replaced Ionia as the intellectual focus of Greece.

1.2 Athens

According to later theorists of rhetoric ('the art of persuading'[19]), including Aristotle, there were three principal subdivisions of the art, corresponding to the different arenas in which persuasion was being exercised: political *(symbouleutikos)*, legal *(dikanikos)* and display *(epideiktikos)*. We ought not to imagine these distinctions as hard and fast: Thoukydides can liken political oratory before the assembly to a sophistic display (3.38), and the (admittedly biased) 'Old Oligarch' describes legal cases as being tried ἐν τῷ δήμῳ, before the people (*Ath.* 1.18). But Aristotle's categories may serve as a rough guide.

Of the three types, display oratory[20] is the least familiar to the modern Western observer, and the one most likely to bring the phrase 'mere rhetoric' to his lips. In a way this reaction is justified: as Aristotle noted (*Rh.* 1358b), the audience at a display—funeral speech, oration given at one of the Games, or whatever—came not to reach a decision, but to admire and contemplate a spectacle. But we should not underestimate the impact which it could have in Greece.

The arrival of Gorgias at Athens in 427 evidently caused the sort of stir which recitals by Paganini or Liszt aroused in more recent times. But it is to political and legal persuasion that we must look if we want to understand the origins of Athens' love-affair with the power of the word.

We may begin by recalling a story which was told about Solon and which, besides being at the very least *bien trouvé*, splendidly illustrates the kind of public and reasoned argumentation that we have sought to link with the developing Greek polis. Plutarch (*Sol.* 10) tells of a dispute between Athens and Megara over possession of the island of Salamis. Some Spartans were asked to arbitrate in the matter; and the Athenian chosen to put his city's case was Solon. Two of the arguments which Plutarch's sources ascribed to Solon may be called arguments from 'authority'. First, Solon was said to have quoted a couplet from the Catalogue of Ships in the *Iliad* (2.557-8), which mentioned the ships of Athens and Salamis as being beached next to each other. (The question of whether or not the couplet is a late concoction by the Athenians is irrelevant: if it is, this merely confirms the assumption that Homer's support was regarded as valuably authoritative.) Second, Solon is said to have quoted the Delphic oracle, which referred to 'Ionian' Salamis—suggesting a connection with 'Ionian' Athens. But Solon is also reported to have used a quite different sort of argument, which would be fully at home in Herodotos. In order to demonstrate that the old graves on Salamis were those of Athenians and not Megarians, he said: the Megarians bury their dead facing east, but the Athenians bury them facing west. The truth or falsity of this claim does not concern us; what does is the deployment of a critical argument about empirically testable phenomena side by side with arguments drawn from the authority of myth. It is this combination—on the one hand, a judicious respect for the authority of mythical tales, on the other, a readiness to argue on the basis of evidence and reason—which typifies the best of Greek thought for almost three centuries after Solon. But, even more than this, we should notice that Solon's arguments are deployed *publicly* and allowed to stand or fall in competition with rival claims offered from the other side. This, as we have already urged, should be seen as deeply characteristic of the Greek, and above all the Athenian, polis.

If there is one figure who can be held to have contributed more than anyone else to the development of arenas for public debate in Athens, that figure is Kleisthenes. That does not mean to imply anything about his intentions, merely something about the consequences of what he did. Whatever the exact details of his reforms, it seems clear that their effect was to diminish the political importance of the noble-dominated 'phratry' to the advantage of the deme. As a result of this shift, instead of simply being born into the clientship of the nobles, the people was henceforth to a small but significant extent prised free of the all-embracing influence of the nobility. The nobles remained the sole repositories of prestige and power, but from the time of Kleisthenes onwards they had to win support by arguing for it against their rivals in front of the people, rather than being able to count on support automatically.[21]

Just as Kleisthenes' reforms were prompted by his rivalry with Isagoras, so the second major step in the direction of democratic government in Athens was taken as a consequence of another internal political dispute. Whether for reasons of ideological preference for rule-by-*demos* over rule-by-nobles, or whether, as seems far more likely, because espousal of the cause of the *demos* was the best tactical way of carrying through a particular anti-Spartan pro-naval-expansionist foreign policy,[22] Ephialtes and Perikles introduced reforms in the late 460s which weakened the power of the nobility as vested in the Areopagos, and strengthened the powers of the popular assembly and council. Through the introduction of pay for attendance in the courts and assembly,[23] the way was open for the Athenian citizen body as a whole to exploit the potential for free debate offered by their public arenas.

Unfortunately, we have no transcripts of what went on in the assembly; but we do have a number of references to what various Athenians thought was going on. We may start with a famous[24] quotation from the comedian Eupolis:

... πειθώ τις ἐπεκάθιζεν ἐπὶ τοῖς χείλεσιν·
οὕτως ἐκήλει καὶ μόνος τῶν ῥητόρων
τὸ κέντρον ἐγκατέλειπε τοῖς ἀκροωμένοις.
(*CAF* I, p. 281, fr. 94. 5-7)

a kind of persuasion sat upon his lips. That is how he, alone among the orators, would bewitch his hearers, and leave his sting in them.

The lips on which persuasion sits[25] are those of Perikles.[26] Plutarch repeats the idea in more pedestrian form centuries later: τὰ μὲν πολλὰ βουλόμενον ἦγε πείθων καὶ διδάσκων τὸν δῆμον ('he was mostly able to win the people's consent by persuasion and instruction', *Per*. 15.3). So when Thoukydides (2.65.8) analyses Perikles' power as based on ἀξίωμα ('reputation') and γνώμη ('intelligence'), we must add, 'and, last but not least, oratorical powers'. For in the face-to-face Athenian democracy,[27] a system which amounted to government by public meeting, the ability to persuade was of paramount importance. In 431 Perikles urged rejection of a Spartan ultimatum; and here is part of what (according to Thoukydides) he said:

ὁρῶ δὲ καὶ νῦν ὁμοῖα καὶ παραπλήσια ξυμβουλευτέα μοι ὄντα, καὶ τοὺς ἀναπειθομένους ὑμῶν δικαιῶ τοῖς κοινῇ δόξασιν... βοηθεῖν...
(1.140.1)

... I see that on this occasion I must give you exactly the same advice as I have given in the past, and I call upon those of you who are persuaded by my words to give your full support to these resolutions which we are making all together...
(tr. R. Warner, Penguin)

To secure the adoption of a policy, Perikles, like every other Athenian politician under the democracy, had to convince a majority of the assembly. Here is Perikles again, this time in the Funeral Speech:

... οἱ αὐτοὶ ἤτοι κρίνομέν γε ἢ ἐνθυμούμεθα ὀρθῶς τὰ πράγματα, οὐ τοὺς λόγους τοῖς ἔργοις βλάβην ἡγούμενοι, ἀλλὰ μὴ προδιδαχθῆναι μᾶλλον λόγῳ πρότερον ἢ ἐπὶ ἃ δεῖ ἔργῳ ἐλθεῖν. (2.40.2)

We Athenians, in our own persons, take our decisions on policy or submit them to proper discussions: for we do not think that there is an incompatibility between words and deeds; the worst thing is to rush into action before the consequences have been properly debated.
(tr. Warner)

This emphasis on debate is corroborated again and again in the course of Thoukydides' narrative: action by the Athenians is shown as unfailingly preceded by discussion, by the efforts of individuals and groups to persuade others. And indeed we can go further than the period covered by the history of Thoukydides: for throughout the duration of the fifth- and fourth-century democracy the use of persuasion was a central feature of Athenian political life. This does not mean that every Athenian was on all occasions content to get his own way by argument alone. The fact that there were attempts forcibly to introduce an oligarchy at the end of the fifth century is enough to eliminate that in any case highly implausible suggestion. Nor does it mean that the Athenians disposed of, in the words of M.I. Finley, 'a free, disembodied rational faculty, that favourite illusion of so much political theory since the Enlightenment':[28] reasoning, cajoling, threatening, arousing, wheedling—each might figure in the repertoire of a public orator. What the fact of reliance on persuasion does imply, though, is that between a given group of people there exists a tacit or openly-acknowledged agreement to exclude the use of violence in favour of the use of language as the approved means of getting one's way.[29]

We should dearly like to know the extent to which the assembly *actually* constituted an arena for free debate amongst Athenian citizens. The right to persuade in public was denied to slaves, women and aliens; yet within the citizen group everyone—rich and poor, noble and nonentity—had in principle the right to stand up and try to sway the assembly. How far the principle was put into practice is much harder to say. In the debate 'reported' in Euripides' *Orestes*, good advice is given by an *autourgos*, 'one who works for himself' (*Or.* 920) — a peasant like the one to whom Elektra was married off in Euripides' *Elektra*. The *Orestes autourgos* gets up and says his piece, in spite of the fact that he is clearly only an ordinary chap[30] ('no great shakes to look at, but a stout fellow, the sort who doesn't waste his time around the agora all day' — 917ff). Was his counterpart in real life equally uninhibited about expressing his views?

By way of an indirect approach to this problem, I offer an ethnographic 'parallel' from Bali. A description by Mark Hobart of local debates amongst the Balinese contains the following passage:

According to the *banjar* (local group) constitution, all householders are equally entitled to contribute to debates, but the majority rarely, if ever, participate actively for a number of reasons. Firstly, a significant proportion of members know little of the current affairs in the community and attend meetings because it is required. Secondly, speakers must effectively possess not only a knowledge of assembly law and custom, but also precedent from past meetings. Thirdly, the rules of procedure and language, as well as the use of indirect means of presenting issues, limit the number of qualified speakers. Finally, and this is perhaps peculiarly Balinese, speakers are expected not to experience *lek* (shame or 'stage-fright' in public)... Spokesmen in meetings who do not possess some or all of these characteristics are liable to ridicule and other diffuse social sanctions.

So, while in principle anyone may address a meeting, several factors tend to restrict the number of major participants and debate in *banjar* assemblies, in Tengahpadang at least, is conducted almost exclusively by about 10% of the members. Villagers with the appropriate requirements are designated as *juru raos* or *tukang munyiang*, a speech-specialist or orator. This role is generally recognised in local society and orators comprise an informal élite within the *banjar* with high prestige or extensive influence in the assembly and community.[31]

There are both similarities and differences between this and the Athenian situation. It is surely *not* the case in Athens that 'a significant proportion of members know little of the current affairs in the community'. The use of lot to select members of the Council of Five Hundred, combined with the provision that a man might not sit on that body for more than two (separated) one-year terms, meant that practical administrative experience was spread very widely through the citizen population. Participation in the running of the deme will have increased still further a man's sense of being involved in the reaching of decisions.[32] But how many people were confidently *au fait* with procedure in the assembly and council? How many could deploy the correct conventions in speaking? Indeed, what were the conventions? (How — when speaking, as opposed to when setting up an inscription—did you introduce an amendment?) We know very little. It is surely possible that procedural formalities ('I beg to move...' 'May I, through the Chair, address...') did indeed deter the ordinary man in the agora—or, like the *Orestes autourgos*, the man out of it—from contributing. And when we come to the point that Hobart makes about the inhibitions felt by the majority, and the gap between them and the 'orators', then the analogy with Athens is unmistakable. *Lek* may be 'perhaps peculiarly Balinese', but it is very reminiscent of *aidos*, the deference-feeling which a Greek was liable to experience in certain competitive situations.[33] In spite of the partial view of the 'Old Oligarch' that 'as things are, any wretch who wants to can stand up and obtain what is good for him and the likes of himself',[34] it seems evident that at Athens a fairly small group of individuals tended to dominate matters in the assembly, and by out-arguing their rivals sought to win, in Hobart's words, 'high prestige and extensive influence in the assembly and community'. Indeed we might even borrow the phrase 'an informal élite' to apply to these 'demagogues'.[35] But, if so, we must bear in mind at the same time that the position they held was acutely unstable: the moment such a leader of the people failed to persuade the assembly to follow his policy, the potential precariousness of his situation became instantly (and, if defeat were to bring with it exile or ostracism, catastrophically) actual.

Thus persuasion was central not only to Athens' own idealized version of her political life, as represented in, e.g., Euripides' *Suppliants*,[36] but to her real life also. As Diodotos says in his second speech about the Mytilene affair, 'When a man insists that words ought not to be our guides in action, he is either wanting in sense or wanting in honesty.'[37] Faith in public argument lay at the root of the Athenian democracy. It is no coincidence that the short-lived law forbidding the teaching of the art of words (λόγων τέχνην μὴ διδάσκειν) was passed not under the democracy but under the brief regime of the Thirty Tyrants.[38]

Law was another area which the Athenians opened up for public debate. If we consider the arbitration scene depicted on the shield of Achilles at *Il.* 18.497ff, we see the people (*laoi*) present only as enthusiastic spectators: it is the elders (*gerontes*) who decide the case. However, as we saw earlier, in archaic Greece a challenge was offered to the powerful word of the noble, a challenge whose practical result was widespread codification of the laws in many parts of colonial and mainland Greece. The logical culmination of this making-public of the law is to be found in the popular juries of fifth- and fourth-century Athens.

Not all Athenian legal disputes went to court: many were settled by an arbitrator, and in that case the litigants required no special powers of oratory in order to put their side of the story. But, as the considerable corpus of extant forensic speeches attests, very many cases did appear before a court. Two characteristics of the conduct of such cases are important for us here. First, in an Athenian court it was the litigants themselves who established (their versions of) the facts of the case: witnesses were only there to corroborate.[39] Thus the outcome of a case hinged very largely on the ability of the contending parties to convince the jury of their credibility. Second, the size of juries—five hundred and upwards—must surely have been daunting to prospective litigants. It is no wonder that the profession of speech-writer developed in Athens: the need for some kind of help was certainly there.

Like political persuasion, forensic persuasion at Athens was intimately related to the complexion, democratic or occasionally otherwise, of the polis. This is shown negatively by the fact that, after the oligarchic coup of 411, the 'Four Hundred' tried criminal cases themselves, instead of leaving them with the mass juries.[40] The obverse of the same point is shown in a passage from Aristotle's *Constitution of Athens* (25.2). Speaking of the constitutional reforms of 462/1, he reports that Ephialtes 'stripped the Areopagos of all the acquired prerogatives from which it derived its status as guardian of the constitution, and assigned some of them to the Council of Five Hundred, and others to the assembly and the law courts (*dikasteria*)'.[41] Whatever specific powers the *dikasteria* actually received here, and whatever the motives behind the reform, Ephialtes' strengthening of the popular courts at the expense of an organ of the nobility represents a placing of yet more decisions *es to koinon* (cf. Otanes at Hdt. 3.80.6), 'into the common space'.

Another arena where issues were placed into the common space was the theatre. Tragedy and comedy were genres whose staging and production involved the active participation of dozens of citizens; the dithyrambic choruses brought in hundreds more; and the spectators who watched in the theatre of Dionysos below the Akropolis numbered many thousands. More important even than the scale of involvement was the fact that none of the actors or chorus-members or producers or musicians fulfilled these roles by virtue of a priestly or in some other way religious authority. The representations in the theatre were by citizens and in front of citizens.

As for the issues explored, these covered an astoundingly wide range. Taking comedy first, we see that Aristophanes makes humour out of an enormous variety of the 'great issues' of his day: peace and war (*Acharnians, Peace*), political leaders and their policies (*Knights*), the generation gap (*Wasps*), alternative societies (*Birds, Ekklesiazousai*), intellectual freaks (*Clouds*), styles in poetry (*Frogs*), and so forth. What is even more remarkable is that this list represents a portion of the output of *one* comic dramatist. Year in, year out, other rival comedians were putting their views of the world 'into the common space' to be judged—and, they hoped, to be judged victorious—against Aristophanes.

Tragedy was an analogous arena. Like the comic dramatists, the tragedians were putting rival views of the world before an audience in the hope of being adjudged the best. There was no question of representing a settled and shared dogma: the aim of the dramatist was to persuade the spectators to accept his view (within the conventions used) of reality. We happen to have three different versions of one theme: Aischylos' *Choephoroi* and the *Elektra* plays of Sophokles and Euripides. There were very many more such reworkings, each offering something more or less new. Some dramatists did it well, others badly; all were engaged in the public exploration of a common set of stories.

1.3 Beyond Athens

In emphasizing Athens' great contribution to the development of the persuasive word, we must not overlook the fact that the Athenian experience formed part of a much wider movement throughout Greece. Two groups—with much in common—are especially relevant here: sophists and doctors.

To account for the growth of the sophistic movement is extremely difficult; but it is clear that any explanation must, if it is to be convincing, include reference to circumstances in Greece as a whole. If we ask what broad generalization will fit the development of many Greek poleis in the sixth and early fifth centuries, the answer is that this period saw a progression from strongly entrenched aristocracy, *via* an interim period of tyranny in which (owing to the greater centralization of power) the ties binding ordinary people to nobles necessarily took second place to the ties binding everyone to the tyrant; to, finally, a situation where nobles could no longer count on the same sort of automatic support from the people as they could in the days before tyranny. As nobles had now to claim and defend their privileges in public, the need for some sort of assistance in mastering the techniques of rhetoric would, it may be argued, come increasingly to be felt. The younger members of noble families constituted an eager, ready-made clientèle for teachers of public speaking; and the teachers who came forward were the sophists.[42]

For their own discourses the sophists chose a variety of contexts. Sometimes these were formal and public: Hippias of Elis, Gorgias of Leontinoi and Prodikos of Keos were official ambassadors for their respective cities,[43] and they spoke in such arenas as the Olympic Games (Gorgias, Hippias), the Athenian theatre (Gorgias) and the Athenian Council (Prodikos). Sophists also gave private lectures and engaged in private debates. (The informal scene recreated by Plato at the beginning of his *Protagoras* presumably gives a good idea of the atmosphere of such disputes.) The historical Protagoras was said by some to have given a reading of his treatise *On the Gods* in a private dwelling, either that of Euripides or Megakleides (Diog. Laert. 9.54). The veracity of such anecdotes is beyond our power to test, but there is no need to doubt the general pattern of activity which they report.

As for the substance of the sophists' teachings, three aspects may be mentioned. First, they continued the tradition of the Presocratics in so far as they attempted to outdo rivals by offering a superior account or theory regarding the subject under discussion. This competitive aspect of sophistry found a philosophical justification at the hands of Protagoras, who 'was the first to assert that on every issue there are two arguments opposed to each other' (Diog. Laert. 9.51), and among his works there was one entitled *Contradictory Arguments (Antilogiai)* (Diog. Laert. 3.37; 3.57; 9.55). This is now lost, but an example of the kind of contradictory argumentation which the sophists might indulge in is given by the *Two-fold Arguments (Dissoi Logoi)*, which is, precisely, a series of double-sided arguments on moral, political and logical matters. In the same antithetical spirit are the 'tetralogies' of Antiphon, a series of model legal speeches in which each case is argued four times, twice by the defence and twice by the prosecution.

The second point concerns the range of issues which the sophists debated. Justice and injustice, truth and falsehood, the nature of language, the existence of the gods, the possibility of teaching moral excellence—all this, and more, is explored even in the relatively meagre collection of fragments which happens to have survived. Equally impressive are the conceptual tools deployed to tackle this diverse material: above all the opposition *nomos* (custom, convention)/*physis* (nature), which can be compared in analytical fertility to the powerful and illuminating polarity nature/culture in the thought of our own day. The variety of intellectual endeavour displayed by the sophists is disappointing only if we relate it to the subsequent achievement of Plato; if we compare it to what was going on in the rest of the Near East (cf. sect. 1.4), the contribution of the sophists is seen in its true and bold colours.[44]

Thirdly, we should notice the connection between the sophists and *peitho*. This will be discussed in sect. 2.3 below.

Besides the speculations of the sophists there is another area of conceptual and above all practical activity which was developing in Greece in the fifth century, and which enables us to see further evidence of the pervasiveness of public debate in Greek intellectual life. The area in question is medicine. Kos and Knidos were the principal centres of medical tradition in the later fifth and fourth centuries; but, just as illness was present throughout Greece, so were doctors. Like sophists, doctors were marginal figures in relation to the social structure of the polis. Like sophists, they travelled from city to city in the performance of their professional duties. Like sophists, they had to drum up a responsive group of clients by 'presenting' themselves as credibly and as persuasively as they could.[45] Plutarch (*vit. dec. or.* 833c) tells an anecdote about Antiphon which neatly illustrates the connection that was felt to exist between professing medicine and professing rhetoric:

> ... getting himself a room near the market place at Corinth he advertised that he had the power of curing those that were in trouble by means of speech; and discovering the causes of their sickness by enquiry he consoled the sick; but thinking that the profession was beneath his dignity he turned to rhetoric.[46]

The author of the treatise *Prognostic* is fully aware of the importance of putting a credible case before one's potential patients:

> I hold that it is an excellent thing for a physician to practise forecasting (πρόνοιαν). For if he discover and declare unaided by the side of his patients the present, the past and the future, and fill in the gaps in the account given by the sick, he will be the more believed to understand the cases (πιστεύοιτο ἂν μᾶλλον γινώσκειν τὰ τῶν νοσεύντων πρήγματα), so that men will confidently entrust themselves to him for treatment. (*Prog.* 1, tr. W.H.S. Jones, Loeb edn of Hippokrates, vol. II)

Thus the meticulous recording of data which characterizes many of the Hippokratic treatises demonstrates not only a devotion to empirical fact but also a sound awareness of where one's best interests lay:

Brilliant and 'debate-effective' (*agonistika*) forecasts are made by distinguishing the way, manner and time in which each case will end, whether it takes the turn to recovery or incurability. (*On Joints*, 58; tr. adapted from Jones, Loeb, vol. III)

The criterion of being effective in an *agon,* a competitive situation in which rival experts put forward contrasting claims before an audience,[47] might affect treatment as well as theory. A little later in *On Joints* (70) the writer commends a procedure on the grounds that it is both medically sound and *agonistikon*:

Dislocation of the thigh at the hip should be reduced as follows, if it is dislocated inwards. It is a good and correct method, and in accord with nature, and one too that has something striking about it (καὶ δή τι καὶ ἀγωνιστικὸν ἔχουσα), which pleases a dilettante in such matters. (tr. Jones)

However proficient the medical practitioners of the rest of the ancient Near East may have been, there was, as far as we can tell, no parallel in these cultures to the situation in Greece, where there took place not only public disputes about medical procedures and treatment, but also public arguments between professionals about the nature of health and sickness.[48] The beginning of *On the Nature of Man* gives us an idea of the form which such disagreements could take. The author criticizes those speakers, evidently philosophers, who propose a unitary account of the nature of man, asserting it to be air, or fire, or water, or earth. According to the author, such assertions are founded on

evidence and proofs (μαρτύριά τε καὶ τεκμήρια) that amount to nothing... The best way to realize this is to be present at their debates (αὐτοῖσιν ἀντιλέγουσιν). Given the same debaters and the same audience, the same man never wins in the discussion three times in succession, but now one is victor, now another, now he who happens to have the most glib tongue in the face of the crowd. (ch.1, tr. Jones, Loeb)

In chapter 2 the author tackles physicians who hold similar sorts of views about human nature and who are wrong (according to the author) in similar ways. But when in chapter 5 the author expounds his own opinion—that man is composed of blood, phlegm, yellow bile and black bile, and that these remain the same and separate by convention (*kata nomon*) and by nature (*kata physin*)—then he is using 'evidence and proofs' quite as sophistical and inconclusive as those which he castigates in the mouths of his opponents. (He is not unlike Aristophanes, who abuses his rivals for cracking crude jokes while cracking them himself.) The author of *On the Nature of Man* is engaged in a context-bound attempt to persuade an audience to his point of view, and is under no obligation to provide a balanced or 'objectively true' account.

The case of the sophists and the doctors, like that of the Presocratics, shows that the increase in the importance of persuasive argument was by no means confined to Athens. But must we then reject the notion that Athens was *particularly* associated with the persuasive word? In his recent important work *Magic, Reason and Experience* G.E.R. Lloyd considers various explanatory hypotheses which have been advanced to account for what may, with misleading simplicity, be called 'the emergence of science' in ancient Greece. Stressing the part which the Greeks' political arrangements ought to play in the framing of any such explanation, Lloyd is led (244ff) to emphasize what was common to the constitutions of the various Greek cities, and what distinguished those Greek cities taken together from the majority of their Near Eastern neighbours. While acknowledging the power and sophistication of Lloyd's account, I would myself wish to place the emphasis somewhat differently. While it may be true that the constitutions of the classical poleis can be located on a spectrum from oligarchy to democracy with a good deal in common between the different shades, it is not the case that each polis offered an equally favourable environment for persuasive argumentation.

The example of Sparta supports this contention. According to a view of Sparta which we find evidenced in many sources, while Athenian political life operated through a process of persuasion, Spartan political life worked on the basis of obedience. In chapter 8 of his *Constitution of the Lakedaimonians* Xenophon puts it like this: 'We all know that in Sparta they are particularly obedient (μάλιστα πείθονται) to the authorities and the laws.' Even the most important men in the city, he goes on to say, bow and scrape before the magistrates in order to set a socially desirable model for everyone else. And perhaps, we are told, this respect for τὸ πείθεσθαι, obedience, lay behind the institution of the ephorate:

It is probable also that these same citizens helped to set up the office of Ephor, having come to the conclusion that obedience is a very great blessing whether in a state or an army or a household. For they thought that the greater the power of these magistrates the more they would impress the minds of the citizens.[49]

The difficulty, of course, is to know how far this picture corresponded with the reality of classical Sparta. In general, conclusions about the role of persuasion in Sparta have to be based on *ex silentio* arguments: we have to use inference and guesswork in order to reconstruct the kind of reasoning used by Spartan leaders as they advocated their political causes. But one guess, based on what we know of the structure and tone of Sparta's government, seems to be fairly plausible: that most decisions had already, to all practical intents and purposes, been taken before they were put to the assembly. To put it another way: the outcome of the average meeting of the Spartan assembly must have been predictable; that of the average meeting of the Athenian assembly must by contrast have been quite hard to predict—one thinks of Mytilene—because the outcome might be altered by discussion.

The generalized comments in the preceding paragraph might suggest that I am accepting the validity of the Athens/Sparta polarity lock, stock and barrel; but to do so without qualification would go too far. It is true that Aristotle (*Pol.* 1273a10) states that the right ἔξεστι τῷ βουλομένῳ ('anyone who likes may speak') did not exist in Sparta in his day; yet Aischines (*Against Timarchos* 180-1) reports an episode in which a kind of Thersites-figure did speak in the Spartan assembly—he was, it is implied, one of the πονηροὶ ἄνθρωποι ('base men'), and was alleged 'to have lived a disgraceful life' to boot.[50] Again, before positing an absolute opposition between classical Athens, characterized by agreed acceptance of shared *nomoi*, and classical Sparta, characterized by uncritical submission to authoritative *rhetrai*, one ought to note the mitigating fact that already Tyrtaios knew of a constitutional provision in case the *demos* should formulate crooked decisions.[51]

Yet it cannot be disguised that Sparta produced neither a

Euripides, nor an Aristophanes, nor a Sokrates, nor a Demosthenes. It will not do to explain this by saying that Athens 'just happened' to be the place where several geniuses in public debate were born within a relatively modest span of time. The point is that Athens offered a wide variety of contexts in which men could publicly explore their common experience. The contexts offered by Sparta were fewer and more restricted.

It may be objected that in arguing for Athenian uniqueness by citing the case of Sparta I have selected a conveniently unrepresentative and extreme 'foil'. But it seems to me that, in spite of the broadly common cultural background shared by the Greek cities, none of them in fact quite matched Athens in the range of contexts which it exhibited for persuasive discourse. Granted, philosophers, sophists and doctors flourished in many parts of the Greek world; yet in the fifth century they tended, increasingly as time went on, to gravitate to Athens. A nice instance—perhaps even an 'exception' who, if he does not prove the rule, at least supports it — is Gorgias. His native land was Sicily, the birthplace, according to tradition, of rhetoric.[52] But it was in Athens that he created such a stir: it was there that his reception had long been prepared for by home-grown developments in political and other debating arenas. Regarding rhetoric as an outside importation into Athens is very nearly as unhelpful as regarding tragedy as something brought in from the Peloponnese.

1.4 Greece and the Near East

The role of persuasive argumentation in classical Greece, and (if the reasoning of the preceding section is found acceptable) *a fortiori* in classical Athens, acquires greater significance, and perhaps becomes more comprehensible in terms of the political conditions which fostered it, if we set the Greek evidence against what happened in the Near East.

Early political developments in Mesopotamia are extremely hard to sketch owing to the nature of our sources, which consist of later mythical stories about the words and deeds of gods. The difficulty of inferring from myth to the supposed historical reality behind it makes any conclusions at best tentative. Nevertheless, one of the leading scholars in this field, Thorkild Jacobsen, has felt justified in suggesting[53] that the political system depicted in the early myths, a system in which the citizen assembly (*unkin*) apparently has the ultimate authority, probably reflects a real situation, 'primitive democracy', which came into being as a consequence of the transition from village to city-state in Mesopotamia.[54] Other scholars have contested Jacobsen's 'optimistic' speculations about early Mesopotamian democracy,[55] but it does seem likely that a greater degree of local involvement in government existed in Mesopotamia before the establishment of warrior empires as compared with after their establishment. But what is not in doubt is that at no time, either before or after the transition to empire, were the rules of political (as opposed to legal) activity formalized or the constitutional role of public debate and argument formulated.[56]

The last point applies with equal validity to Egypt. Egypt was a monarchy in which there was no central popular assembly to pass judgement on the king's decisions. The monarch ruled by divine right. He had his advisers, and in addition presided over a traditional bureaucracy of unguessable antiquity. Not surprisingly, Egypt offered nothing comparable to the formalized arenas for public debate which were available in the classical Greek polis.

In Achaemenid Persia the king's power was absolute, and that power received theological buttressing when Zoroastrianism became the established creed in the empire. A doctrine which recurs insistently in Zoroastrianism is that of the absolute divide between the Truth and the Lie, the former being associated with the good order presided over by Ahuramazda, the latter espoused by all who threaten that order. This absolute distinction between Truth and Lie plainly offered an ideal symbol by which the established political authority (the king) could justify itself. To rebel was to side with the agents of the Lie; to deviate from the straight path of political obedience meant not only going against temporal authority, but also putting oneself into the iniquitous company of the opponents of Ahuramazda. 'Do not leave the right path; do not rise in rebellion!' was Darius' advice.[57] The king had his advisers but, with the politico-religious system so strongly favouring a monopolistic—even proprietorial—view of truth, there emerged no ethos of the value of debate and dispute for its own sake, and certainly no range of contexts for public argument to match Greece.

The kings of ancient Israel were considered neither divine nor above criticism. On the contrary: they were subject to constant judgement in the light of their fidelity to the people's covenant with Yahweh.[58] As no one in political authority could claim automatically to possess the truth there was room for debate, indeed for outspoken disputation, on political, moral and religious issues. Yet the framework of disputation was not negotiable: it rested on the bedrock assumption of the supreme power of Yahweh and his moral involvement in the course of human affairs. The last point comes out clearly if we look at the individuals who were the most vociferous in their criticisms of contemporary ways, namely the prophets. How free they could be in expressing their views is illustrated by the rebuke delivered by Nathan to David over the question of Bathsheba (2 Sam. 12: 1-15).[59] Sometimes they might act on their own initiative in proffering advice, sometimes they were summoned to give it,[60] but always their authority derived from the simple fact that they were believed to be giving voice to the word of Yahweh.[61] The word of Yahweh was powerful: when he said, let there be light, there was light (Gen. 1:3).[62] As transmitters of the powerful word of Yahweh the prophets were *eo ipso* powerful in their own speech. Not, of course, that their words were unchallengeable—there might be false prophets as well as true (Jeremiah 14:14);[63] and there might even be disputes between prophets, such as the one recorded at Micah 2: 6-11.[64] But the basis of such claims to truth and falsity, and such disputes, was that there was a truth, embodying a right understanding of the purposes of Yahweh. The framework of the debate was unquestioned, and persuasion lay not in appeals to 'reasoned argument' but in 'the general agreement of a prophet's preaching with Yahweh's will, thoughts, and purpose...'.[65] Herein, of course, lies an important contrast with Greece, where one of the most astonishing features of public, speculative argumentation was the radical nature of the questions asked and the religious and philosophical pluralism of the answers given.

On the whole,[66] evidence from other Near Eastern cultures supports the picture which I have been trying to give, according to which classical Greece was remarkable both for its range of contexts for public debate and for the radical nature of the issues open to argumentation. But in spite of the Greeks' achievement in developing uses of the persuasive word for the purpose of rational argument, the power which they called *peitho* retained in their eyes potent non-rational qualities. The next chapter will examine some of the complexities inherent in the notion of *peitho*.

PEITHO

2.1 Approaching the evidence

In chapter 1 we examined the evidence through the mediation of such modern concepts as 'debate', 'argument' and 'persuasion'. In the present chapter we shall try to arrive at a better understanding of how the Greeks themselves perceived 'persuasive' speech and behaviour by exploring the notion of *peitho*, a word which, while it may conventionally be rendered 'persuasion', is by no means always comparable with that English 'equivalent'. I shall first (sects. 2.2, 2.3) review the evidence which we have about *peitho* in its various aspects, and then go on (sect. 2.4) to place it, as one term among contrasting terms, within a functioning system of thought.

It may be useful to preface my own account by mentioning some methodological issues raised by previous writers on the subject. The nearest thing we have to a comprehensive general treatment of *peitho* is a dissertation by George M. Pepe.[1] This scholar deals with most of the available material down to the end of the fifth century, but with hardly anything later than that; nor does he include the visual arts in his survey. Amongst earlier discussions, the most valuable are the entries *s.v.* 'Peitho' in Roscher and Pauly-Wissowa by Weizsäcker and Voigt respectively.[2] Both bring in the visual arts, but in another respect their articles are incomplete: they are principally concerned with mythological aspects of *peitho* — i.e. with the goddess — so that what one might describe as the 'secular' aspects of the concept are inadequately treated. The same is true of Otto Jahn's account.[3]

None of these writers successfully executes the double task which a student of *peitho* must set himself: to do justice to *peitho's* diversity, yet at the same time to avoid creating the impression of a bewildering collection of disparate phenomena lumped together under one head. Weizsäcker's article is a case in point. He multiplies sub-headings so freely that the personality of the goddess Peitho turns out to be an absurdly split one:

1. Peitho, the daughter of Okeanos and Tethys.

2. Peitho, the wife of Phoroneus and mother of Aigialeus and Apis.
3. Peitho linked with the Graces.
4. (i) Peitho as epithet of Aphrodite.
   (ii) Peitho as an independent goddess, but in the train of, and closely associated with, Aphrodite.
5. Peitho's importance in civic life.

Near the beginning of his article Voigt takes Weizsäcker to task on just this point, yet in his own account he too puts undue emphasis on a category-distinction, that between Peitho as goddess of love and Peitho as goddess of rhetoric.[4] It is precisely the fact that Peitho embraced both of these to us separate areas of experience that constitutes one of the interesting things about her.

A particularly awkward problem, apparently minor but important in its implications, concerns whether or not one should distinguish in exposition between the goddess and the 'abstract noun'. In Aischylos' *Suppliants* the Argive king leaves the scene with the words:

πειθὼ δ᾽ ἕποιτο καὶ τύχη πρακτήριος. (523)

Let *peitho* follow, and fortune (or 'success') in action.

Are Peitho and Tyche to be regarded here as divine? That they could be is shown by a passage in Alkman (quoted by Plutarch at *de fort. Rom.* 318a = *PMG* 64) where the deities Peitho and Tyche are described as sisters. Nevertheless, Aischylos 'could', one might argue, have intended simply the 'abstract' qualities denoted by the two nouns. From the point of view of a modern editor the dilemma is a real one: do we print πειθώ or Πειθώ, τύχη or Τύχη? But for Aischylos and his audience the dilemma would have been meaningless. There was no orthographical distinction between capital and lower-case lettering, and *a fortiori* no semantic distinction based on such orthography. The polarity 'Personification'/'Abstract' is always fluid in classical antiquity.[5] There is no hard and fast dichotomy between Πειθώ and πειθώ: at most they may be thought of as occupying two ends of a spectrum.

It is true, though, that sometimes one end of the spectrum predominates over the other. When, in describing Pheidias' statue of Zeus at Olympia, Pausanias mentions that on the base of the throne there was a relief portraying the birth of Aphrodite, greeted by Eros and 'crowned by Peitho' (5.11.8), the reference has to be to a goddess. Equally indisputably, when Thoukydides gives the following words to the representatives of the Plataians:

χαλεπῶς δὲ ἔχει ἡμῖν πρὸς τοῖς ἄλλοις καὶ ἡ πειθώ. (3.53.4)

But we find ourselves confronted by a further difficulty, in that we have to convince you.

then *peitho* appears to be used as what we should call an abstract noun. Thus I hope little harm will be done if, for exegetical purposes, I deal first with Peitho as a goddess (when Peitho/Πειθώ will be printed, with an initial capital), and afterwards with the remainder of the evidence. But, as a reminder that *peitho* is really a unity, we may recall the use which Gorgias makes of it in his *Encomium of Helen*. (See also below, p. 53.) For Gorgias, *peitho* is the instrument used by every speaker in ordinary contexts. Yet it is also a quasi-divine force:

λόγος δυνάστης μέγας ἐστίν, ὃς σμικροτάτῳ σώματι καὶ ἀφανεστάτῳ θειότατα ἔργα ἀποτελεῖ. (*Enc.* 8)

Language is a powerful ruler who with a tiny and invisible body accomplishes deeds most divine.

Again, *peitho* is the seductive persuasion which may have been what induced Helen to go off with Paris. Yet it is also the power used and the effect produced by oratory in contexts which we would regard as non-erotic—but to Greeks *all peitho* was 'seductive'. *Peitho* is a continuum within which divine and secular, erotic and non-erotic come together.

2.2 The goddess

Peitho was a divinity whose province was the alluring power of sexual love. But in addition to this erotic function she had wider associations which linked her more directly with the public life of the community. Evidence for this general role comes mostly from literary texts, but it is not wholly absent from our piecemeal sources for cults of Peitho or from artistic representations of her. It will be convenient to take these three types of evidence in turn.

Cult

Our information here is difficult to assess, for a number of reasons.

Firstly, Peitho is sometimes an autonomous deity, sometimes the epithet of another—and not always the same—deity. Second, the source which records a cult of Peitho often fails to make clear the characteristics of the goddess; or rather, not 'fails to', but 'does not need to', since to a person making a dedication at the neighbourhood shrine the divinity's local qualities and functions are so well known that they do not have to be mentioned explicitly. A further problem stems from the fact that cults of Peitho are attested in places where little or no corroborative literary material survives; so we may be obliged simply to report the existence of a cult without being able to say anything about its character.

We may begin with these observations by Pausanias about his trip to Megara:

And next to the temple of Dionysos is the shrine of Aphrodite, and a statue of the goddess in ivory, under the title *Praxis* (Action). This is the oldest statue in the shrine. And *Peitho* (Persuasion) and another goddess whom they call *Paregoros* (Coaxing) are by Praxiteles; and by Skopas *Eros* (Love) and *Himeros* (Desire) and *Pothos* (Yearning)... (1.43.6)[6]

The context could hardly be more explicitly erotic, since the most probable explanation of *Praxis* is that it refers to the sexual act.[7]

At Olynthos Peitho may have had similarly erotic associations. In 1933 D.M. Robinson published[8] an inscription from the base of a votive statue of Peitho, dedicated by officials called *agoranomoi*. Robinson suggested that these men fixed the salaries of *hetairai* (prostitutes), and he could well be right. The Suda records that 'the *agoranomoi* determined how much each *hetaira* should receive';[9] and Aristotle (*Ath.* 50) reports that in his own day the Athenian *astynomoi*—closely related to the *agoranomoi*[10]—had to watch that flute-girls and their business colleagues did not price themselves out of the reach of their potential clients.[11] It looks as if the *agoranomoi* at Olynthos may have had the same duty.[12]

In addition to the above cases we know of places where 'Peitho' is used as an epithet[13] to define the particular aspect of Aphrodite to which appeal is being made: Pharsalos,[14] Knidos[15] and Mytilene.[16] In the last-mentioned city we have inscriptional evidence for a cult association between 'Aphrodite Peitho' and Hermes. This certainly does not contradict the idea that the context is erotic: at *Peace* 456 Aristophanes' Trygaios prays to 'Hermes, the Charites, the Horai,

Aphrodite and Pothos'; and Plutarch (*praec. coni.* 138c-d) links Hermes, Aphrodite, Peitho and the Charites when describing the love between man and wife.[17] However, bearing in mind Plutarch's words, we might guess that it was a marriage cult that linked 'Aphrodite Peitho' and Hermes at Mytilene. If so, this is importantly different from Peitho's role at, say, Olynthos, where she is associated with love outside marriage. As we shall see later, this is one of the most significant ambivalences of *peitho*.

Attica offers two instances of a connection between Peitho and Aphrodite. At Daphni a votive inscription to Peitho[18] was found on the site of the temple of Aphrodite. If this is a coincidence, it is a striking one; if not, it indicates a link between the cults of the two deities. More important is the association between the two at Athens. The source is Pausanias (1.22.3) who refers to a temple of Aphrodite Pandemos and Peitho. Whether or not it had been, as was alleged, founded by Theseus, the shrine was certainly old: 'In my time', relates Pausanias, 'the ancient images were gone, but the existing images were by no obscure artists';[19] and the antiquity of the cult has been confirmed by the discovery of an inscription dating from the late sixth or early fifth century and implying the cult's existence.[20]

The meaning of 'Pandemos' is disputed. That it specifies an erotic function of Aphrodite is a view advocated by Frazer in his note on the passage.[21] He translates 'Pandemos Aphrodite' as 'Vulgar Aphrodite', implicitly connecting the Athenian cult with those at Megalopolis and Thebes, where there were images of both a Heavenly ('Ourania') and a Common ('Pandemos') Aphrodite (Paus. 8.32.2; 9.16.3-4). An alternative and overtly political interpretation is given by Erika Simon.[22] She identifies the two figures on certain 'double-headed' coins from late archaic (late sixth-/early fifth-century) Athens with Aphrodite Pandemos and Peitho.[23] In view of the fact that these coins with (supposedly) Aphrodite and Peitho on one side have (unmistakably) Athene on the other, Simon suggests that we have here a sort of pre-echo of the end of the *Oresteia*, where Athene relies on the power of Peitho. The identification on which this hypothesis rests is highly speculative, but Simon's arguments for the political character of Peitho in the joint cult at Athens are largely independent of these speculations. First, she cites the historian Apollodoros of Athens, quoted in an entry in

Harpokration's *Lexicon*. According to Apollodoros, the epithet 'Pandemos' derived from the fact that the temple was built close to the agora where 'all the people', *panta ton demon,* used to assemble (*FGrH* (Jacoby) 244 F 113). Then Simon refers to the Pausanias passage already noticed (1.22.3) where it is said that Theseus established the joint cult at the time of the unification of Attica—a supremely 'political' context. The second part of the Harpokration entry, which gives Nikandros of Kolophon's version of the founding of the cult—that it was established on the profits of prostitution—is relegated by Simon to the status of a later 'Platonic' misinterpretation, since it suggests a 'vulgarly erotic' origin for the cult.

Which account, Frazer's or Simon's, is the more satisfactory? It has been argued that Frazer's sublime/vulgar distinction is Platonic and so cannot illuminate the origins of the cult.[24] But the *origins* of the cult are in any case inaccessible to us. What is more significant is that, as Apollodoros and Nikandros testify, people told two stories about Pandemos-Peitho: according to one story, the cult had to do with prostitutes, i.e. erotic seduction; according to the other, it had to do with the agora, i.e. the arena where people gathered for public discussion. The range of activities covered by *peitho* could not be more neatly illustrated.

Apart from the joint cult with Aphrodite Pandemos, Peitho was—as we might expect of a city where the persuasive word was so preeminent—also worshipped at Athens independently as a goddess of all persuasion. Isokrates (*Antid.* 246-50, esp. 249) complains about the citizenry's ambivalent attitude to persuasion:

But as a symptom, not only of their confusion of mind, but of their contempt for the gods, they recognize that Peitho is one of the gods, and they observe that the city makes sacrifices to her every year, but when men aspire to share the power which the goddess possesses, they claim that such aspirants are being corrupted, as though their desire were for some evil thing. (tr. after Norlin, Loeb)

He would not have made his point in this way if the Peitho to whom sacrifice was offered was exclusively a goddess of love within or outside marriage. The Prytaneis sacrificed to her, presumably in view of her connection with the persuasive speech which they would hope to employ;[25] and maybe it was in virtue of this same role that, later on,

Peitho's priest had a special seat in the theatre of Dionysos,[26] the arena where Athens and her priorities were on display to the rest of the Greek world.

Of the other cities in which Peitho may have had the character of a 'general' persuader,[27] Argos constitutes the most interesting case. Pausanias (2.21.1) relates that there was a temple of *Artemis* Peitho in the city: 'The sanctuary of Artemis, surnamed Peitho, was also dedicated by Hypermestra, after her acquittal at the trial to which she had been brought by her father on account of Lynkeus' (tr. after Frazer). Hypermestra was the one Danaid who, instead of complying with her father's murderous command, spared the life of her new husband on their wedding night. She had, so the story went, won the ensuing court case; what more natural than that Peitho, goddess of persuasive speech, should be honoured as a result?

It has, however, been argued that the 'rhetorical' explanation for this cult is simply the product of later rationalization. (As with Aphrodite Pandemos, the 'original' nature of a cult has often proved irresistibly fascinating to scholars.) Voigt[28] maintains that Artemis Peitho in Argos[29] was a marriage goddess. Plutarch (*quaest. Rom.* 264b) names Artemis and Peitho as two of the five divinities to whom marriage torches are lit; the same writer gives Peitho a role in cementing the conjugal bond (*praec. coni.* 138c-d); and Nonnos (θαλαμηπόλος... Πειθώ, 'Peitho, attendant at the bridal chamber', 3.84; γαμοστόλος ... Πειθώ, 'Peitho, attendant at marriage', 42.530) and Kollouthos (καὶ στέφος ἀσκήσασα γαμήλιον ἤλυθε Πειθώ, 'There came also Peitho, who had made a bridal wreath', 30) reflect a tradition in which Peitho figures in marriage.[30] Moreover, the myth recounted by Pausanias exalts the bond of marriage through the union of Hypermestra and Lynkeus.[31] In any case, whether or not we follow Voigt over the Argive marriage cult, the myth of Artemis Peitho in Argos is important, since it shows Peitho at work within marriage in contrast to her role as patroness of *hetairai*.

We should certainly like to know more about Peitho at Argos, especially in view of two tantalizing items of mythographical information which have been preserved. We are told (schol. E. (Schwartz) *Ph.* 1116, quoting Pherekydes) that Peitho married Argos; alternatively (schol. E. *Or.* 1246), that she married Phoroneus. Now Phoroneus was an Argive culture-hero, responsible for bringing men together into a civilized, community existence:[32] thus the two versions of Peitho's marriage are structurally equivalent, their logic being that *peitho* is a central quality in a civilized polis. Whether there is any link between these myths and the democratic tradition in historical Argos[33] is hard to say, though such a connection is not at all improbable.

Literature

There are no explicit allusions to the goddess Peitho in Homer: although the verbal form πείθειν occurs numerous times, the noun is absent. However, the power, if not the word, is certainly present, especially in the 'Deception of Zeus' in the *Iliad*. This part of the story is highly relevant to the erotic role elsewhere attributed explicitly to Peitho, since the plot is dealing with the role of seductiveness in marriage. In order to deflect her husband's attention from warfare, Hera gets from Aphrodite the magic girdle in which all the charms of sexual allurement reside:

> ἔνθ' ἔνι μὲν φιλότης, ἐν δ' ἵμερος, ἐν δ' ὀαριστὺς
> πάρφασις, ἥ τ' ἔκλεψε νόον πύκα περ φρονεόντων. (*Il.* 14.216-17)

> ...in it is delight, desire, and whispered enticement, which steals away the mind even of the wise.

πάρφασις is here practically synonymous with πειθώ.[34]

With Hesiod we have a little more substantial ground to go on. There is a direct allusion in the *Theogony*, where Peitho is said to be one of the progeny of Tethys and Okeanos (349). She herself is not given an individualized function, although all the Okeanids, together with Apollo and the Rivers, are said to 'tend men in their youth' (ἄνδρας κουρίζουσι, 347). But in the only other Hesiodic passage to mention her she does have her own peculiar sphere of influence. In the account of Pandora near the beginning of *Works and Days* Peitho is listed among her divine benefactors:

> ἀμφὶ δὲ οἱ Χάριτές τε θεαὶ καὶ πότνια Πειθὼ
> ὅρμους χρυσείους ἔθεσαν χροΐ · (73-4)

> Around her, the Charites and the lady Peitho adorned her skin with golden necklaces.

Two matters concerning these lines are worth pursuing here. First, 'golden necklaces'. These were traditional instruments of erotic enticement. Aphrodite wore them when she encountered Anchises (*H. Aph.* 5 (Allen) 88-90)—perhaps the very ones which the Horai had given her at birth (*H. Aph.* 6 (Allen) 10-13). Necklaces were powerful, and their power might be dangerous and evil if they seduced women into immoral sexual behaviour. The famous necklace of Harmonia brought destruction on Amphiaraos, Eriphyle, and eventually Alkmaion. It was with a golden necklace that Minos corrupted the daughter of Nisos (A. *Cho.* 613ff). And Helen—delightful, destructive Helen—was given a necklace by Aphrodite (Ath. 6 (232f)). So both because they were alluring and because they were dangerous, necklaces were a suitable adornment for Pandora. And for the same two reasons necklaces were a suitable present for Peitho to give. In the right place—marriage—Peitho brings men and women harmonious delight; in the wrong place—illicit sexual relationships—Peitho can be an agent of discord and catastrophe.

In commenting on ὅρμους χρυσείους, 'golden necklaces', in *Works and Days* the scholiast hits one particular nail squarely on the head:

...ἐπειδὴ ἡ γυνὴ κεκοσμημένη πείθει τὸν ἄνδρα πρὸς συνουσίαν τάχος.

Because the woman, finely adorned, quickly persuades the man to have sex.

He correctly assumes that in this passage it is the woman who persuades the man. Yet a number of scholars have persisted in identifying Peitho exclusively with the pattern: man persuades woman.[35] This quite simply flies in the face of the evidence. Athenaios tells us of a prostitute named 'Peitho' (13 (577a)); and it is hardly masculine persuasion which is in question there. Just before this, the same author quotes a snatch of Pindar:

Πολύξεναι νεάνιδες, ἀμφίπολοι
Πειθοῦς ἐν ἀφνειῷ Κορίνθῳ... (Ath. 13 (574a) = Pi. fr. 122 (Snell))
Hospitable girls, servants of Peitho in rich Corinth.

The allusion is to sacred prostitution in the temple of Aphrodite at Corinth.[36] Erotic persuasion of the man by the woman is again under Peitho's tutelage.[37] There are, of course, many cases where Peitho does represent the pattern 'man persuades woman'—compare the role of the goddess in the Helen story, which we shall be examining below. All I am saying is that Peitho was thought to be operative both in this and in the reverse pattern.

The second thing to arise from the Hesiodic lines concerns the 'status' of Peitho: is she here an autonomous goddess or is she, as C. Robert suggests,[38] simply synonymous with Aphrodite? The argument is that at 65-6 Zeus tells *Aphrodite* to bestow *charis* and *pothos* on Pandora, yet at 73 *Peitho* is carrying out the instruction. Thus to remove the supposed contradiction we must assume that 'Peitho' is actually 'Aphrodite Peitho'. But this is absurdly over-logical. It is perfectly feasible for Aphrodite to be in overall erotic command, while the beauty treatment is administered by other (and perhaps, should we be determined to rationalize, subordinate) goddesses whose special functions suit them for the business in hand.

In erotic poetry from early lyric to the Hellenistic epigrammatists Peitho has a place in the mythology of love. A fragment of Ibykos preserved by Athenaios (13 (564)) gives us Peitho in her usual surroundings:

> Εὐρύαλε γλαυκέων Χαρίτων θάλος ⟨Ὡρᾶν⟩
> καλλικόμων μελέδημα, σὲ μὲν Κύπρις
> ἅ τ' ἀγανοβλέφαρος Πει-
>   θὼ ῥοδέοισιν ἐν ἄνθεσι θρέψαν. (*PMG* 288)
> (Ὡρᾶν Page, following Bergk)

> Euryalos, child of the blue-eyed Charites, delight of the lovely-haired Horai, Kypris and Peitho of the tender glances nurtured you in rose-flowers.

Sappho's first poem mentions the power of sexual persuasion:

> τίνα δηὖτε πείθω
> †..σαγην† ἐς σὰν φιλότατα; (*PLF* 1.18-19)

> Whom am I to persuade this time [to be drawn?] into your love?

Here, in spite of the poor state of the text, it seems on balance more likely that we have πείθω (verb) than Πειθώ (noun): that is, Aphrodite herself is exercising the power. Rather as in the case of the relationship between Aphrodite and Helen in *Iliad* 3, we are glimpsing the intimate relationship between goddess and protégée—third parties are unnecessary.[39]

In the extant verses of Pindar Peitho occurs four times. Twice the relevant passage is recorded by Athenaios. We have just met the hospitable ladies of Corinth, 'servants of Peitho'. The second quotation (fr. 123 (Snell)) is of special interest, in that it shows how Peitho was perceived to be at work not only in relations between a man and a woman and (cf. Sappho's poetry) between two women, but also in relations between two males—specifically, between a man and a boy:

> Χρῆν μὲν κατὰ καιρὸν ἐρώ-
>   των δρέπεσθαι, θυμέ, σὺν ἁλικίᾳ·
> τὰς δὲ Θεοξένου ἀκτῖνας πρὸς ὄσσων
> μαρμαρυζοίσας δρακείς
> ὃς μὴ πόθῳ κυμαίνεται, ἐξ ἀδάμαντος
> ἢ σιδάρου κεχάλκευται μέλαιναν καρδίαν
> ψυχρᾷ φλογί, πρὸς δ' Ἀφροδί-
>   τας ἀτιμασθεὶς ἑλικογλεφάρου
> ἢ περὶ χρήμασι μοχθίζει βιαίως
> ἢ γυναικείῳ θράσει
> ψυχρὰν† φορεῖται πᾶσαν ὁδὸν θεραπεύων.
> ἀλλ' ἐγὼ τᾶς ἕκατι κηρὸς ὣς δαχθεὶς ἕλᾳ
> ἱρᾶν μελισσᾶν τάκομαι, εὖτ' ἂν ἴδω
> παίδων νεόγυιον ἐς ἥβαν·
> ἐν δ' ἄρα καὶ Τενέδῳ
> Πειθώ τ' ἔναιεν καὶ Χάρις
> υἱὸν Ἁγησίλα.

You ought to cull the flowers of love, my heart, at the right moment, in the season of youth. But whoever, having seen the rays flashing from the eyes of Theoxenos, is not tossed upon a sea of desire, must have a black heart, forged in a cold flame from adamant or iron; spurned by Aphrodite of the quick-glancing eyes, he either toils violently for riches or (?) through the boldness of a woman he is borne along subservient to her in every way (?). But I, for the sake of her (sc. Aphrodite), like the wax of the sacred bees when it is bitten by the sun's heat—I melt when I look at the fresh-limbed youth of boys. So in Tenedos too there dwelt Peitho and Charis [near?] the son of Hagesilas.

Unfortunately the text at the end is not quite certain; but it is evident that Pindar is not wishing that Peitho were in Tenedos, he is stating that there is an actual link between Peitho and the island. In other words Peitho is a quality displayed by the boy: it describes an aspect of the influence he has over his older lover.

The context of the third Pindaric passage is heterosexual: it evokes the love between Jason and Medea:

> ...μαινάδ᾽ ὄρνιν Κυπρογένεια φέρεν
> πρῶτον ἀνθρώποισι, λιτάς τ᾽ ἐπαοιδὰς
> ἐκδιδάσκησεν σοφὸν Αἰσονίδαν·
> ὄφρα Μηδείας τοκέων ἀφέλοιτ᾽ αἰ-
> δῶ, ποθεινὰ δ᾽ Ἑλλὰς αὐτὰν
> ἐν φρασὶ καιομέναν δονέοι μάστιγι Πειθοῦς. (*Pyth.* 4. 216-19)

She, the Cyprian, first brought the bird of madness to men, and taught the wise son of Aison the charms of entreaty; that he might remove the shame Medea felt before her parents, and that the Hellas she yearned for might excite her with the lash of Peitho, as her heart burned.

ἐπαοιδάς, 'charms', suggests an almost magical quality in the act of influencing another person—just the kind of thing against which Aischylos' Prometheus is resolute:

> καί μ᾽ οὔτι μελιγλώσσοις πειθοῦς
> ἐπαοιδαῖσιν θέλξει... (*P.V.* 172-3)

He will not bewitch me with the honey-sweet charms of *peitho*...

Indeed in the passage from *Pythian* 4 the metaphorical sense shades into the literal, since Pindar's context does actually refer to magic. Another expression worth noticing is μάστιξ Πειθοῦς, the 'lash of Peitho'. This is poetic imagery rather than an allusion to a traditional iconographical appurtenance of Peitho's (so Voigt, rightly); and it generates the satisfying *frisson* of oxymoron, since Peitho is normally opposed to force-compulsion.[40]

Finally there is the delightful opening of the ninth *Pythian*. Apollo chances on Kyrene, and consults Cheiron about the morality of taking her there and then. Cheiron's reply begins thus (39-40):

> ...κρυπταὶ κλαῖδες ἐντὶ σοφᾶς Πειθοῦς ἱερᾶν φιλοτάτων,
> Φοῖβε...

Secret are the keys of wise Peitho to love's holy sanctuaries, Phoibos...

The image, again poetical not iconographical, evokes the sense of intimacy where Peitho is at home.

The passages so far considered provide a consistent and probably representative sample of how the earlier Greek poets saw Peitho the goddess of love. Much the same picture emerges from poetry down to Hellenistic times and beyond: the goddess is regularly found in the company of Kypris/Aphrodite, Eros, the Charites, Pothos, Himeros, and so forth.[41] Instead of multiplying corroborative examples, then, we may now consider what might be called the 'political' or 'public' aspect of Peitho's power.

As we saw earlier, Alkman sang the genealogy of the goddess Tyche in these terms:

Εὐνομίας ⟨τε⟩ καὶ Πειθῶς ἀδελφὰ
καὶ Προμαθήας θυγάτηρ... (Plu. *de fort. Rom.* 318a = *PMG* 64)

Sister of Eunomia and Peitho, daughter of Prometheia ...

We cannot be sure about the significance of Prometheia: *qua* 'personification', as opposed to *qua* festival of Prometheus, she is practically unattested; although Ehrenberg[42] sees her as representing the 'cautious reluctance' which often appeared to be the predominant psychological disposition informing Spartan policy. Tyche herself presumably connotes something like 'Success': we recall that the Argive king at A. *Supp.* 523 prays that *peitho* and *tyche* may go with him in his attempt to persuade the assembly; while Pindar (fr. 39 (Snell)) referred to Τύχα φερέπολις, 'Tyche who upholds the city'.[43] Eunomia (see below, pp. 47-8) presides over the 'good order' of a city. As for Peitho, Ehrenberg[44] translates her as 'Obedience', since he 'cannot think of any section of the social or political world of Sparta, even of the Sparta of the seventh century which had not yet the rigidity of the post-Chilonian State, that could be governed by Persuasion'. This interpretation may be right for, although the meaning 'obedience' is much rarer than Ehrenberg suggests,[45] it could be significant that the only known classical instances are in Xenophon, a writer much influenced by Sparta. On the other hand, Alkman's own *Partheneion* shows us a world so apparently unlike the later 'obedient' Sparta in atmosphere that we cannot be confident that Ehrenberg has the truth. However, more important than such matters of detail is a general point to be made about the way in which Alkman presents the relationship between what we would call 'political' concepts. Perhaps the best commentary on the Alkman couplet is given by Pindar (*Ol.* 13.6ff):

ἐν τᾷ γὰρ Εὐνομία ναίει, κασίγνηταί τε, βάθρον
    πολίων ἀσφαλές,
Δίκα καὶ ὁμότροφος Εἰρήνα, τάμι' ἀνδράσι
    πλούτου,
χρύσεαι παῖδες εὐβούλου Θέμιτος.

> Within her [sc. the city of Corinth] there dwells Eunomia, her sister
> Dike, secure foundation-stone of cities, and her sister Eirene,
> assigners of wealth to men—the golden children of Themis of the
> Good Counsel.

Politics is here, as in Alkman, not a separate conceptual area: it is
rooted in, and imagined in terms of, a world of natural growth and
human relationships. Thus if we say that the Alkman lines present us
with a 'political' Peitho this must be taken as implying no radical
break with Peitho's role in the area of love between individuals. At
most it represents a shift of emphasis.

Yet there is some evidence to suggest that in time, and at any rate
by the middle of the fifth century, the political dimension of Peitho
became more prominent. In this connection a story told by Herodotos
is instructive:

> ...and the Greeks, now that it was decided neither to continue the chase nor to
> sail to the Hellespont to break the bridges, invested the island with the
> intention of taking it. The Andrians were the first of the islanders to refuse
> Themistokles' demand for money; he had put it to them that they would be
> unable to avoid paying, because the Athenians had the support of two
> powerful deities, Persuasion and Necessity (Πειθώ τε καὶ Ἀναγκαίην), and
> the Andrians had replied that Athens was lucky to have two such useful gods,
> who were obviously responsible for her wealth and greatness; unfortunately,
> however, they themselves, in their small and inadequate island, also had two
> deities in permanent possession of their soil—and by no means such useful
> ones, for their names were Poverty and Impotence (Πενίην τε καὶ
> Ἀμηχανίην); consequently no money would be forthcoming: for Athens'
> power could never be stronger than Andros' inability to pay. (Hdt. 8. 111; tr.
> after de Sélincourt, Penguin)

Themistokles meant that, if the Athenians could not get what they
wanted by persuasion, they could get it by violence.[46] Peitho is
identified with a mode of political behaviour, the use of spoken
arguments as opposed to compulsion.[47]

In the writings of some of the Presocratics Peitho figures as a
goddess of 'general' persuasion. The most famous instance is

probably in Parmenides:

> ...ἣ μὲν ὅπως ἔστιν τε καὶ ὡς οὐκ ἔστι μὴ εἶναι,
> Πειθοῦς ἐστι κέλευθος (Ἀληθείῃ γὰρ ὀπηδεῖ)... (DK fr. 2.3-4)
>
> One way, that it-is and cannot not-be, is the path of Peitho (for she attends upon Truth)...

The logic, put into its simplest terms, is: the way of 'is-and-cannot-not-be' is true; but Peitho attends necessarily[48] upon truth; therefore the way of 'is-and-cannot-not-be' is the 'path of Peitho' — i.e. it must produce conviction in those who understand it.[49] In other words, it is on the rhetorical sense of Peitho that Parmenides draws here, as elsewhere do Empedokles (DK fr. 133) and Demokritos (DK fr. 181, cf. fr. 51).

Comedy offers a number of passages relevant to Peitho's more general aspect. The most famous is from *Frogs:*

> Ευ. ʻοὐκ ἔστι Πειθοῦς ἱερὸν ἄλλο πλὴν λόγος.ʼ
> Αι. ʻμόνος θεῶν γὰρ Θάνατος οὐ δώρων ἐρᾷ.ʼ
> Δι. μέθεσθε μέθεσθε· καὶ τὸ τοῦδέ γ᾽ αὖ ῥέπει·
> θάνατον γὰρ εἰσέθηκε βαρύτατον κακόν.
> Ευ. ἐγὼ δὲ πειθώ γ᾽ ἔπος ἄριστ᾽ εἰρημένον.
> Δι. πειθὼ δὲ κοῦφόν ἐστι καὶ νοῦν οὐκ ἔχον. (1391-6)

> Eurip. 'Persuasion has no shrine but language.'
> Aisch. 'For alone among the gods Death does not love gifts.'
> Dion. Let it go, let it go! Aischylos' side is heavier! It's because he put in death, the heaviest misfortune of all!
> Eurip. I put in persuasion—and well said too!
> Dion. Persuasion is a light and fickle thing.

The context is the 'weighing of lines' episode in which the Aristophanic 'Aischylos' sets Death against Persuasion, hence implicitly belittling the power in which 'Euripides' places reliance. Not for the first time, an Aristophanic creation does not square with the historical figure on whom it was based: as we shall see, the real Aischylos by no means devalued the power of Peitho. But for the moment we may simply note one point: Dionysos' verdict (1396) evidently only makes sense if Peitho is being employed in the sense of rhetorical persuasion. Against the solid, military figure of Aischylos, Euripides is presented as an arch-democrat and lover of sophistries, so it is appropriate that Peitho should be the goddess whom he cites.

In two other passages from comedy the erotic and the more general senses of Peitho are juxtaposed, and the juxtaposition exploited. At *Lys.* 203-4, when the women are about to swear their oath to renounce sex, the heroine makes the following appeal:

> δέσποινα Πειθοῖ καὶ κύλιξ φιλοτησία,
> τὰ σφάγια δέξαι ταῖς γυναιξὶν εὐμενής.

> O Peitho Our Mistress,[50] O Loving Cup, look favourably on these women and receive their sacrifice.

Why is Peitho invoked? First, the women have assembled in opposition to the men and have taken a political decision — to do everything possible to stop the war. Having achieved ostensible unanimity amongst themselves they must now persuade their menfolk to comply and to alter *their* political position — hence the need to call upon a goddess of rhetoric. But Peitho also has a more precisely erotic reference, for the means by which the women will get their way is by arousing and then cheating their husbands. And who better to appeal to in the matter of arousal than Peitho? With her help, the women influence first the physical and then the political stance of the men.

In Menander's *Epitrepontes* at 555-6 (lineation as in Sandbach's OCT), Habrotonon, the music-girl with a heart, and with whom we are clearly meant to sympathize, invokes Peitho in order to add weight to her desire for freedom:

> φίλη Πειθοῖ, παροῦσα σύμμαχος
> πόει κατορθοῦν τοὺς λόγους οὓς ἂν λέγω.

> Dear goddess Peitho, come and help me—grant that my words succeed![51]

Capps[52] misses half the point by saying, 'Habrotonon is not thinking of Aphrodite's handmaid, but of the goddess who bestows the power of convincing speech...' Not so: Peitho's role as goddess of rhetoric is of course relevant, but it is equally pertinent that, in as much as Peitho is a goddess of love, she is that much more likely to favour a lady of Habrotonon's calling. Both ends of the Peitho 'spectrum' must be taken into account if the passage is to yield its full meaning.[53]

Visual arts[54]

We have already mentioned Pheidias' statue of Zeus at Olympia, with the representation of Aphrodite, Eros and Peitho on the base of the throne. Unfortunately this fabled work has not survived, but we do have a number of others which show Peitho in similar company. On a mid-fifth-century Attic pyxis in Ancona[55] Peitho is linked with the birth of Aphrodite, and is seen together with Zeus, Hera, Eros and Charis (all inscriptionally secure). From Eretria comes an Attic 'onos' or 'epinetron'—wool-carder's knee-guard—(Pl. 1)[56] which again depicts Peitho in an aphrodisiac setting. Present as well as Peitho and Aphrodite are Eros, Harmonia, Kore, Hebe, Himeros (all inscriptionally secure). Unfortunately, the inscriptions are situated in a way that makes identification of two of the three central figures doubtful. Harmonia (seated) is flanked by Peitho and Kore (a 'maiden'). One of these figures is standing, holding a mirror; the other leans towards Harmonia, and the two look at each other. The proximity of the inscription 'Kore' to the figure on the right of Harmonia leads one to think that Peitho must, by a process of elimination, be the one with the mirror; and a mirror is a highly appropriate thing for her to carry since mirrors are connected in myth with seductiveness.[57] On the other hand, it might be argued that it is more suitable for a named mythological figure, Peitho, to be involved closely with Harmonia, while the anonymous 'Kore' should be standing passively by: i.e. 'Kore' has the mirror, Peitho leans forward.[58] Whichever view is right, the erotic context is indisputable.

This context is repeated in several vase-paintings where Peitho appears in the company of Aphrodite, Pothos, Himeros or related figures. Usually there is nothing in the attributes, attitude or gestures of Peitho to characterize her specifically as the goddess of *persuasion* in love: she either remains impassive, or at most performs some act of (presumably) cult significance, e.g. carrying a box of trinkets or a dish or a receptacle for ointment.[59] But there are some works in which the character of the myth being depicted makes it likely that the reason for the goddess' presence is precisely her role as the embodiment of erotic persuasion. These works portray the legend of Helen.

On a Boston skyphos[60] (Pl. 2(a)) dating from 490–480, made by

Hieron and painted by Makron, we have on one side the abduction of Helen: Paris takes her by the wrist, Aphrodite extends her hand over Helen's head as if in blessing, and Peitho (inscriptionally secure) follows, holding a flower—a symbol of her erotic function.[61] Equally clear for our present purpose is a Berlin amphora[62] (Pl. 2(b)) dating from the later fifth century. Helen sits on the knees of Aphrodite, and among others present—Paris, Himeros, Nemesis, Heimarmene are all certain—is Peitho, who represents figuratively the power at work on Helen.[63]

So far we have dealt with instances where either Peitho is present at an erotic scene in which there is no specific act of 'persuasion', or else she presides over the persuasion of a woman by a man (or by Aphrodite on behalf of a man).[64] But—to corroborate an observation already made—the man too can be on the receiving end of Peitho's power. On a Vatican oinochoe of 430-425[65] (Pl. 3) the story of Helen has reached a later stage. Menelaos is chasing Helen, who flees in panic towards a statue of Athene. But Menelaos is himself discomfited: Aphrodite stands before him, and a winged Eros is presenting him with a garland. Menelaos has clearly succumbed to this pressure, since his sword has fallen from his grasp. Left of the main action and slightly apart from it stands Peitho, holding up a flowering shoot. The action can, as Jahn saw, be most aptly glossed with Peleus' scornful words to Menelaos in *Andromache* (627-31):

> ἑλὼν δὲ Τροίαν—εἶμι γὰρ κἀνταῦθά σοι—
> οὐκ ἔκτανες γυναῖκα χειρίαν λαβών,
> ἀλλ', ὡς ἐσεῖδες μαστόν, ἐκβαλὼν ξίφος
> φίλημ' ἐδέξω, προδότιν αἰκάλλων κύνα,
> ἥσσων πεφυκὼς Κύπριδος, ὦ κάκιστε σύ.

> When you had captured Troy—I'll be on your traces there, too!—
> you took your wife prisoner, but did not kill her. No: you dropped your
> sword as soon as you saw her breast. You took her kisses, and petted
> the treacherous bitch. Kypris mastered you, you worthless creature.[66]

On the oinochoe Peitho is far more than a decorative addition relevant only by virtue of belonging to Aphrodite's female *entourage*. Rather, she draws together the meaning of the whole scene. In her, the artist has found an imagistic realization of the power of Aphrodite over Menelaos.[67]

If we turn our attention to the 'political' end of the Peitho spectrum, we find little iconographical material that is of direct relevance to us. Nevertheless we do have some likenesses which, while erotic in situation, yet link the goddess to a wider frame of reference. In these cases Peitho is accompanied by Eunomia,[68] Eukleia[69] or Harmonia.[70]

Eunomia has been described[71] as a personification of *'legalità'*, but her functions are in fact much broader. We can see this already in a passage in the *Odyssey* (17.485-7) where Antinoos is being warned not to threaten the beggar in the palace, since the gods

ἐπιστρωφῶσι πόληας,
ἀνθρώπων ὕβριν τε καὶ εὐνομίην ἐφορῶντες.

...go abroad amongst cities, watching men's violence and their good-order.

εὐνομίη is contrasted with anti-social violence, and presumably has the sense of 'orderly behaviour' such as would imply respect for vital customs like hospitality.[72] According to Hesiod, Eunomia was one of the three Horai, the others being Dike and Eirene (*Th.* 901ff).[73] (The rich significance of the trio is made clear by Pindar at *Ol.* 13.6ff, the passage already noticed in which Eunomia, Dike and Eirene are presented as profoundly important for the well-being of a polis.) In a state where the citizens practise εὐνομία there will be social order as opposed to lawlessness and violence:[74] Solon used the word to describe the 'good order' of the city.[75] Nor is the political significance of Eunomia restricted to archaic Greece: Demosthenes connects her with 'justice' and affirms her importance for the maintenance of the social fabric.[76] Thus, though on vases she is usually in the company of Aphrodite and other erotic figures,[77] Eunomia has more far-reaching implications than such colleagues might be taken as implying.[78]

When Eukleia appears on vases she is usually in erotic company; but not always. On an oinochoe in Budapest she is with Eunomia and Apollo, and Schefold[79] interprets the role of the two goddesses in a political sense as representing qualities bestowed by Apollo upon the city. Eukleia was worshipped at Athens jointly with Eunomia,[80] and the pair of them shared a priest.[81] From the description of Eukleia's shrine given by Pausanias at 1.14.5 ('Further on is the temple of Eukleia, this too being an offering from the spoils of the Medes who landed at Marathon') it is quite certain that the significance of the cult extended beyond the erotic.[82] Clearest of all, perhaps, is the passage (*Arist.* 20)[83] where Plutarch says that one Euchidas, who brought glory upon his community, is buried in the sanctuary of Artemis Eukleia at Plataiai, and then goes on to mention that amongst the Boiotians and the Lokrians Eukleia is a marriage goddess—a fine illustration of the inseparability of the two 'sides' of Eukleia.

Harmonia too had both an erotic and a wider political role. In the *Homeric Hymn to Apollo* (194-6) she is linked with Hebe, Aphrodite, the Charites and the Horai; and at A. *Supp.* 1040 with Aphrodite, Pothos, Peitho and the Erotes. But the following passage from Plutarch concerning homosexuality at Thebes indicates that Harmonia's influence extended to more political questions, in similar (if far less politically crucial) fashion to her Roman counterpart Concordia:

It is for the same reason that they have also—and rightly—enshrined in their city the goddess said to be the daughter of Ares and Aphrodite, in the belief that where warlike and aggressive natures have most intercourse with Peitho and the Charites, the state enjoys, thanks to Harmonia, the most balanced and perfect organization. (Plu. *Pel.* 19.2)[84]

It has been argued that when Eunomia, Eukleia, Harmonia and Peitho appear on vases in erotic contexts their significance is limited and unserious. Thus Tillyard, commenting[85] on the red-figure hydria with Peitho and Eukleia,[86] says: 'The scene is of course purely domestic, the artist having given the pretty pet-names Peitho and Eukleia to what he thinks are pretty figures.' Körte expresses much the same view about lekythoi[87] showing, among others, Peitho and Harmonia, since he regards their names as concealing nothing more serious than 'a light-hearted game with poetical ideas and images'.[88] One's reaction to such comments is ambivalent. It would of course be risky to read too much into pictures of pretty girls on ornament boxes. Yet it is impossible to ignore the consistent pattern which we have seen emerging: the characteristics of Eunomia, Eukleia and Harmonia, like the characteristics of Peitho, span the erotic and public spheres. Seductiveness resides not only in Persuasion, but also in Good Order, Noble Reputation, and Harmony.

2.3 'Secular' *peitho*

Of the word-group πείθω/πείθομαι/πειθώ, the verbal forms are much commoner than the nominal form, and, of the verbal forms, the middle is commoner than the active. Linguistic discussion of the trio has tended to centre on the problem of whether the active or the middle is etymologically prior.[89] But what is important to us is not the external observer's 'objective' view of the development of these words but the meaning they were felt to have by the Greeks who spoke and wrote them: not etymology, but usage. The middle πείθομαι can usually be translated by one of the three English words 'obey', 'trust' or 'believe'. All three have in common the notion of acquiescence in the will or opinions of another. Correspondingly, the active πείθω, conventionally translated as 'persuade', can perhaps best be understood as a factitive, meaning 'get (someone) to acquiesce in (some belief or action)', or, more explicitly, 'get one's way over someone in such a way that they πείθεσθαι'.[90] A good instance of the relevance of the idea of 'getting to acquiesce' is the end of the *Oresteia*, where, as will be seen in detail later, Athene's winning-over of the Furies is openly described as a triumph of *peitho*. But what she does goes beyond what we would call 'persuading': she uses a veiled threat, promises, argument, and so forth. If we recognize that the main sense of πείθω is 'I get (someone) to acquiesce', then the character of the scene is more adequately conveyed.

The nominal form πειθώ is a member of the class of Greek nouns which end in -ώ, which were, as Gusmani's study shows,[91] in a high proportion of cases originally proper names designating a quality thought to be typical of the character concerned: Ἀργώ, Ἐρατώ, Θαλλώ, Καλλιστώ, Κλωθώ, etc. Πειθώ comes squarely into this category: Πειθώ is the name given to her who πείθει. Later, as Gusmani again points out, the form in -ώ is extended to appellatives as well as proper names; and here too πειθώ fits the general pattern. For, although early on it was—it seems—exclusively a 'proper' noun, it later became applied not only to the divinity believed to embody a given quality of behaviour but also to that behaviour itself.

As regards the mode in which *peitho* was believed to operate, it is important to realize that there is no necessary connection between *peitho* and language. As H. Fränkel rightly argued,[92] πείθειν should be rendered 'willig machen' rather than 'überreden', since it may function by other means than persuasive words—by bribery, for instance (Hdt. 9.33.3: μισθῷ... πείσαντες, 'having won them over with a bribe'). Gifts can speak louder than words, as Medea was well aware:

> πείθειν δῶρα καὶ θεοὺς λόγος·
> χρυσὸς δὲ κρείσσων μυρίων λόγων βροτοῖς. (*Med.* 964-5)[93]

The story goes that gifts win over even gods; while for mortals gold is more powerful than ten thousand words.

and Nestor's advice at *Il.* 9.112-13 is that an attempt should be made to win Achilles over 'by gentle gifts and sweet words':

> ...μιν... πεπίθωμεν
> δώροισίν τ' ἀγανοῖσιν ἔπεσσί τε μειλιχίοισι.

Sometimes, too, *peitho* worked through the nudge, the wink and the breath of perfume.[94] Throughout the period we are dealing with, relationships between lovers had the qualities which they have always had since the birth of Aphrodite:

> παρθενίους τ' ὀάρους μειδήματά τ' ἐξαπάτας τε
> τέρψιν τε γλυκερὴν φιλότητά τε μειλιχίην τε. (Hes. *Th.* 205-6)

...young girls' chatter, smiles, deceptions, sweet enjoyment, love, tenderness.

Lovers 'prevailed upon' each other; and when they did so, *peitho* was at work. In exceptional circumstances *peitho* might be resisted. Thus, while Aphrodite has power over all others, she cannot *peithein* Athene, Hestia or Artemis:

> τρισσὰς δ' οὐ δύναται πεπιθεῖν φρένας οὐδ' ἀπατῆσαι. (*H. Aph.* (5 Allen) 7)

Three there are whose wits she cannot persuade or beguile.

Occasionally a mortal too might be steadfast: 'Kalypso', says Odysseus, 'did not *peithein* me' (*Od.* 9.33). Yet usually the power of love was too great (Ἔρως ἀνίκατε μάχαν..., 'Love, unconquered in battle ...', S. *Ant.* 781), its charms too heady (Ἔρως δέ νιν μόνος θεῶν θέλξειεν ..., 'Love, alone of the gods, bewitched him (sc. Herakles) ...', S. *Tr.* 354-5), its *peitho* too winning:

> τίνα δηῦτε πείθω
> †.. σαγηντ† ἐς σὰν φιλότατα; τίς σ' ὦ
> Ψάπφ' ἀδικήει;

1 Peitho as companion of Aphrodite. For identifications see p. 45.

2(*a*) *Centre:* Paris leads off Helen. *Left:* Paris' companion Aineias.
Right: Aphrodite extends a protective hand over Helen.
Extreme right: Peitho, flower in hand.

2(*b*) Helen on the knees of Aphrodite. To the right is Paris with Himeros;
to the left, Peitho. For the other figures see ch. 2, n. 63.

3 *Left:* Peitho holding a flowering shoot.
Centre: Menelaos, discomfited before Aphrodite.
Right: Helen at a statue of Athene.

4 Abduction of the daughters of Leukippos from a sanctuary of Aphrodite and the Dioskouroi.

καὶ γὰρ αἰ φεύγει, ταχέως διώξει,
αἰ δὲ δῶρα μὴ δέκετ', ἀλλὰ δώσει,
αἰ δὲ μὴ φίλει, ταχέως φιλήσει
κοὐκ ἐθέλοισα. (*PLF* 1.18-24)

Whom am I to persuade this time [to be drawn?] into your love? Who is doing you wrong, Sappho?

For, if she is running from you, soon she will be pursuing you; if she spurns your gifts, soon she will be offering them herself; if she doesn't love you now, she *will* soon — even if she doesn't wish it.

The paradox is evident: love is aroused by *peitho* yet the victim is under the influence of something as powerful as any *bia* or *ananke* (κοὐκ ἐθέλοισα).

No story illustrates the power of erotic *peitho,* and its opposition to *bia,* better than the encounter between Odysseus and the Sirens in the *Odyssey.* The Sirens exercise irresistible attraction over all mortals who come within ear-shot:

αἴ ῥά τε πάντας
ἀνθρώπους θέλγουσιν, ὅτις σφέας εἰσαφίκηται. (*Od.* 12.39-40)[95]

who charm all mortals who approach them.

As Kirke makes clear, no human decision to resist can stand up to the Sirens' seductiveness; force alone—the tying of Odysseus to the mast of his ship—can prevail. The power of love is delightful, but dangerous, an ambiguity perfectly captured in the visual image which characterizes the Homeric scene: that of Odysseus begging to be allowed to go to the shore on which are scattered the bones of others who have made the same request.

The episode of the Sirens contains no explicit reference to *peitho,* but it includes a word which is semantically very close to it: *thelgein,*[96] meaning 'bewitch' or 'charm'. As these translations imply, the word can be used in magical contexts. Thus the wand of Hermes ἀνδρῶν ὄμματα θέλγει, 'bewitches the eyes of men' (*Il.* 24.343; *Od.* 5.47), and the same term is applied to the power of enchantment which Kirke wields.[97] But θέλγειν, like θελξίμβροτος, θελξίφρων etc., is regularly associated with the charms and enchantments of love,[98] so that Kalypso's attempts to seduce Odysseus into staying for ever with her are described thus:

αἰεὶ δὲ μαλακοῖσι καὶ αἱμυλίοισι λόγοισι
θέλγει, ὅπως Ἰθάκης ἐπιλήσεται... (*Od.* 1.56-7)

and constantly with soft and wheedling words she seeks to bewitch him
into forgetting Ithaka...

In addition, θέλγειν can refer to the effect of words in general, as
when Gorgias applies it (*Enc.* 10) to the spell which incantatory
language can exert. Like πειθώ, θέλγειν covers other magic than the
magic of love.

As the examples of bribery and love show, *peitho* does not work
through language alone; but language is its principal mode of
operation. The best evidence for this comes from the fifth and fourth
centuries.

We may begin with the sophists. To set up as a teacher of any
subject argues a certain faith in the ability of one individual to
persuade another. But the sophists' involvement with *peitho* was
closer than that. As Professor Guthrie puts it: 'Though some of [the
sophists] taught many other things as well, all included political
advancement in their curriculum, and the key to this, in democratic
Athens, was the power of persuasive speech.'[99] One of the things
which young men hoped to derive from the sophists' teaching was
competence in the art of arguing. That, at any rate, is what the chorus
expects Pheidippides to have learned (*Clouds* 1397-8):

σὸν ἔργον ὦ καινῶν ἐπῶν κινητὰ καὶ μοχλευτὰ
πειθώ τινα ζητεῖν, ὅπως δόξεις λέγειν δίκαια.

It is your job, O mover and wrencher of novel expressions, to hit on
some *peitho* to prove the apparent justice of your argument.

Many sophists occupied themselves with technical or philosophical
aspects of language, and some wrote *technai*, 'arts' of rhetoric,
forerunners of Aristotle's brilliant analysis of modes of argumentation, also called the 'art of rhetoric'.[100]

Gorgias stands out from the others as regards his importance for
our theme. He argued, it seems, as follows (DK fr.3):
 (i) that nothing exists;
 (ii) that, even if something did exist, no one could comprehend it;
 (iii) that, even if anyone could comprehend it, he could not pass that
       comprehension on to anyone else.

On the consequences of this startling challenge to the arguments advanced by Parmenides and his successors I quote Professor Guthrie again:

We live in a world where opinion (*doxa*) is supreme, and there is no higher criterion by which it can be verified or the reverse. This leaves the Sophist-orator, master of the art of persuasion both private and public, in command of the whole field of experience, for opinion can always be changed. Only knowledge, based on unshakeable proof, could withstand the attacks of *peitho*, and there is no such thing.[101]

In fact Gorgias propounded what amounts to the most radical confession of faith in *peitho* known to us from Greece. It is in the *Encomium of Helen* (see above, p. 31) that this confidence is at its most explicit, especially in the following famous passage about the power of *logos*:

λόγος δυνάστης μέγας ἐστίν, ὃς σμικροτάτῳ σώματι καὶ ἀφανεστάτῳ θειότατα ἔργα ἀποτελεῖ · δύναται γὰρ καὶ φόβον παῦσαι καὶ λύπην ἀφελεῖν καὶ χαρὰν ἐνεργάσασθαι καὶ ἔλεον ἐπαυξῆσαι. (*Enc.* 8)

Logos is a mighty lord. With a most tiny and invisible body it effects deeds most divine: it can put an end to fear, remove grief, produce joy, increase pity.

This is one point on which the Platonic Gorgias coincides with the real one: 'Many times, Sokrates, I have heard Gorgias maintain that the art of persuasion far surpasses all others and is far and away the best, for it makes all things its slaves by willing submission, not by violence' (*Phlb.* 58a-b).[102]

Sokrates evidently rated *peitho*'s importance highly. In *Kriton* the opposition *peitho/bia* recurs in a way which contrasts utterly with the levity of Gorgias' *Encomium*. For Sokrates and Plato the issue is: how may one rightly live and die in a polis? The answering of this question is a matter of the utmost moral earnestness. Sokrates, and later 'The Laws', urge that political conduct must be based on persuasion, a theme which is raised at 49e-50a:

Sok. 'Look at it this way. If we leave here without having persuaded (μὴ πείσαντες) the city, shall we be doing some people wrong—and those, at that, whom we ought least of all to be harming—or not?'

and is continued by 'The Laws' at 51b:

'...you must either persuade (πείθειν) your country or do what it tells you ...'

and *ibid*.:

'...in war, in court and everywhere else you must do what your city and native land tell you, or else persuade (πείθειν) it according to justice; but the use of force (βιάζεσθαι) is impious against one's mother and father, and much more so against one's native country.'

Finally, at 51e, with 'The Laws' still speaking, the theme receives its fullest treatment. It is worth quoting complete in view of the interesting play on τὸ πείθειν (persuasion) and τὸ πείθεσθαι (obedience), both being deemed to have a role in the well-governed city:

'On the other hand, if any one of you stands his ground when he can see how we administer justice and the rest of our public organization, we hold that by doing so he has in fact undertaken to do anything that we tell him; and we maintain that anyone who disobeys is guilty of doing wrong on three separate counts: first because we are his parents; and secondly because we are his guardians; and thirdly because, after promising obedience (πείσεσθαι), he is neither obeying nor persuading us (οὔτε πείθεται οὔτε πείθει) to change our decision if we are at fault in any way; and although all our orders are in the form of proposals, not of savage commands, and we give him the choice of either persuading (πείθειν) us or doing what we say, he is actually doing neither.'[103]

Sokrates has in mind the moral obligation upon the citizens of the Athenian democracy to effect change by reasoned argument.

A similar faith in *peitho* is reflected in the writings of Lysias and Isokrates, both of whom shared a deep commitment to the spoken word. In the course of the *Funeral Oration* attributed to Lysias there occurs a quite lengthy eulogy of language and persuasion. After mentioning, during a rehearsal of the glorious Athenian past, how the city championed the rights of the fallen 'Seven against Thebes' and succoured the children of Herakles in their flight from Eurystheus, the author asserts a connection between, on the one hand, such struggles for justice, and, on the other, democracy, the rule of argument, and the power of persuasion:

[Our ancestors] were the first and only people in that time to drive out the ruling groups of their state and to establish a democracy, believing the liberty of all to be the strongest bond of agreement; by sharing with each other the hopes born of their perils they had freedom of soul in their civic life, and used law for honouring the good and punishing the evil. For they deemed that it was the way of wild beasts to be held subject to one another by force (βίᾳ), but the duty of men to delimit justice by law, to convince by argument (λόγῳ...πεῖσαι), and to serve these two in act by submitting to the sovereignty of law and the instruction of reason (λόγου). (*Fun. Or.* 18-19; tr. after Lamb, Loeb)

For Isokrates too the possession of persuasive speech is the necessary foundation upon which civilized human social life rests. Animals, he argues, have the advantage over us in many merely physical respects, but

...because there has been implanted in us the power to persuade each other (τὸ πείθειν ἀλλήλους) and to make clear to each other whatever we desire, not only have we escaped the life of wild beasts, but we have come together and founded cities and made laws and invented arts; and, generally speaking, there is no institution devised by man which the power of language has not helped us to establish.[104]

Naturally, Isokrates recognizes that *peitho* has a place in, for example, a monarchy;[105] but its special association is with Athens and Athenian democracy. At *Antid.* 230-6 he maintains that four of the heroes of the Athenian democratic past relied on their eloquence and their power to persuade;[106] while later in the same work he establishes a hierarchy of users of language, from beasts at the bottom, through barbarians, to Greeks in general, and then to the summit, Athens:

Therefore, it is proper for all men to want to have many of their youth engaged in training to become speakers, and you Athenians most of all. For you, yourselves, are preeminent and superior to the rest of the world, not in your application to the business of war, nor because you govern yourselves more excellently or preserve the laws handed down to you by your ancestors more faithfully than others, but in those qualities by which the nature of man rises above the other animals, and the race of the Hellenes above the barbarians, namely in the fact that you have been educated as have been no other people in wisdom and in speech (τῷ καὶ πρὸς τὴν φρόνησιν καὶ πρὸς τοὺς λόγους ἄμεινον πεπαιδεῦσθαι τῶν ἄλλων). (293-4; tr. after Norlin, Loeb)

Athenian self-idealization is often expressed in terms of polarities, of a contrast between Athens on the one hand and the rest of the Greek world, or barbarians, or animals, or Spartans, on the other.[107] In this case the focus of the contrast is the opposition between *peitho* (skill with *logoi*) and its (here implied) contrary, *bia*.

Although on chronological grounds we cannot use Isokrates to help us reconstruct the conceptual background to fifth-century tragedy, it may reasonably be argued that he is merely making explicit that which is implicit in certain views expressed already in the fifth century. (Pheidippides might have agreed: 'But wasn't this law originally made by a man like you and me? And didn't he make it by persuading our ancestors through his arguments (λέγων ἔπειθε)?' *Clouds* 1421-2.) In the case of Plato, however, one can never assume that he is making explicit something implicit in someone else's thoughts or words: he is too idiosyncratic a genius to be representative of anyone but himself. What he says about *peitho* cannot be divorced from the philosophical context in which he says it. In some of his dialogues Plato deals with the relation between rhetoric and truth, and in so doing sets out his position *vis-à-vis* that of Gorgias. If, in contradistinction to Gorgias, you maintain that there are absolute criteria for assessing human behaviour, then the view that there are no finally convincing arguments, but only stronger or weaker ones whose effectiveness depends in practice upon the power of *peitho* — that view will be anathema to you. Plato did believe in such absolute criteria; and consequently he expresses himself as a vigorous opponent of the glorification of *peitho*.

Appropriately enough, this opposition is most fully developed in his *Gorgias*. After the Platonic 'Gorgias' has argued (*a*) that the kind of *peitho* produced by oratory concerns right and wrong (454b),[108] and (*b*) that the kind of *peitho* concerning right and wrong produced by oratory is the kind which engenders *belief*, not knowledge (454e), the Platonic 'Sokrates' attacks him by a devious outflanking movement. He seeks to undercut the value of rhetoric by 'placing' it in terms of an elaborate series of analogies. For example: as cookery is to the body, so rhetoric is to the soul (465d). Rhetoric is a branch of flattery (κολακεία); and of flattery 'Sokrates' says this:

...it is not an art (τέχνη) but a knack (ἐμπειρία), since it has no account to give of the real nature of the things it applies (*text obscure*), and so cannot tell the cause of any of them. I refuse to give the name of art (τέχνη) to anything that is irrational (ἄλογος). (465a)

Here is a measure of the difference between Plato and Gorgias: for Plato, the rhetoric of the sophist-orator can without absurdity be said to be *alogos*, irrational; for Gorgias, the power of *peitho* is the power of *logos*, and neither is to be judged by any higher criterion of truth.

Here we must confront a paradox. On the one hand Plato, in *Gorgias* and elsewhere, displays contempt for the art of the professional persuader; yet, on the other hand, his dialogues are nothing if not attempts to arrive at philosophical truth by *peitho*, one character endeavouring to convince another and, by extension, Plato's audience too. However the paradox disappears on closer inspection; for Plato's position is consistent. The essential point is that, for Plato, the validity of an argument depends on its relationship to an absolute and universal truth. That he is prepared to entertain the possibility of a 'true rhetoric' is clear from *Phaidros*, but such a rhetoric is only conceivable if the orator possesses knowledge of the truth (*Phdr.* 278b-d). For Plato an ideal rhetoric could be 'co-extensive with philosophy'.[109]

In *Timaios*[110] the paradox over *peitho* is resolved in an analogous way. At 51e, in characterizing the distinction between true opinion and intelligence, Plato is dismissive about persuasion:

One (sc. intelligence) is produced by teaching, the other (sc. true opinion) by persuasion; one always involves truth and rational argument, the other is irrational; one cannot be moved by persuasion, the other can; true opinion is a faculty shared, it must be admitted, by all men; intelligence by the gods and only a small number of men. (tr. from H.D.P. Lee, Penguin)

Yet a few pages earlier persuasion was given an august role in the constitution of the universe: intelligence controls necessity by persuading it (47-8). But again there is no inconsistency. Since intelligence is controlling the persuasion, it is *eo ipso* that true or philosophical persuasion which we met in *Phaidros*. It is only persuasion divorced from knowledge for which Plato reserves his contempt.

In the *Statesman*, too, Plato recognizes a type of rhetoric which 'persuades men to do justice and helps in guiding the helm of the state' (303e); but it is in the *Laws* where we find persuasion most securely embedded in the running of the state. Plato's 'Athenian' advocates for the hypothetical Cretan colony whose legal system is being considered the prefacing of laws with preambles, designed to cause the populace to acquiesce voluntarily in the factual provisions of the laws. Once more Plato is very far from advocating the free and critical use of persuasion which the Athenians of the democracy believed in and the Sokrates of the *Apology* embraced; on the contrary, Plato's persuasion is a tool used by the knowledgeable legislator in order to produce and maintain a general conviction that the laws are right and proper and just. For public debates about the justice of the laws there is no room in this 'ideal' state.[111]

2.4 Categories and structures: *peitho* in Greek thought

'peitho' and 'bia'

In order to understand how *peitho* fitted into the system of categories through which Greeks perceived experience, we may start with the main polarity in which it figured, that which opposed it to *bia* ('force' or 'violence').

It will be recalled how in Lysias' *Funeral Oration* (18-19) *peitho* is represented as a characteristic which distinguishes men from (violent) beasts;[112] whereas in Plato's *Kriton* the use of *peitho* is applauded, while that of *bia* is argued to be morally reprehensible.[113] In these cases as in many others, *peitho* is a mark of civilized, *bia* of uncivilized behaviour. This is graphically illustrated on a London hydria[114] (Pl. 4) by the late-fifth-century Meidias painter. It portrays the abduction of the daughters of Leukippos from a sanctuary of Aphrodite and the Dioskouroi. The violent act is regarded with unconcern by Aphrodite, but Peitho (inscription) is hurrying in panic towards the right: a striking visual expression of the *peitho/bia* opposition.

While *peitho* characterizes conduct within a civilized community, *bia* characterizes conduct outside such a community. 'Outside' may be a matter of either geography or chronology. In his *Antidosis* (293-4) Isokrates dwells on a geographical distinction between *peitho*-using and *peitho*-lacking societies: Greeks employ *peitho*; those outside—barbarians — do not.[115] By contrast, in a passage from Kritias (DK fr. 25, esp. 10) *pre*-civilized life is described as being subservient to brute force. The geographical and chronological distinctions are combined in another passage from Isokrates (*Panegyr.* 39-40). He asserts that Athens was the first city to have set down *nomoi* (laws) and established a *politeia* (political constitution), an assertion whose validity 'is apparent from the fact that those who in the beginning brought charges of homicide and desired to settle their mutual differences by *logos,* and not by *bia*, tried their cases under our laws'.[116] Thus a city which relies on *logos* is contrasted both with what went before ('Athens was the first...') and with what happened (spatially) outside.

This extract from *Panegyrikos* associates *nomoi* with *peitho*; and the connection is not fortuitous. In *Kriton,* it will be recalled, it is 'The

Laws' themselves who urge the value of *peitho*. In fact there is a strong parallelism between the oppositions *nomos*/absence-of-*nomos* and *peitho/bia*. Just as the presence of *peitho* distinguishes Greeks from barbarians, so the presence of *nomos* separates Greeks from their lawless barbarian foes (e.g. Hdt. 7.104). Likewise, just as the presence of *peitho* distinguishes humans from animals, so the presence of *nomos* amongst humans sets them apart from animals (e.g. Isokr. *Nikokl.* 5-9, *Antid.* 253-6; Dem. *Against Aristog.* 1.20). A third aspect of the homology between *peitho/bia* and *nomos*/absence-of-*nomos* relates to types of political organization within the framework of the polis. A society which operates without the benefits of *peitho* suffers either from the violence (from 'above') of the tyrant, or from the violence (from 'below') of the intolerant and domineering majority (Xen. *Mem.* 1.2.40ff; cf. Aristot. *E.N.* V. 1134b). Similarly, a society without *nomos* suffers either from an excess of order, as in a tyranny (τὸ δεσποτούμενον, A. *Eum.* 527, 696) or from a deficiency of order, a state of anarchy (τὸ ἄναρχον, A. *Eum.* 696; cf. 526). The presence of *nomos* and *peitho* permits people to live in a civilized intermediate position between the two extremes (Isokr. *Panegyr.* 39). 'Men should have *nomos* for king and *logos* as guide', says Lysias (*Fun. Or.* 19), illustrating the close relationship between the concepts.[117]

A comment by Theognis enables us further to widen our frame of reference. Complaining about the upstart rulers of Megara, he maintains that before coming to power they 'knew neither *dikai* nor *nomoi*' (54), for 'they wore to tatters the goatskins that covered their sides and pastured outside the city like deer' (55-6).[118] Thus the following characteristics are linked together: lack of *dike* (fairness, right order); lack of *nomos*; being 'outside'—in this case, before—civilization; behaving like animals instead of men. This pattern is confirmed by, for example, Herodotos' account (4.106) of the Androphagi, who do not practise 'justice' and have no use for law. These people are geographically rather than chronologically 'outside', but the structural similarity between their case and that of the Megarian rulers is plain. (Analogous too is the behaviour of the Homeric giant Polyphemos. His attitude towards the helpless and puny mortals who find their way to his geographically remote home is violent and unjust; he knows no *themistes*, customary laws (*Od.* 9.

215), and various aspects of his social life, not least his readiness to practise cannibalism and his solitary extra-societal existence, mark him out as uncivilized.[119]) The structural parallel between *peitho* and *dike* can clearly be observed if we confront the extract from Lysias' *Funeral Oration,* already noticed more than once, with a passage from Hesiod's *Works and Days.* For Lysias *peitho,* opposed to *bia,* distinguishes men from beasts.[120] For Hesiod (*W.D.* 274ff), it is *dike* which distinguishes men from beasts, and which is, as a mode of conduct, opposed to *bia:*

> ὦ Πέρση, σὺ δὲ ταῦτα μετὰ φρεσὶ βάλλεο σῇσιν,
> καί νυ δίκης ἐπάκουε, βίης δ' ἐπιλήθεο πάμπαν.
> τόνδε γὰρ ἀνθρώποισι νόμον διέταξε Κρονίων,
> ἰχθύσι μὲν καὶ θηρσὶ καὶ οἰωνοῖς πετεηνοῖς
> ἔσθειν ἀλλήλους, ἐπεὶ οὐ δίκη ἐστὶ μετ' αὐτοῖς·
> ἀνθρώποισι δ' ἔδωκε δίκην, ἣ πολλὸν ἀρίστη
> γίνεται·

> Perses, put this into your heart: give heed to *dike,* forget *bia* altogether. For such is the law which the son of Kronos established for men: that the fish and the beasts and the winged birds should eat each other, since they have no *dike;* but to men he gave *dike,* far the greatest of blessings.

An analogy which has been alluded to several times is *peitho: bia ::* men: beasts. The particular form in which this proportional equation is expressed is in fact only a special case of a more general feature of Greek thought, namely the idea that *language* is something which marks men off from animals.[121] The *locus classicus* is Aristot. *Pol.* 1253a7-18, where man is said to be distinguished from animals because he possesses *logos.* Whereas animals too possess a voice, enabling them to transmit sounds indicating, e.g., pleasure or pain, man alone has language, which enables him to communicate an awareness of moral values; and it is, in turn, shared notions of such values which lie at the basis of household and polis. Before Aristotle arrived at this clear and comprehensive formulation, several other writers, in widely differing contexts, had been using a virtually identical set of ideas. The chorus of Sophokles' *Antigone,* reflecting that 'there are many marvels, but nothing is more marvellous than mankind', included the possession of *phthegma,* 'speech' (354), as one of man's special characteristics. In Euripides' *Suppliants* (201ff)

Theseus describes the transition from pre-civilization to civilization thus:

αἰνῶ δ᾽ ὃς ἡμῖν βίοτον ἐκ πεφυρμένου
καὶ θηριώδους θεῶν διεσταθμήσατο,
πρῶτον μὲν ἐνθεὶς σύνεσιν, εἶτα δ᾽ ἄγγελον
γλῶσσαν λόγων δούς, ὥστε γιγνώσκειν ὄπα...

I praise the god who brought our life out of confusion and beastliness, and gave it order. First, he gave us reason; then a tongue, carrier of words, so that we might recognize [the articulate communication of] the voice...

Speech comes second only to intellect in this account of humanity's origin. Protagoras, too, according to Plato (*Prt.* 322a), ascribed to language a significant place in the transition from nature to culture:
And now that man was partaker of a divine portion, he, in the first place, by his nearness of kin to deity, was the only creature that worshipped gods, and set himself to establish altars and holy images; and, secondly, he soon was enabled by his skill to articulate speech and words (φωνὴν καὶ ὀνόματα ταχὺ διηρθρώσατο τῇ τέχνῃ), and to invent dwellings, clothes, sandals, beds, and the foods that are of the earth...[122]
In Xenophon, not only is mankind's unique possession of *logos* given a physiological basis (*Mem.* 1.4.12: '... though all creatures have a tongue, the tongue of man alone has been formed by them to be capable of contact with different parts of the mouth, so as to enable us to articulate the voice and express all our wants to one another'),[123] but also the importance of speech for men living in a polis is brought out: '...and think of the power of expression (sc. given us by providence), which enables us to impart to one another all good things by teaching and to take our share of them, to enact laws (*nomoi*) and to administer states (*politeuesthai*)' - *Mem.* 4.3.12. To such accounts[124] may be added Lys. *Fun. Or.* 18-19 and Isokr. *Nikokl.* 6 (= *Antid.* 254), where *peitho* is specified as the type of *logos* which is associated with men but not beasts. In short: mankind has the power of articulate speech, and can thus communicate moral values, act politically, acquire knowledge, teach, persuade. Beasts lack this ability. They are, in fact, *aloga zoa*, 'creatures without *logos*' (Xen. *Hier.* 7.3; often in Aristotle).[125]

To draw inferences from metaphors used by individuals to the category-structure of an entire society is a hazardous procedure; but it can on occasions be justified and rewarding. Now several times in Greek poetry we find a metaphorical equivalence between the speech of 'barbarians' and the twittering of birds.[126] A Greek finds it impossible to understand a barbarian, just as a human finds it impossible to understand a beast; or, expressing it more formally:

Greeks : barbarians : : mankind : beasts

If a single metaphor seems a flimsy base on which to erect such an analogy, we may recall that for Isokrates wisdom and speech are qualities in which mankind is superior to animals and Greeks are superior to barbarians (_Antid._ 294). Equally suggestive is the passage in Isokrates' _To Philip_ (16) where Philip needs to possess τὸ πείθειν, 'persuasion', for his dealings with Greeks, but τὸ βιάζεσθαι, 'force', for his dealings with barbarians. So it would seem reasonable to construct a three-fold analogy:

Greeks : barbarians :: mankind : beasts :: _peitho_ : _bia_.

Perhaps, it may be argued, Isokrates' obsession with the importance of speech, and his political concern to emphasize what makes Greek and barbarian different from one another, make him a special case. There is some truth in the objection, but evidence supporting the proportional equation is not restricted to Isokrates.[127] One need only think of Aischylos' _Suppliants,_ in which the Greeks of Argos behave in a way which respects _peitho,_ while the barbarian sons of Aigyptos rely on _bia._[128]

We have now considered a range of polarities which may be seen as homologous with _peitho/bia:_

peitho	_bia_
civilized	uncivilized
inside polis	outside polis
nomos	absence of _nomos_
dike	absence of _dike_
mankind	animals
Greeks	barbarians

It must be emphasized that this table is not a record of a rigid mental system dominated by starkly and invariably opposed contraries. So far from being rigid, the distinctions we have pointed to were supple and manipulable. _Peitho_ and _bia_ are usually opposed to one another; yet a poet can, if he wishes, speak of violent _peitho_ (A. _Ag._ 385-6). _Nomoi_ usually exclude _bia;_[129] yet Hippias can assert (Pl. _Prt._ 337d) that *nomos* is a 'tyrant' that forces (*biazetai*) people to act against their nature.[130] 'Greeks' and 'barbarians' are usually opposed to one another, yet we have the remarkable passage in Plato's *Statesman*, where distinguishing humanity into Greeks and barbarians is likened to separating 'number' into '10,000' and 'all other numbers'—and might not cranes split the world into 'cranes' and 'all other creatures (including mankind)'? (262d-263d).[131] In all three cases the effect of what is being said depends on the fact that an expected opposition is being challenged.

Nor should our table of opposites be taken as implying that 'the Greeks' were a homogeneous group, free from variety and change. On the contrary, different individuals in different places at different times emphasized different aspects of *peitho/bia*. The fact that for Hesiod it is *dike* which distinguishes men from beasts, while for Lysias one of mankind's distinguishing characteristics is the power of persuasive speech, cannot simply be explained by the assumption that *dike* and *peitho* are 'structurally equivalent' in Greek thought. We must also note that Hesiod's poem is centrally concerned with the place of 'justice' in a harsh world, while Lysias, as a speech-writer, has a professional interest in the power of language; in other words, the social context and the individual intention of the writer must be taken into account in the explanation.

All our table is intended to be is a heuristic device which draws attention to certain parallelisms and analogies frequently found in Greek thought. *Peitho/bia* and its homologies are evidenced from a very wide range of contexts, and they tell us a good deal about discriminations which were important in Greek culture. We may turn now to consider the other concept with which *peitho* is often found in relationships of opposition or complementarity.

'peitho' and 'dolos': the ambiguities of persuasion

The closest we can get in English to a translation of *dolos* is 'cunning trick'; but perhaps a better appreciation of its connotations can be gained if we recall a particular *dolos* described in detail by a Greek writer. The *Homeric Hymn to Hermes* portrays the theft of Apollo's cattle by the infant Hermes. The first thing to notice is that Hermes' trickery permits one who is weaker to outwit one who is stronger — as Hermes admits (469), Apollo is 'valiant and strong'. Next, the quality which permits this circumvention of the normal ordering of power-relations is the cunning intelligence, the *metis,* of Hermes (13; 317ff). Third, the trickery is carried out at night, which marks it off from those normal forms of social activity which take place in day-time. (Compare *Il.* 10, which narrates the night episode involving the appropriately-named spy Dolon; and Ajax's night *dolos* in Sophokles' *Ajax*—cf. 47, νύκτωϱ... δόλιος ὁϱμᾶται...) Fourth, the notion of *dolos* is linked closely with that of *apate,* 'deceit', exemplified by Hermes' driving of the stolen cattle backwards in order to confuse possible pursuers, and by his disguising of the traces of his own progress by wearing foliage on his feet.

It is clear that *dolos* is a subversive form of activity. It is often used in situations where one person wishes to get the better of another who is superior in power: if your antagonist will not be persuaded, and his superior strength rules out force, then your only resort is cunning. Thus women were frequently imagined in Greek myth as overcoming their inferiority to men by means of cunning.[132] Deianeira attempted to reassert her position in the house of Herakles by means of the ruse of the supposed love-charm (S. *Tr.*). Medea, inferior by virtue of being a barbarian as well as a woman, got her way over Jason by means of a trick (E. *Med.*).[133] Phaidra deceived Theseus into falsely accusing Hippolytos (E. *Hipp.*). At the end of Euripides' *Hekabe,* the Trojan queen tricked her enemy Polymestor and managed to blind him.[134] The daughters of Danaos treacherously agreed to marry the sons of Aigyptos and then murdered them on the wedding night.[135] Skylla, daughter of Nisos of Megara, treacherously cut from his head the lock of hair on which his life depended (e.g. A. *Cho.* 613ff). Kreousa, seeking revenge on the innocent Ion, conceived a *dolos* by which to poison him (E. *Ion*). And of course the deed of the Lemnian women was notorious (e.g. Ap.Rhod. 1.609ff, where we hear it was done 'in bed', i.e. at night). In short, *dolos* functions as a sort of mirror-image of *bia*: while *bia* is used by one who is superior in power to subdue one who is inferior, *dolos* enables an inferior to subvert the prevailing power of a superior.

The distinction between *dolos* and *peitho* is much more variable and ambiguous than that between *bia* and *peitho*. Sometimes, to be sure, the two are clearly separated, and are used to designate mutually exclusive types of conduct; but sometimes *peitho* is used in a way that makes it virtually identical with *dolos*. We may begin with the former type of case.

In Sophokles' *Philoktetes*, the discussion between Odysseus and Neoptolemos about *how* Philoktetes is to be won over so that he will go to Troy is conducted in terms of a choice between *peitho, bia* and *dolos. Bia* simply means the use of brute force; *dolos* means lying and deception; *peitho* means putting one's cards on the table openly and trying to *convince* Philoktetes that going to Troy is best. Half a century earlier, in Aischylos' *Eumenides,* Athene invokes the power of Peitho to preside over a scene of open argument and public dispute, which has replaced not only the multiple acts of *bia* presented earlier in the trilogy, but also the *dolos* employed by Klytaimestra in entangling Agamemnon in the (metaphorical) net, and by Orestes in similarly deceiving and ensnaring his mother. In these two dramas *peitho* is opposed to *dolos* as frankness is to cunning deceit.[136]

With *Philoktetes* and *Eumenides* we may contrast a passage from *Choephoroi*. The chorus, in its passionate involvement in Orestes' cunning plot to kill his mother, calls for help from two deities, Peitho and Hermes. Hermes is invoked as νύχιος, 'of the night' (728), while Peitho is invoked as δολία, 'tricky' (726).[137] This is far from being the only example of the intimate connection between *peitho* and *dolos*. The Hesiodic *femme fatale* in the adorning of whom Peitho was said to have participated[138] is described elsewhere by Hesiod as a *dolos* (*Th.* 589, *W.D.* 83).[139] Again, it is no coincidence that the episode in the *Iliad* which depicts Hera's seduction of her own husband is often referred to as the *apate Dios*, 'deception of Zeus': for Hera's action is perfectly summed up in the phrase *peitho dolia*, 'tricky persuasion', her aim being to deceive Zeus into forsaking his favourites.

In some contexts, then, *peitho* is characterized by frankness, and is opposed to *dolos* and indeed to any subversion of the normal values of the polis. This is the socially desirable *peitho* which cements the legitimate union of man and wife, and the harmonious agreement of citizen with citizen. But other contexts emphasize that *peitho* can have another face, which retains the seductiveness of its twin, but uses that seductiveness to put the values of the polis in jeopardy. So far from being opposed to *dolos*, this *peitho* may become virtually indistinguishable from it. In the right place *peitho* deserves 'holy reverence' (A. *Eum.* 885); in the wrong place it can be baneful (cf.

τάλαινα, *Ag.* 385), a 'child of Ruin' (*Ag.* 386).[140] This ambiguity is one of *peitho's* fundamental qualities. It is also one of the features explored in tragedy, the genre which, above all others, exposed the ambivalences generated by the cultural world of Greece.

3

AISCHYLOS

Introduction

In the first chapter we saw that the importance of debate, argument and public persuasion is a distinguishing characteristic of the Greek polis in contrast to other earlier or contemporary cultures of the Near East; and we saw that it was in Athens that this distinguishing characteristic achieved its greatest prominence. In the second chapter we found that the Greek concept of *peitho* exhibits features that take us beyond the bald equation *peitho* = 'persuasion', and into the areas of magic and seduction as well as those of rhetoric and politics. It is my aim to show that in the light of these investigations some of the surviving fifth-century Athenian tragedies will make fuller sense.

3.1 *Suppliants*

The generally agreed redating of *Suppliants* to 467-456[1] is of more than passing interest to our enquiry. Political conditions at Athens in the 460s were, even by Greek standards, extremely volatile. We cannot trace this in any detail; but the fact that within a short space of time the Athenians had Kimon ostracized and saw Ephialtes assassinated gives an idea of the chill winds of political acrimony blowing through Athens. One of the foci of these strong passions was the struggle for and against the democratic reforms which were championed first by Ephialtes and then by Perikles. Democracy was under threat. Who knew what the murder of Ephialtes might precipitate? Reading between, and occasionally on, the lines of the *Oresteia,* one guesses that one of the things which might have eventuated was civil war. At any rate, as we look at *Suppliants* it is worth keeping in mind that a dramatic enquiry into the roles of *peitho* and *bia* in a city might have seemed uncomfortably topical to Aischylos' audience.

Since one of the central strands of meaning in *Suppliants* relates to the place of *peitho* and *bia* in personal (particularly sexual) and in political relationships, we have a good opportunity to study a dramatic exploration of both poles of the *peitho* spectrum. As was made clear earlier,[2] we shall be concerned, not with what Aischylos may have 'thought' about *peitho/bia,* but with how these modes of behaviour receive precise and unique theatrical examination. So from now on we shall be engaged in literary interpretation; and, since the only truly satisfying interpretation of a play is that which respects its possession of a gradually unfolding structure with a given direction, rhythm and pace,[3] our analysis will begin at the beginning and end at the end.[4]

The chorus' opening words are Ζεὺς μὲν ἀφίκτωρ, 'Zeus, god of suppliants'. Both here in the parodos and elsewhere later, the name of Zeus is often mentioned. How Aischylos wanted his audience to see the relationship between Zeus's will and the Danaids' actions is a complex question, the answer to which alters in the course of the play; but at the outset his being invoked as ἀφίκτωρ merely adds weight and legitimacy to the maidens' case. But what is that case? What are they running away from?

> οὔτιν' ἐφ' αἵματι δημηλασίαν
> ψήφῳ πόλεως γνωσθεῖσαι,
> ἀλλ' αὐτογενεῖ φυξανορίᾳ
> γάμον Αἰγύπτου παίδων ἀσεβῆ τ'
> ὀνοταζόμεναι ⟨   ⟩.[5] (6-10)

... not because we have been condemned to exile by the people, on the vote of the polis, for having shed blood, but because, in an act of fleeing from men of our own kin (?), we abhor marriage with the sons of Aigyptos, and [we abhor] their impious [...].

The first part of this is plain in import: just as Orestes hastens to reassure Athene that he has not brought pollution to Athens (*Eum.* 445ff), so the Danaids are anxious to affirm that they are ritually pure. More generally, they begin as they mean to go on: for they scotch any fears that they have behaved in an 'anti-polis' way — fears which might bar their reception into Argos.[6] But over lines 8-10 there has been more controversy: what *is* the girls' motivation?[7] For the moment we may simply notice that the only word which can with certainty hint at why they have run to Argos is ἀσεβῆ: their suitors are 'impious'. Lines 11ff begin to fill out the contrast between the wild and lawless sons of Aigyptos and the law-abiding and reasonable Danaids. Danaos is 'leader in counsel', βούλαρχος (contrast 108, the

Aigyptioi with their δυσπαραβούλοισι φρεσίν, 'minds impervious to persuasion'), and he reflects on his conduct like one moving pieces at draughts (12). By contrast the sons of Aigyptos are an ἑσμὸς ὑβριστής, 'insolent swarm' (30), threatening to 'climb upon unwilling marriage beds' (37-9). The proposed union would be, in their view, a negation of marriage: an act of violence and violation.

Imagery soon enforces the same point: the voice of the suppliant crying out for help is like that of the κιρκηλάτου ἀηδόνος, the nightingale driven by the hawk (62). After further implicit appeals for sympathy (70, etc.) the maidens state their claim with greater confidence and urgency: the gods of their ancestors must do the just thing, namely loathe the men's *hybris,* 'insolent violence' (81). The picture of the Aigyptioi as the incarnation of *bia* against both persons and cities is beginning to be built up.

From the wanton aggression of the suitors the mood alters again at 86ff, with the mysterious evocation of Zeus's dark purposes. True, Zeus deals ruthlessly with human aggression, but he does so without *bia*: βίαν δ' οὔτιν' ἐξοπλίζει, 'he musters no violence' (99). This easy strength must, the Danaids implore, be sent against their suitors, for they are violent (104), impervious to persuasion (108), and crazed (109). Naturally enough the girls invoke Artemis, Διὸς κόρα, 'the maiden daughter of Zeus' (145), to succour them as they defend their virginity. With her their relations are directly opposite to those with the Aigyptioi, being based on mutual acceptance and consent (θέλουσα... θέλουσαν, 144). Then comes a further sustained plea to Zeus—their ancestor through Io—and with that the subtly-controlled opening movement draws to a close. The parodos has served to highlight the violence which characterizes the Aigyptioi in their pursuit of sex—violence which seems the more despicable by being set against a background of divine agents who do *not* rely on violence.

Dust in the distance indicates that the maidens' arrival has not passed unnoticed, so Danaos quickly instructs his daughters in how to make the best impression:

> καὶ μὴ πρόλεσχος μηδ' ἐφολκὸς ἐν λόγῳ
> γένῃ...(200-1)

And do not be forward or laggardly in your speech...

Success will depend on the persuasiveness of the Danaids'

demeanour and speech. A little later Danaos couples further advice
with an affirmation of the justice of their cause, mainly in terms of an
image already used in the play:

πάντων δ' ἀνάκτων τῶνδε κοινοβωμίαν
σέβεσθ'· ἐν ἁγνῷ δ' ἑσμὸς ὡς πελειάδων
ἵζεσθε κίρκων τῶν ὁμοπτέρων φόβῳ,
ἐχθρῶν ὁμαίμοις καὶ μιαινόντων γένος.
ὄρνιθος ὄρνις πῶς ἂν ἁγνεύοι φαγών;
πῶς δ' ἂν γαμῶν ἄκουσαν ἄκοντος πάρα
ἁγνὸς γένοιτ' ἄν; (222-8)

Revere the common altar of all the rulers here. Be seated in the holy
place like a flock of doves, in fear of the hawks of like plumage,
enemies of their kin and defilers of their race. How could the bird
which eats a bird be pure? And how could he be pure who marries an
unwilling girl [taking her from] an unwilling father?

Once more the figurative language brings out the Danaids' role as
helpless victims of violence, that of the Aigyptioi as brutal
perpetrators of it. It is worth noticing ἄκουσαν ἄκοντος πάρα,
'unwilling (girl) from unwilling (father)', another reference to the
absence of consent on one side of the proposed union—contrasted
verbally with the relationship with Artemis (θέλουσα... θέλουσαν
ἁγνά... κόρα, 144-5; cf. ἁγνός, 228). At this stage the Danaids'
objection to marriage surely resides in the fact that the particular
union with which they are faced is indissolubly linked with force.[8]

There follows a confrontation between the suppliants and the
representative of the polis from which protection is asked. The
Argive king identifies himself, at length; the chorus does the same, in
brief:

μακράν γε μὲν δὴ ῥῆσιν οὐ στέργει πόλις. (273)

The city has no love of a long speech.

The king is surprised to hear that the girls are of Argive ancestry: had
they been armed with bows he would have taken them for

τὰς ἀνάνδρους κρεοβότους τ' Ἀμαζόνας... (287)

the manless, flesh-eating Amazons...

(Over the extent to which this should be seen as an appropriate analogy, the commentators have differed. Some emphasize the similarities between Danaids and Amazons;[9] others with equal justice remind us that the Amazons were thorough-going warriors in a way the Danaids certainly were not,[10] and that the Amazons' usually manless existence by no means excluded the possibility of occasional liaisons.[11] But no analogy is exact; and the central point is that the Amazons, like the Danaids, are fundamentally hostile to men (ἀνάνδρους, after all).[12])

But Argive the Danaids are; and in an unhurried and regrettably corrupt passage of stichomythia they describe how Zeus and Io originated their branch of the family. But again, *why* are they suppliants?[13] This brings us to what has become the most notorious crux in the play, lines 335-9. I give them as in Page's OCT, with his apparatus:

> Χο. ὡς μὴ γένωμαι δμωὶς Αἰγύπτου γένει.
> Βα. πότερα κατ' ἔχθραν ἢ τὸ μὴ θέμις λέγεις;
> Χο. τίς δ' ἂν φίλους ὄνοιτο τοὺς κεκτημένους;
> Βα. σθένος μὲν οὕτως μεῖζον αὔξεται βροτοῖς.
> Χο. καὶ δυστυχούντων γ' εὐμαρὴς ἀπαλλαγή.
> 337 φιλοῦσ' Marckscheffel   ὄνοιτο Robortello: ὤνοιτο M et M^Σ;
> fort. γ' ὄνοιτο (M. Schmidt)

The notion of subservience in δμωίς, 'slave-woman', adds bite to the chorus' reply to the king at 335, and the line may be rendered: 'That I may not become a slave to the offspring of Aigyptos.' The violence with which the conduct of the Aigyptioi has been characterized so far in the play makes the metaphor of domination quite natural. The king's reply can equally certainly be given as: 'Do you mean that you hate them, or is the marriage against what is right?' At this stage, instead of having the chorus-leader answer: 'The former', or: 'The latter', or: 'Both', Aischylos kept generations of future scholars in work by giving the Danaids *another question*. Line 338 makes it plain that 337 is a rhetorical question, one which amounts to a further (or repeated) reason for not marrying the suitors. But the direction of the rhetorical question is disputed. Reading ὄνοιτο, we get the sense: 'Who would find fault with masters who were dear to one?'[14] In this case the Danaids are saying, 'We are running because we hate them.' With ὤνοιτο we introduce a totally new, socio-legal motive: 'Who would *buy* masters who were one's relations?' This adds an unexpected twist to the girls' argument; but it receives confirmation from the next two lines, which we may translate as follows:

King.   That is how people's families grow in strength.   338
Chorus.   And if things go badly, a separation (= divorce) 339
            is easy.

That is to say, in a marriage between cousins, the women would have no kinsmen of their own to whom they could appeal if their husbands wanted to divorce them. So, 'separation is (too) easy'; while on the other hand to keep the women (and their dowries) within the *oikos* by marrying them to kinsmen might enable the *oikos* to 'grow in strength'. In short, ὄνοιτο squares more happily with 335-6, ὠνοῖτο with 338-9.

This is well-trodden ground, of course, and I have no original solution to offer. It may be that Friis Johansen's assumption (following Wilamowitz) of a two-line lacuna (between 337 and 338) is correct — although, as some critics[15] have suggested, the ambiguity about the Danaids' motivation may here be intentional. But in any event there is one point which must on no account be missed, namely that even if *here* the girls are drawing attention to a social disadvantage for women inherent in cousin-marriage, nevertheless *this is, from the standpoint of the play as a whole, of minimal dramatic significance.*[16] But what does recur, in imagery, particular statement and generalization, and what has already been prominent in imagery, particular statement and generalization hitherto, is the presentation of the proposed marriage as an act of *bia:* that is why the union is rejected, and why until almost the end of the play Aischylos directs his audience's sympathies towards the victims and away from the agents of violence.[17]

When the appeal in iambics fails, the chorus changes key into lyric. Again the Danaids cast themselves in the role of a hunted quarry: they are like a heifer pursued by wolves (351-2). The king keeps to iambics, and his reply leads us into the second area where *peitho* and *bia* operate in this play: politics. We have already seen the king in his opening addresses to the chorus (234-45, 249-73) use an unmistakably monarchical tone: ἀρχηγέτης, 'leader' (251); κρατῶ, 'I rule' (255, 259). Yet Aischylos, writing under the Athenian democracy, has invested the regime in his dramatic Argos—a city evidently offered to us as morally admirable—with traits familiar from the audience's own polis.[18] And that polis operated through the exercise of public persuasion:

οὔτοι κάθησθε δωμάτων ἐφέστιοι
ἐμῶν· τὸ κοινὸν δ' εἰ μιαίνεται πόλις,
ξυνῇ μελέσθω λαὸς ἐκπονεῖν ἄκη.
ἐγὼ δ' ἂν οὐ κραίνοιμ' ὑπόσχεσιν πάρος,
ἀστοῖς δὲ πᾶσι τῶνδε κοινώσας πέρι. (365-9)

It is not my house at whose hearth you sit as suppliants. But if, as a community, the polis is being defiled, then let the people, as a community, take care to work out some remedy. For my part, I would ratify no promise before I have taken counsel with the citizens in this matter.

The chorus will have none of this: while in favour of the seeking of consent in matters of love, they see no objection to the uncomplicated exercise of command in public affairs:

σύ τοι πόλις, σὺ δὲ τὸ δήμιον·
πρύτανις ἄκριτος ὤν
κρατύνεις βωμόν, ἑστίαν χθονός,
μονοψήφοισι νεύμασιν σέθεν,
μονοσκήπτροισι δ' ἐν θρόνοις χρέος
πᾶν ἐπικραίνεις· ἄγος φυλάσσου. (370-5)

But *you* are the polis; *you* are the people. As leader unjudged you rule the altar, the land's hearth, by your single-voting nod; on your single-sceptred throne you determine everything. Avoid defilement.

They invoke Justice and the anger of Zeus (381-6), but against this (387ff) the king most significantly sets 'the law of the polis': 'If by your country's laws (νόμῳ πόλεως) the sons of Aigyptos are your masters, since they claim to be your next of kin, who could oppose their plea?[19] By your own laws you must be tried, and prove these men have no right over you.' The king stands for the *nomos* of the polis, and for decisions reached by consensus.

In the next phase of the argument, both parties are concerned with *kratos*, power.[20] For the Danaids this means domination in love; for the king, political authority. The girls rehearse their refrain-like motif:

μή τί ποτ' οὖν γενοίμαν ὑποχείριος
κράτεσιν ἀρσένων· (392-3)

Might I never become subject to the power of [the] males.

—power exercised in what would be an 'evil-minded marriage' (394).
Pelasgos, on the other hand, is thinking of a *kratos* which is at once
absolute and based on consent:

εἶπον δὲ καὶ πρίν, οὐκ ἄνευ δήμου τάδε
πράξαιμ' ἄν, οὐδέ περ κρατῶν... (398-9)

I said it before: I would not do this without the people, even though I
am ruler...

The Danaids again place their faith in Zeus (402ff), yet for the
mortal, Pelasgos, the choice between war and pollution is none the
less a real one. Indeed, the issue of human choice between two almost
equally undesirable alternatives is soon revealed as the central
dramatic turning-point, as also happens at a comparable point in the
dramatic structure of nearly all Aischylos' other surviving works.[21]
For, when the maidens have sung once more of the *hybris* and *bia* of
the Aigyptioi and have expressed once more their ultimate faith in
Zeus (418-37), in the following scene the crisis, in its full
etymological sense, is reached.

The king's speech at 438ff is in a poor state of repair, but one thing
is clear enough: in order to support his decision to avoid bloodshed
(by refusing the request of asylum) he employs a distinction between,
on the one hand, financial loss and injury caused by inappropriate
words, both of which may be put right; and, on the other hand,
kindred murder, which cannot be remedied. The rhetorical structure
is triple ('money... and a word...; but *blood* ...'); yet within it we see
the opposition so central to our play, that between violence and the
almost magical power of language:

γένοιτο μύθου μῦθος ἂν θελκτήριος· (448 Page)

a word might be the enchanter of a word...

The epithet with μῦθος recurs almost identically with Peitho at the
end of the play (1040); and in fact our present context is another
variation on the *peitho/bia* opposition.

As it turns out the connection between language and violence is much closer than the king's analogy allows. Since the girls have so far failed in their attempt to persuade him by words, they resort to a more direct form of action by threatening suicide at the images of the gods. At 478-9 he accepts the weight of the case which the maidens have been pressing all along:

ὅμως δ' ἀνάγκη Ζηνὸς αἰδεῖσθαι κότον
ἱκτῆρος· ὕψιστος γὰρ ἐν βροτοῖς φόβος.

But still, one must respect the anger of Zeus, god of suppliants — for that is the highest dread amongst mortals.

Linguistically as well as morally he appropriates the Danaids' stance and makes it his own: his words are a complex echo of earlier prayers by the girls,[22] and, correspondingly, he echoes the girls' own judgement of their suitors as displaying *hybris* (487).

Once the king has been won, the next matter is how to persuade the people. A concerted attempt at political *peitho* is needed, in which both the Danaids' demeanour and the king's oratorical *savoir faire* play a part. He invites them to leave the altar and to move to a 'level precinct' (508). The maidens' fear of abduction is expressed in terms of the by now familiar animal imagery (509-11); but eventually the king manages to still their anxieties sufficiently to allow Danaos himself to vacate the scene. Their joint aim will be political:

ἐγὼ δὲ λαοὺς συγκαλῶν ἐγχωρίους
σπεύσω, τὸ κοινὸν ὡς ἂν εὐμενὲς τιθῶ,
καὶ σὸν διδάξω πατέρα ποῖα χρὴ λέγειν. (517-19)

(σπεύσω is a conjecture by Martin, but the sense is not really in doubt.)

I shall hasten to call together the local people, so that I may make the community well-disposed [to you], and I shall teach your father what sort of things to say.

And the king's last line before his exit invokes the power on which a favourable outcome depends:

πειθὼ δ' ἕποιτο καὶ τύχη πρακτήριος. (523)

Let *peitho* follow, and success in action.

The function of the ensuing choral song is to raise the issues generated by the action so far to a higher level of generality so that, when a return is subsequently made to dramatic particularity, the action will quite simply mean more, and more resonantly, than before. The opening strophe (524-30) resumes the maidens' faith in the power of Zeus, and restates their loathing of the impending marriage:

> ἄλευσον ἀνδρῶν ὕβριν εὖ στυγήσας· (528)

> Ward off the men's insolent violence, rightly loathing it.

Hitherto the prime claim which the Danaids have had on Zeus's attention has been in virtue of their role as suppliants and his role as protector of suppliants. But by now they have left the altar, and their appeal for sanctuary stands a fair chance of succeeding. Understandably, then, the ground of their prayers to Zeus changes. They have a further basis for expecting Zeus's blessing: consanguinity.

One of the most intriguing strands of meaning running through the play is that relating to Io.[23] It first appears at the outset of the parodos as the Danaids describe their long journey from Egypt to Argos:

> ... Ἄργους γαῖαν, ὅθεν δὴ
> γένος ἡμέτερον τῆς οἰστροδόνου
> βοὸς ἐξ ἐπαφῆς κἀξ ἐπιπνοίας
> Διὸς εὐχόμενον τετέλεσται. (15-18)

> ... to the land of Argos, whence our race, claiming descent from the gadfly-stung cow through the touch and breath of Zeus, had come to completion.

The Danaids, maidens, flee in anguish from Egypt to Argos; Io, a maiden, fled in anguish from Argos to Egypt. The story is ostensibly invoked in order to establish the Danaids' claim on Argive help; but its effect is also to hint at parallels, and differences, between the fates of the 'victims' concerned. A little later in the parodos the Io story is once more mentioned, and the hint in ἐξ ἐπαφῆς κἀξ ἐπιπνοίας Διὸς ('through the touch and breath of Zeus') is made explicit. The Io legend is useful for the Danaids to cite since it exemplifies Zeus's kindness and gentleness to their race. When Io's wanderings ended, the product of the touch and breath of Zeus was Epaphos, personification or incarnation of the act itself (45ff). Already the Io myth stands at some distance from the Danaids' own plight, since *her* wanderings ended in union and birth. Surely the Danaids' story will not end the same way? The next time Io is mentioned, during the dialogue between the chorus-leader and the Argive king at 291ff, the facts of the case are set out in matter-of-fact narration: Io was keeper of keys at Hera's temple in Argos when Zeus conceived a passion for her; Hera turned her into a cow, setting the watcher Argos over her as guardian; Hermes killed Argos, but Hera sent the gadfly, which pursued the maiden to the Nile. There Zeus touched her in gentleness, and Epaphos was born. What the story shows is a pursued victim whose fate is to have union, and give birth, in an atmosphere of reconciliation.

As we said, the Danaids appeal to Zeus in virtue of his kinship with them through his union with Io (535-7); and once more the story of Io's persecution, wanderings and eventual relief is evoked, this time not in bare iambic but in richer choral language. Now Aischylos is a writer with the ability to compress meaning to such an extent that sometimes Greek practically bursts under the pressure: he is rarely otiose, or repetitive, without purpose. So we must do him the respect of assuming that the Io myth is repeated so often for a special dramatic reason or complex of reasons. This is not hard to find. Io is an innocent victim of male violence; she, like the Danaids, has the audience's sympathy (ἀθλίαν, 'poor', 572). Most important is the implication behind 576ff:

† βία † δ' ἀπημάντῳ σθένει
καὶ θείαις ἐπιπνοίαις
παύεται...

She was stayed by painless strength (?) and divine breaths...

Whatever the precise text, it is plain that it is the non-violence of Zeus's power which is being referred to (cf. *P.V.* 849, about the same episode: ἐπαφῶν ἀταρβεῖ χειρὶ καὶ θιγὼν μόνον, 'laying a gentle hand upon you, merely touching'). We heard earlier in *Suppliants* (99: βίαν δ' οὔτιν' ἐξοπλίζει '[Zeus] musters no violence') that Zeus is *not* a user of *bia*; now we learn that a term which describes what Zeus's power is like is *thelgein* (571), a word whose sphere of reference we found to be intimately related to *peitho*. Here, then, is a possible scenario from which the Danaids' own story may diverge, or to which it may correspond: *bia* is replaced and transfigured by consent and reconciliation.

Danaos returns, and describes a scene which must have resembled an assembly in democratic Athens at the period when the play was put on—an arena where decisions were taken on a basis of public *peitho*:

> εὖ τὰ τῶν ἐγχωρίων
> δήμου δέδοκται παντελῆ ψηφίσματα. (600-1)

Authoritative decrees have been passed by the local people — and to good effect.

ψήφισμα is unambiguously political, and δήμου δέδοκται recalls the formula ἔδοξε τῷ δήμῳ, 'the people resolved'. The chorus replies with a question which suggests not only the ideology of democratic method but even its practical realization:

> ἔνισπε δ' ἡμῖν ποῖ κεκύρωται τέλος,
> δήμου κρατοῦσα χεὶρ ὅπῃ πληθύνεται. (603-4)

Tell us what way the decision has gone, and on what side the victorious hands of the people were in a majority.

Then at 605-24 Danaos provides a resumé of the functioning of the assembly. He begins with the outcome (ἔδοξεν Ἀργείοισιν, 'the Argives resolved', 605), and then describes the voting process in vivid pictorial terms (607-8). At 614 the consequences to anyone disobeying the city's decision are made explicit: he who fails to help the Danaids in time of need 'is to be deprived of civic rights, and exiled by the people' (ἄτιμον εἶναι ξὺν φυγῇ δημηλάτῳ). We remember 6-7, where the Danaids said they had 'not been condemned to exile by the people, on the vote of the polis, for having shed blood' (οὔτιν' ἐφ' αἵματι δημηλασίαν ψήφῳ πόλεως γνωσθεῖσαι...). Then as now the Danaids' behaviour is in accordance with the laws of, and is sanctioned by, the polis. (Of the Aigyptioi, as we shall see, the reverse is true.) Danaos continues by recounting the process of persuasion which led to the vote:

> τοιάνδ' ἔπειθε ῥῆσιν ἀμφ' ἡμῶν λέγων
> ἄναξ Πελασγῶν... (615-16)

Such was the persuasive speech made by the lord of the Pelasgians on our behalf...

and:

δημηγόρους δ' ἤκουσεν εὐπειθὴς στροφὰς
δῆμος Πελασγῶν, Ζεὺς δ' ἐπέκρανεν τέλος. (623-4)²⁴

The Pelasgian people was easily won over as it heard the oratorical
turns of speech; and Zeus added his ratification.

For the moment, political *peitho* is supreme.

Danaos' last words referred to Zeus, and the chorus develops the
theme of the gods' relation to the action in the next ode. Not
surprisingly, Zeus himself is the divinity to whom they allude most
often here, twice under the explicit heading Zeus Xenios (627,
671-2), and four times more too. But for the first time another god
begins to make his presence prominently felt: Ares. One of the
functions of the ode is to convey the chorus' prayers of thanksgiving
to Argos, and one of the prayers they repeat most often is that the
violence of war may keep far from the city. War is evoked through
images which, though lacking the unforgettable precision, resonance
and pathos of the χρυσαμοιβὸς δ' Ἄρης σωμάτων ('Ares the
gold-changer of bodies') lines in *Ag.* (437ff), still produce,
cumulatively, a telling effect. At first, Ares is μάχλος, 'lustful',

τὸν ἀρότοις θερίζοντα βροτοὺς ἐναίμοις· (636)²⁵

he that reaps mortals in bloody fields.

Then the image becomes more exact and—because the object of
comparison in the metaphor is now something delicate and
vulnerable—more moving:

ἥβας δ' ἄνθος ἄδρεπτον
ἔστω, μηδ' Ἀφροδίτας
εὐνάτωρ βροτολοιγὸς Ἄ-
ρης κέρσειεν ἄωτον. (663-6)

May the bloom of [Argos'] youth be unplucked, and may the
bed-fellow of Aphrodite, man-killing Ares, not cull its flower.

Goddess of love with god of war; love is (as we saw²⁶) associated with
flowers, while Ares destroys them: the coupling is in every way an
oxymoron. Why does Aischylos recall their mythical union here?
First, because the Danaids recoil from both these divinities, from sex
no less than war; second (perhaps) in order to suggest that even the

power of pure violence is connected with a more benign, positive and creative force: even when force has the upper hand—as it will shortly in the drama—there is still a hope that love and reconciliation may replace it.

In the third passage to mention Ares he is represented as an enemy of all social and literal harmony, and as a friend of violence and discord:

> μηδέ τις ἀνδροκμὴς λοιγὸς ἐπελθέτω
> τάνδε πόλιν δαΐζων,
> ἄχορον ἀκίθαριν δακρυογόνον Ἄρη
> βίαν τ᾽ ἔνδημον ἐξοπλίζων· (679-83)

> And let no man-slaying destruction come upon this city to tear it,
> arming dance-less, music-less, tear-bringing Ares, and civil violence.

As in *Pythian* I, he who opposes order and harmony is opposed to music also. But the Ares of *Pythian* I, βιατάς ('violent') though he be, succumbs to music (10-12); the Ares of the chorus' imagination in *Suppliants* is not so amenable.

What *bia* means for human beings will very shortly be enacted on the scene. In political terms, *bia* is the mortal enemy of a city; when *bia* is present, *peitho* is banished, and with *peitho* go law and justice. It is precisely this contrast between the lawful city and the power of violence that the Danaids build into one of their last prayers for Argos:

> φυλάσσοι τ᾽ ἀτρεμαῖα τιμὰς
> τὸ δάμιον, τὸ πτόλιν κρατύνει,
> προμαθὶς εὐκοινόμητις ἀρχά·
> ξένοισί τ᾽ εὐξυμβολούς,
> πρὶν ἐξοπλίζειν Ἄρη,
> δίκας ἄτερ πημάτων διδοῖεν· (698-703)

> And may the people, who rule the polis by thoughtful and
> jointly-deliberating wise government, retain their privileges firmly;
> and to strangers may they grant, before mustering Ares, the right of a
> fair hearing without harm.

Since Danaos' return the action of the play has been dominated by politics: by the exercise of political *peitho,* and by the threat of political *bia* to come. Now the erotic joins the political as the focus of dramatic interest: the Aigyptioi, violent in both regards, are about to land.

Danaos advises the girls to behave non-violently (724); but perhaps envoys might come from the suitors who would behave oppositely, 'laying their hands on you as prizes', ῥυσίων ἐφάπτορες (728).[27] Having already observed Aischylos' sensitivity to language, we may suspect that the repetition of a word from the same root as 'touching' (ἐπαφή/Ἔπαφος) is unlikely to be innocent. Until now the act of 'touching' and 'laying hands upon' has been associated with Zeus in the Io story; this time it is associated with the Aigyptioi, whose position in the analogous story of the pursuit of the Danaids corresponds to that of Zeus. By delicately hinting at the parallelism between the divine suitor and his fifty human counterparts, Aischylos begins to suggest that this union may, perhaps, eventually end, as that one did, in reconciliation and harmony. But the Danaids' thoughts are far from harmony: as the Aigyptioi are birds of prey, so their ships are 'swift-winged' (734); indeed they are *bia* incarnate:

> ἐξῶλές ἐστι μάργον Αἰγύπτου γένος
> μάχης τ᾽ ἄπληστον. (741-2)

The wild race of Aigyptos is abominable, insatiable of battle.

They have sailed here κότῳ (744), 'in wrath'; another typically Aischylean linguistic resonance, since hitherto (347, 385, 478, 616, and cf. 427) it has been Zeus whose κότος has been mentioned. Against this attack the Danaids need help, for they do not have Ares in them (749)—force is on the side of their adversaries, who are 'like crows' (751) in their disrespect for sanctity, like dogs in their recklessness (758, 760), and like 'bloodthirsty and ungodly monsters' (αἱματηρῶν ἀνοσίων τε κνωδάλων, 762; cf. the 'uncivilized' associations of κνώδαλα at 264) in their general savage behaviour.

Once more Danaos leaves on an errand of political *peitho*:

> ἄγγελον δ᾽ οὐ μέμψεται
> πόλις γέρονθ᾽, ἡβῶντα δ᾽ εὐγλώσσῳ φρενί. (774-5)

The polis will find no fault with a messenger who is old in years, but young in the skill of his oratory.

The Danaids meantime are left to sing of their fear. So dominant is their obsession with the impending assault that their language is quite literally coloured by it: they seek some 'dark' (κελαινόν) refuge in the earth (778); they would like to become 'black' smoke (μέλας, 779); and their hearts are 'black' with fear (κελαινόχρως, 785). Hitherto blackness has been a quality by which the Danaids have contrasted themselves with the Aigyptioi (e.g. τὰν μελανόζυγ' ἄταν, 530; μελαγχίμοις γυίοισι, 719-20); but now the men are so close that they infect even the girls' imaginings. 'Anything', they cry, 'rather than suffer a marriage which tears my heart by violence' (πρὶν δαΐκτορος βίᾳ καρδίας γάμου κυρῆσαι, 798-9). And again they characterize the Aigyptioi with the qualities of *bia* and *hybris* (812, 821; 817), invoking Zeus's wrath to punish them (811ff).

In spite of the desperate corruption of 825-902, it is at least clear that a herald of the Aigyptioi arrives and behaves as we have been led to expect: he threatens to abduct the suppliants by force. Words for violence, outrage and assault recur like a nightmarish refrain: βιαίων, 'violent deeds' (830); τιλμοὶ τιλμοὶ καὶ στιγμοί, 'pluckings, pluckings and brandings' (839); δεσποσίῳ ξὺν ὕβρει, 'with a master's insolent violence' (845); βία (in some case or other), 'violence' (849); βίᾳ βίᾳ τε πολλᾷ, 'with violence, with much violence' (863); ὑβρίζοντα... ὕβριν, '[your] insolent violence' (880-1). The threat of immediate assault (884) elicits animal imagery still more monstrous than hitherto: the assailant is an ἄραχνος, 'spider' (887); a δίπους ὄφις, 'two-legged snake' (895); an ἔχιδνα, 'viper' (896); a δάκος, 'biting creature' (898). But this verbal defence does no good, and presently the dragging threatened at 884 is on the point of being converted (909) into scenic action, when the king of Argos returns.

As before he upholds the rule of *nomos* in the polis. As aliens the Aigyptioi should have acted through local representatives (πρόξενοι, 919); why did they not do so? Such niceties are not to the taste of the herald:

> οὔτοι δικάζει ταῦτα μαρτύρων ὕπο
> Ἄρης, τὸ νεῖκος δ' οὐκ ἐν ἀργύρου λαβῇ
> ἔλυσεν, ἀλλὰ πολλὰ γίγνεται πάρος
> πεσήματ' ἀνδρῶν κἀπολακτισμοὶ βίου. (934-7)

This is not a case that Ares decides after hearing witnesses, nor does he settle the quarrel upon receipt of silver; no, first there are many fallen bodies of men, many kickings-off of life.

But the advocate of *bia* is immediately countered by the disciple of *peitho:*

> ταύτας δ᾽ ἑκούσας μὲν κατ᾽ εὔνοιαν φρενῶν
> ἄγοις ἄν, εἴπερ εὐσεβὴς πίθοι λόγος·
> τοιάδε δημόπρακτος ἐκ πόλεως μία
> ψῆφος κέκρανται, μήποτ᾽ ἐκδοῦναι βίᾳ
> στόλον γυναικῶν· (940-4)

As for these girls, you could take them if pious argument were to persuade them to go willingly and with free consent; but such is the unanimous popular vote that came ratified from the polis, that this group of women never be surrendered under compulsion (*bia*).

With words of war and violence still on his breath, the discomfited herald departs, and the king reiterates his and his people's championing of the suppliants in 'political' terms:

> προστάτης δ᾽ ἐγὼ
> ἀστοί τε πάντες, ὧνπερ ἥδε κραίνεται
> ψῆφος. τί τῶνδε κυριωτέρους μένεις; (963-5)

I am your protector, and so are all the citizens, whose authoritative vote this was. What greater authority than these do you await?

The maidens react with an anapaestic hymn of blessing and thanksgiving. Taplin has argued[28] with disturbing cogency that these lines bring into the play very grave dramatic-structural weaknesses —weaknesses which may suggest the drastic conclusion that a 'proper exit speech' for the Argive king and 'a full strophic act-dividing song' have fallen out to be replaced by interpolated anapaests.[29] Until the points raised by Taplin are settled one way or the other, any interpretative remarks offered on the content of the lines must remain provisional. But, with that in mind, we may note one intriguing detail. The Danaids apparently give instructions to their servant-girls[30] in these words:

> τάσσεσθε, φίλαι δμωίδες, οὕτως
> ὡς ἐφ᾽ ἑκάστῃ διεκλήρωσεν
> Δαναὸς θεραποντίδα φερνήν. (977-9)

Take up your positions, handmaidens, according as Danaos allotted to each of us a dowry of servants.

The important detail is φερνήν, 'dowry': that the maidens have (metaphorical) dowries hints at the possibility that some day they may marry.

When Danaos returns, his long speech completes the action so far and prepares for and prefigures what is to come. After expressing thanks to Argos, he turns to a matter which he has already spoken about at length, namely the impression which the Danaids are to seek to make in their adopted home. His words relate interestingly to some of the main themes of the play:

> ὑμᾶς δ᾽ ἐπαινῶ μὴ καταισχύνειν ἐμέ,
> ὥραν ἐχούσας τήνδ᾽ ἐπίστρεπτον βροτοῖς·
> τέρειν᾽ ὀπώρα δ᾽ εὐφύλακτος οὐδαμῶς·
> θῆρές σφε κηραίνουσι καὶ βροτοί· τί μήν;
> καὶ κνώδαλα πτεροῦντα καὶ πεδοστιβῆ
> †καρπώματα στάζοντα † κηρύσσει Κύπρις
> †καλωρα κωλύουσαν θωσμένειν ἐρῶ†
> καὶ παρθένων χλιδαῖσιν εὐμόρφοις ἔπι
> πᾶς τις παρελθὼν ὄμματος θελκτήριον
> τόξευμ᾽ ἔπεμψεν ἱμέρου νικώμενος·
> πρὸς ταῦτα μὴ πάθωμεν ὧν πολὺς πόνος,
> πολὺς δὲ πόντος οὕνεκ᾽ ἠρόθη δορί,
> μηδ᾽ αἶσχος ἡμῖν, ἡδονὴν δ᾽ ἐχθροῖς ἐμοῖς
> πράξωμεν. (996-1009)

> I counsel you not to bring shame upon me: for this youth of yours makes people's eyes turn to look at you. Delicate fruit is not easy to guard. Beasts spoil it—men too. How could they not? Animals winged and land-walking alike... Kypris proclaims... *[text obscure]* When a man goes by lovely, shapely girls, he shoots at them a bewitching (*thelkterion*) arrow-glance from his eye, conquered by desire. So, let us not suffer that which we have avoided with so much labour, with a sea-crossing of such length in our ship. Let us not shame ourselves, nor bring joy to our enemies.

Hitherto the metaphor of bestiality has been used to describe the Aigyptioi; and the demeanour of their herald has confirmed the appropriateness of the comparison. Now for the first time it is normal sexual desire which is linked with violence (κηραίνω) and savagery (θῆρες, κνώδαλα). Is Danaos going too far here? Does Aischylos want us to see the father's concern for his daughters' virginity as overstated? Or would the audience have regarded his advice as perfectly reasonable, a part of his and the Danaids' continuing desire to behave properly in the polis? Perhaps it could be played either way. At any rate the girls agree to comply, although they do so in terms which show that Aischylos is again preparing the ground for a *union* later on:

εἰ γάρ τι μὴ θεοῖς βεβούλευται νέον,
ἴχνος τὸ πρόσθεν οὐ διαστρέψω φρενός. (1016-17)

Unless the gods have devised some new plan, I shall not turn from my mind's former pathway.

The final scene is an antiphonal lyric coda in which two contrasting sets of voices are heard, usually identified as those of the Danaids and their maidservants.[31] Being inclined to excise 966-79 (and in particular 977-9), Taplin[32] sees no reason to retain the maidservants. But how, then, account for the contrasting voices? Taplin's first suggestion is that the chorus could divide into two hemichoruses, since 'an Aischylean chorus has no rigidly uniform outlook; it will change its attitudes to suit the context and to further the dramatist's larger purposes' (*Stagecraft* 231). But if in what followed *Suppliants* (see below, p. 88) the Danaids divided 49/1 (? or 48/2) on the issue of murder *vs* marriage—the exception(s) being Hypermestra and Amymone[33]—then surely to have the chorus divide *equally* in this play is, from the dramatic point of view, rather odd? Alternatively, Taplin suggests, we might follow Friis Johansen[34] in replacing the maidservants by a Bodyguard. If the anapaests are indeed to go, then there may be something to be said for this view. Thirdly, there is Taplin's preferred solution, that it is with Danaos that the chorus sings. To my mind this does not work, especially if (*Stagecraft* 232 n. 2) Hermann's distribution is retained. For: (i) Why should Danaos sing 1038-42? These lines, a continuation of 1034-7 about Aphrodite's power (so Page in OCT), are peculiar in Danaos' mouth: they cannot be a *warning* against erotic desire, yet that is what we should expect in view of 996ff. (ii) Why should Danaos advocate marriage, as he does, on this distribution, in 1050-1? Unless this is a deliberately false trail, then the recommendation would come more naturally from a neutral observer. In short it seems to me that while the question of the anapaests is unresolved as a whole we may as well retain the maidservants; and in any case most of the observations I shall make could stand with little change even if the voice which contrasts with the Danaids' own is not that of their maids but of some other group.

We may begin with a textual crux at 1030ff. Page's OCT has this:

(Χο.)   ἐπίδοι δ' ᾿Άρτεμις ἀγνὰ
               στόλον οἰκτιζομένα, μηδ' ὑπ' ἀνάγκας
               γάμος ἔλθοι· Κυθερείᾳ
               στυγερὸν πέλοι τόδ' ἆθλον.
<Χορὸς θεραπαίνων>
               Κύπριδος <δ'> οὐκ ἀμελὴς ἑσμὸς ὅδ' εὔφρων...

Κυθερείᾳ στυγερὸν Burges: Κυθερείας· στύγειον Μ; στύγιον Stephanus.

Chorus: May pure Artemis look upon our company in pity; and
               may marriage not come [upon us] by compulsion — may
               such a struggle be hateful to Aphrodite.
(?) Chorus of
handmaidens: Yet this friendly swarm (band, group) is not heedless of
               Aphrodite.

In adopting Burges' solution to the problem caused by the nonsensical στύγειον Page prints a text in which the chorus prays to both Artemis and Aphrodite. This strikes me as highly improbable: it is the maidservants (or 'the alternative voice') who will urge the claims of sexual love, and if the Danaids themselves pray to Aphrodite the point of this disagreement is lost. Just as at the start of the play, the Danaids invoke 'their' goddess as protectress of chastity: θέλουσα δ' αὖ θέλουσαν ἀγνά μ' ἐπιδέτω Διὸς κόρα... ('May the pure maiden-daughter of Zeus look willingly upon me, willing too...', 144-5) is echoed by ἐπίδοι δ' ᾿Άρτεμις ἀγνά ('May pure Artemis look upon...', 1030). In the first passage chastity is associated for the Danaids with consent, the prospective union being implicitly (and of course elsewhere explicitly) presented as violent and a product of compulsion. So in 1030-1 any connection between the power of Aphrodite and compulsion would be, bearing in mind that it is the Danaids speaking, entirely suitable. This is just what we get with the following reading:

ἐπίδοι δ' ῎Αρτεμις ἁγνὰ
στόλον οἰκτιζομένα, μηδ' ὑπ' ἀνάγκας
γάμος ἔλθοι Κυθερείας·
στύγιον πέλοι τόδ' ἆθλον.

May pure Artemis look upon our company in pity; and may marriage not come [upon us] under the compulsion of Aphrodite: may such a struggle be as death itself.[35]

To this the servant-girls, voicing what is, in terms of the development of the plot, a 'progressive' sentiment, urge that the power of sexual love need not be uniquely associated with violence: for Peitho is one of the children of Aphrodite:

μετάκοινοι δὲ φίλᾳ ματρὶ πάρεισιν
Πόθος ᾷ τ' οὐδὲν ἄπαρνον
τελέθει θέλκτορι Πειθοῖ·
δέδοται δ' ῾Αρμονίᾳ μοῖρ' ᾿Αφροδίτας
†ψεδυρὰ τρίβοι τ' † ᾿Ερώτων. (1038-42)

And accompanying their dear mother are Pothos ('Desire') and she to whom nothing is denied, bewitching (*thelktori*) Peitho; and to Harmonia[36] has been given the (?) whispering share of Aphrodite's work, and the paths of the Erotes ('Loves').

Thus the positive, delightful features of sexual love, neglected for dramatic reasons (except in the Io story) until now, are given due emphasis, in such a way that the Danaids' own attitude is seen now to be a biased and one-sided one. To their mistresses' prognostication of war and bloodshed as the inevitable concomitants of union the servant-girls oppose a contrary view of the future: one sealed by reconciliation. They do so by calling on the name of Zeus—not only as ally of the Danaids *qua* Zeus Hikesios, but also as lover of Io:[37]

ὅ τί τοι μόρσιμόν ἐστιν, τὸ γένοιτ' ἄν·
Διὸς οὐ παρβατός ἐστιν
μεγάλα φρὴν ἀπέρατος.
μετὰ πολλᾶν δὲ γάμων ἅδε τελευτὰ
προτερᾶν πέλει γυναικῶν. (1047-51)

That which is fated, would happen; the great, uncrossable mind of Zeus cannot be gainsaid; this end—marriage—you share with many women before you.

Understandably reluctant to hear Zeus invoked against their own
case, the Danaids call immediately upon him themselves at 1052-3;
but after their servants have again advised prudence, the Danaids at
last admit the possibility of an harmonious outcome:

> Ζεὺς ἄναξ ἀποστεροί-
>   η γάμον δυσάνορα
> δάιον, ὅσπερ Ἰὼ
> πημονᾶς ἐλύσατ' εὖ
>   χειρὶ παιωνίᾳ κατασχεθών,
> εὐμενῆ βίαν κτίσας,
>
> καὶ κράτος νέμοι γυναι-
>   ξίν. τὸ βέλτερον κακοῦ
> καὶ τὸ δίμοιρον αἰνῶ
> καὶ δίκᾳ δίκας ἔπε-
>   σθαι ξὺν εὐχαῖς ἐμαῖς λυτηρίοις
> μηχαναῖς θεοῦ πάρα. (1062-73)

May lord Zeus keep away hateful marriage with men who are our foes
— Zeus, who in kindness freed Io from pain, checking her with healing
hand, establishing benevolent force (*bia*) — and may he assign power
to the women. I approve the better part of woe, the 'two-thirds' *[text
uncertain]*, and agree that justice should follow the just, according to
my prayers, by saving measures from god.

Once more the Io story—a coda offering a mythical paradigm of
benediction and hope.

That *Suppliants* was part of a connected trilogy, and that, if so, it
was first in that trilogy, are likely but not finally provable
hypotheses.[38] About what may have followed *Suppliants* we can
make a few guesses, for which *Prometheus Bound* offers a useful
point of departure. At 853ff Prometheus, in discussing Io's progeny,
relates how the Danaids will, with one exception, kill their new
husbands. Beyond mentioning that the odd Danaid out gave birth to a
race of kings, Prometheus says nothing about the sequel to the
murderous night's work. Now it is very probable that, if there was a
connected Danaid trilogy, it dealt with the killings by the many and
the mercy of the one—because that is one of the few features of the
myth 'which are common to all the versions, or at least not
contradicted by one or more of them'.[39] But how was the conflict of
attitude between the many and the one resolved? Our only real clue is

provided by Athenaios (13 (600b)), who quotes a fragment from Aischylos' *Danaids,* the most plausible candidate for third play in the trilogy.[40] In this fragment Aphrodite exalts the power of *eros*:

ἐρᾷ μὲν ἁγνὸς Οὐρανὸς τρῶσαι χϑόνα,
ἔρως δὲ Γαῖαν λαμβάνει γάμου τυχεῖν,
ὄμβρος δ' ἀπ' εὐνάεντος Οὐρανοῦ πεσὼν
ἔκυσε Γαῖαν, ἡ δὲ τίκτεται βροτοῖς
μήλων τε βοσκὰς καὶ βίον Δημήτριον,
δενδρῶτις ὥρα δ' ἐκ νοτίζοντος γάμου
τέλειός ἐστι· τῶν δ' ἐγὼ παραίτιος.

Holy Heaven desires to penetrate Earth; the desire to achieve union seizes Earth. The sperm from Heaven's lust fell, and impregnated Earth; and she bore for mortals flocks of sheep and Demeter's corn; and the fruit of trees came to full growth as a result of that moist union. All this I helped to cause.

The lines seem to be an authoritative expression of a point of view about one of the central dramatic issues set up in *Suppliants*: namely, were the Danaids right to run away from marriage with the Aigyptioi? Specifically, the lines sound like a divine seal of approval on the conduct urged by the maidservants at the end of the first play. If, further, the lines belong to a place in the text as dramatically important as the end, then they might be part of a climax of harmony and reconciliation, perhaps involving the remarriage of the Danaids to a new set of men,[41] or anyway involving their reconciliation to the *idea* of marriage.[42] And if—further again—we suppose the lines to have been delivered in a trial scene (as many have believed and believe), then we have the perfect end to our analysis: erotic and rhetorical *peitho* combine triumphantly in the defeat of *bia*.

However, it is all too easy to fall into the trap of forcing the Aischylean works we do *not* have to fit the model of reconciliation offered by the *Oresteia*. Instead of such speculations[43] it will be more profitable briefly to review the role of *peitho* in *Suppliants*. I would argue that the complex thematic unity of *Suppliants* becomes much clearer in the light of the fact that *peitho* and *bia* span both the erotic and the political spheres. To say that the play is *about* the implications of *peitho/bia* would be greatly to overstate the matter. But that this opposition is important in the work is uncontestable. If we were to reduce what Aischylos is 'saying' to a proposition, I suppose it would amount to this: both in sexual relations between individuals and in the handling of a city's political affairs, persuasion is preferable to violence. Even such a simple affirmation as this would have carried considerable weight in the troubled political atmosphere of Athens in the 460s; but *Suppliants* is far more than the assertion of a simple proposition. It is the *realization* of that proposition in precise and concrete dramatic terms.

3.2 *Prometheus Bound*

With a few exceptions[44] the recent scholarly literature on this play has been chiefly concerned with questions of authorship and date. Griffith,[45] Taplin[46] and West[47] have advanced arguments which must give pause to anyone who believes either that *Prometheus Bound (P.V.)* is by Aischylos, or that it has poetic merits, or both. More important for the subject of this book, however, is the fact that there are considerable thematic resemblances between *P.V.* and the undisputed Aischylean corpus. Whoever wrote *P.V.*, it is clear that the play deals seriously with issues relating to *peitho/bia* in various spheres of human and divine life. When I speak of the author as 'Aischylos', this should be taken to imply no greater certainty about 'authenticity' than the fluidity of the present debate permits. In any case, even if *P.V.* was either wholly or partly *not* by Aischylos, it is not without interest that *peitho/bia* figured in the dramatic vision of (at least) one other playwright than the great three.

The theme of *peitho* in *P.V.* has three main aspects. The first might be described as political or, in view of the huge scale of the action, cosmic. It concerns the question of whether the universe is to operate on the basis of harmonious agreement or violent struggle. This issue is close to the heart of the drama, bearing as it does on the 'problem' of Zeus's despotic (*bia*-dominated) rule, and on the related matter of whether that despotism grew milder (more responsive to *peitho*) later in the trilogy.

The second aspect of *peitho* is erotic. As in Aischylos' *Suppliants,* there is an exploration of the opposition between *peitho* and *bia* in love. The principal character through whose fate this theme is examined is Io. Since she, like Prometheus, is a victim of Zeus's violence, her story is linked with and adds resonance to the main conflict between the god and the Titan; and the eventual reconciliation between Io and Zeus under the sign of erotic *peitho* will almost certainly have prefigured the subsequent (though in *P.V.* still distant) reconciliation between Prometheus and Zeus under the sign of political/cosmic *peitho.*

While the preceding two facets of *peitho* suggest strong similarities with *Suppliants*, the third constitutes rather a link with the dramatic world of Sophokles. In *P.V.*, as in many of Sophokles' plays, compliance or obduracy in the face of persuasion is a variable used by the playwright to shape the audience's attitude towards the characters' moral behaviour. In particular, Prometheus' total deafness to all attempts to deflect him is employed to powerful effect, as it lends individual force and precision to the general atmosphere of intransigence which broods over the play.

P.V. begins, as it ends, with an act of violence: Kratos and Bia bring on Prometheus, whom Hephaistos is to fetter to a rock. The punishment has been commanded[48] by the new tyrant (10 and *passim*) of the universe, Zeus. The significance of the fact that his two special constables are Kratos and Bia becomes apparent if we compare our play with the *Theogony,* which the playwright evidently had in mind as he worked.[49] Hesiod recounts (383ff) that four of the offspring of Styx—Zelos, Nike, Kratos and Bia—were a permanent part of Zeus's entourage. That 'Might' and 'Violence' should reside with the supreme god is natural; having defeated Kronos by force, Zeus rules in power:

> ὃ δ᾽ οὐρανῷ ἐμβασιλεύει,
> αὐτὸς ἔχων βροντὴν ἠδ᾽ αἰθαλόεντα κεραυνόν,
> κάρτει νικήσας πατέρα Κρόνον· (*Th.* 71-3)

He rules in heaven, himself holding the thunder and the blazing bolt, having conquered by his power his father Kronos.

But we have only to continue this quotation to see that Hesiod's Zeus does not rely on force alone:

> εὖ δὲ ἕκαστα
> ἀθανάτοις διέταξε νόμους καὶ ἐπέφραδε τιμάς.

And fairly did he in all respects assign rules and fix privileges for the immortals.[50]

In the *Theogony* Zeus's force is counterbalanced by the positive and enriching divinities with whom he is associated: Metis, Themis, Eunomia, Dike, etc.[51] And similarly in other plays of Aischylos Zeus's *kratos*—in itself neither a positive nor a negative word—is more than once explicitly associated with his *dike (Supp.* 437, *Cho.* 244-5, cf. fr. 734 M). But in *P.V.* the situation is different. In contrast to the Zeus of *Supp.* 673, ὃς πολιῷ νόμῳ αἶσαν ὀϱθοῖ, 'who sets destiny upright according to his ancient law', the power of Zeus of *P.V.* is recent:

> ἅπας δὲ τραχὺς ὅστις ἂν νέον κρατῇ. (35)
>
> One whose power is recent is always cruel.

It is highly appropriate that his minions should be 'Might' and 'Violence'.

Two further points are worth noting in the speech in which Hephaistos replies to Kratos and then turns to Prometheus. First there is the remark at 26-7:

> ἀεὶ δὲ τοῦ παρόντος ἀχθηδὼν κακοῦ
> τρύσει σ', ὁ λωφήσων γὰρ οὐ πέφυκέ πω.
>
> Unceasingly the pain of your present woe will torture you; for the one who will relieve you has not yet been born.

The reference to future 'relief', even though phrased negatively, is to be taken as a first hint that the present conflict may end in reconciliation. But, secondly, the road to be travelled before any such reconciliation is hard and long:

> Διὸς γὰρ δυσπαραίτητοι φϱένες... (34)
>
> For Zeus's mind is hard to sway...

Our play is a chronicle of hard-headedness, of unsuccessful attempts at *peitho*; and the first to be characterized as intransigent is Zeus.

Like the guard in *Antigone*, Kratos, Bia and Hephaistos reveal through their attitudes and behaviour what it is like to serve a despot. It is superfluous to mention that the fettering is *described* as an act of *bia* (15,74): the simulated driving of a wedge through the Titan's body will have created an impression beyond the power of any words.[52] Eventually, abandoned alike by the vicious Kratos, the compassionate but obedient Hephaistos and the wordless Bia,

Prometheus is left to his fate.

With the arrival of the chorus of Okeanids new light is cast on the impasse between the Titan and Zeus:

> νέοι γὰρ οἰ-
> ακονόμοι κρατοῦσ' Ὀλύμ-
> που, νεοχμοῖς δὲ δὴ νόμοις
> Ζεὺς ἀθέτως κρατύνει,
> τὰ πρὶν δὲ πελώρια νῦν ἀιστοῖ. (148ff)

New helmsmen hold power in Olympos; Zeus, with fresh laws, rules as a despot; the Mighty Ones of old he now obliterates.

On one side is the new regime, politically unjust and based on force, and led by him whose mind is ἄγναμπτος, 'inflexible' (164). True, there is a reference to the future, and to a possible relenting by Zeus:

> οὐδὲ λήξει
> πρὶν ἂν ἢ κορέσῃ κέαρ ἢ παλάμᾳ τινὶ
> τὰν δυσάλωτον ἕλῃ τις ἀρχάν. (165-7)

...nor will he relent until his anger is satiated, or else someone by some stroke wrests from him that unassailable empire.

Here Thomson's note (on 178-9 in the lineation of his edition) is good:

παλάμη is properly the palm of the hand, hence a deed wrought by sleight of hand, a device, artifice, also a deed of violence. The Okeanids, like Hephaistos in 27, have nothing definite in mind, but their language suggests to the audience the contingency in which the secret of Prometheus (of which he is at once reminded...) consists, not explained at length till 939ff [=907ff in OCT].

There is no suggestion of a harmonious reconciliation: if Zeus ever relents, it will be because his temper is sated (κορέσῃ) or because events in heaven have taken another turn in the same sort of direction which brought Zeus himself into power (παλάμᾳ).

If that is Zeus's attitude, Prometheus, who is literally unmoving and immovable, affirms that his mind is similarly steadfast:

> καί μ' οὔτι μελιγλώσσοις πειθοῦς
> ἐπαοιδαῖσιν θέλξει... (172-3)

He will not bewitch me (*thelgein*) with the honey-sweet charms of
peitho...

Peitho, with its usual accompaniment of 'honeyed' words and
bewitching enchantments, is explicitly rejected. Prometheus indeed
knows of a 'new plan' which will result in Zeus's downfall (170-1),
but will disclose nothing until Zeus frees him. This is a classic
stalemate: neither party will be the first to give way. The chorus puts
this into words at 178ff. On the scene is Prometheus, Ajax-like in
his stubbornness:

> σὺ μὲν θρασύς τε καὶ πικραῖς
> δύαισιν οὐδὲν ἐπιχαλᾷς...

> You are brazen, and yield not at all to your bitter anguish...

Behind it is Zeus, unmovable and unresponsive to *peitho*:

> ἀκίχητα γὰρ ἤθεα καὶ κέαρ
> ἀπαράμυθον ἔχει Κρόνου παῖς. (184-5)

> The son of Kronos has a temper that is not to be moved; his heart
> cannot be won over.

One last time Prometheus looks ahead over the centuries to a
reconciliation with Zeus:

> οἶδ᾽ ὅτι τραχὺς καὶ παρ᾽ ἑαυτῷ
> τὸ δίκαιον ἔχων Ζεύς· ἀλλ᾽ ἔμπας
> μαλακογνώμων
> ἔσται ποθ᾽, ὅταν ταύτῃ ῥαισθῇ·
> τὴν δ᾽ ἀτέραμνον στορέσας ὀργὴν
> εἰς ἀρθμὸν ἐμοὶ καὶ φιλότητα
> σπεύδων σπεύδοντί ποθ᾽ ἥξει. (186-92)

> I know that Zeus is harsh; that he keeps justice in his own possession;
> yet he *will* one day grow mild, when, in the way I have said, he is
> broken. Then, calming his stubborn anger, he will come to loving
> reconciliation with me: and there will be eagerness on both sides.

Two things are worth noting here. The first is the phrase παρ᾽ ἑαυτῷ
τὸ δίκαιον ἔχων, 'keeping justice in his own possession'. Just like
Kreon in *Antigone*, who treats his own private edicts as if they were
nomoi of the city (cf. *Ant.* 211ff), Zeus has justice 'in his
possession'. This is worlds away from δίκαια Διόθεν κράτη, 'Just is

the power that comes from Zeus' (A. *Supp.* 437): it is in fact the auto-legality of the tyrant, the only free man in his kingdom (*P.V.* 50). The second point is that, even though he can foresee a time when he and Zeus will come together in 'love' (φιλότης), Prometheus believes that this will only be after his adversary has 'broken' (ῥαισθῇ): foreknowledge in no way weakens the Titan's resolve to hold out till the last.

The long narration which starts at 197 evokes the war in heaven and Prometheus' role in it. Once more a comparison with Hesiod is illuminating. In *P.V.* the Titan begins abruptly with the words,

> ἐπεὶ τάχιστ' ἤρξαντο δαίμονες χόλου
> στάσις τ' ἐν ἀλλήλοισιν ὠροθύνετο... (199-200)
>
> As soon as the gods began their anger and factions sprang up amongst them...

— there is no suggestion about where right lies. By contrast, Hesiod makes clear (*Th.* 472) that the quarrel between Zeus and Kronos is closely linked with the crimes which Kronos had committed against his father and children, and for which he must pay. It is a small difference,[53] but one which serves to weaken the moral authority of Zeus as against that of his opponents.

When the dispute developed, says Prometheus, he was at first on the side of his fellow Titans:

> ἐνταῦθ' ἐγὼ τὰ λῷστα βουλεύων πιθεῖν
> Τιτᾶνας...
> οὐκ ἠδυνήθην. (204-6)
>
> Then I tried to persuade the Titans by giving them the best advice... but I failed.

Prometheus offered them stratagems (206), but they rejected his aid, relying instead on *bia* (208). Now Prometheus' mother Themis-Gaia had told him that the victory would be won not through force (212) but through guile (213). Thus he changed sides, and gave his *advice* (219) to Zeus. This connection between Prometheus and mind—indeed, in view of Prometheus' name it is more than just a 'connection'—is significant. Whereas in the *Theogony* Zeus's victory had been achieved through the force of the 'hundred-handers', in *P.V.* the decisive help came from Prometheus' wits.[54] So while in the

Theogony Zeus attains power through force alone but later tempers that force in a spirit of just rule, in *P.V.* Zeus has won power by using the aid of intelligence yet is trying to retain it without any such assistance.[55] We may well guess that a resolution of the conflict explored in the play will only come if the lord of the universe agrees to base his government on something more than mere force.

As Prometheus' narration proceeds, the picture of Zeus's regime gains in definition and emphasis. τύραννος and τυραννίς ('tyrant', 'tyranny', 222, 224) recur; Zeus's ingratitude is stressed; and in particular the desire to destroy humanity—although mitigated by a willingness to create a new race (232-3) — is presented as entirely unmotivated: there is no suggestion that humanity had *done* anything to incur Zeus's wrath. The aggressor (cf. the Aigyptioi) appears in a very bleak light; and Prometheus' gifts to mortals—although the giving of them was admittedly a 'mistake' (260, 266)—can seem nothing but generous altruism in the face of a despot.

The next scene, like the prologue, shows up the characteristics of the government by portraying the contrasting attitudes of those subject to it. This time the conflict is between unflinching rebel and shameless trimmer. Okeanos, because of his 'permanent' status as World-Stream, has to reach an accommodation with whoever happens to be ruling the universe; and, having done so, he urges Prometheus to do likewise:

> ὁρῶ, Προμηθεῦ, καὶ παραινέσαι γέ σοι
> θέλω τὰ λῷστα καίπερ ὄντι ποικίλῳ.
> γίγνωσκε σαυτὸν καὶ μεθάρμοσαι τρόπους
> νέους...
> ἀλλ', ὦ ταλαίπωρ', ἃς ἔχεις ὀργὰς ἄφες,...
> σὺ δ' οὐδέπω ταπεινός, οὐδ' εἴκεις κακοῖς... (307-20)

I see, Prometheus; and, cunning though you are, I want to give you the best advice I can. Know yourself, adopt new ways... Poor wretch, cast away your present anger... Still you are not humble, you do not yield to misfortune...

The tone is familiar from Sophokles (notably *Ajax, Antigone, Elektra*): in spite of entreaties to εἴκειν, 'yield', the hero remains adamant.[56] The obstinacy of Prometheus and Zeus is reaffirmed through insistent verbal repetition: the words hurled by the Titan are τραχεῖς, 'harsh' (311), just like the temper of the tyrant (324). Okeanos offers to intervene on Prometheus' behalf, but Prometheus knows that the enterprise will fail:

> πάντως γὰρ οὐ πείσεις νιν· οὐ γὰρ εὐπιθής. (333)

> You will be wholly unable to persuade him — he is not easily persuaded.

He reinforces this view in a long speech; but Okeanos still retains his confidence that words can heal the quarrel:

> οὔκουν, Προμηθεῦ, τοῦτο γιγνώσκεις, ὅτι
> ὀργῆς νοσούσης εἰσὶν ἰατροὶ λόγοι; (377-8)

> Do you not know, Prometheus, that words are healers of the disease of wrath?

Prometheus accepts the medical metaphor, [57] but grimly adapts it: 'You cannot reduce a swelling before it has reached its moment of ripeness.' Having listened to Prometheus' argument that the attempt to *peithein* Zeus would be fruitless, Okeanos reaches the same conclusion about the present interview — and off he goes.

Far less superficial is the involvement and sympathy of his daughters. Their description of Zeus's behaviour is one with which Prometheus himself could concur:

> ἀμέγαρτα γὰρ τάδε
> Ζεὺς ἰδίοις νόμοις κρατύνων
> ὑπερήφανον θεοῖς
> τοῖς πάρος ἐνδείκνυσιν αἰχμάν. (402-5)

> By this unhappy example Zeus, ruling by his own private laws, demonstrates his arrogant spear-power over the gods who ruled before.

Zeus's 'spear-power' is secured by 'private laws'. When the ode (397-435) is ended there follows silence, after which Prometheus amplifies the significance of his punishment, and justifies the 'crime' which has led to it, by describing what benefits he brought to man. More important than the details is the generalization with which he begins:

> ...σφας νηπίους ὄντας τὸ πρὶν

ἔννους ἔθηκα καὶ φρενῶν ἐπηβόλους. (443-4)

Whereas before they were witless, I gave them mind, and the ability to think.

Just as the source of Prometheus' bargaining power with Zeus is something in his mind—a secret; and just as his role in the battle in heaven was to supply intellectual assistance; and just as his very name identifies him with a capacity for thought; so Prometheus' characteristic gift to men is *nous*. Once more there is a direct contrast with Zeus, who wanted to exterminate mankind: the ultimate act of *bia*. In *P.V.* there is no suggestion of gifts bestowed on mortals by Zeus; Prometheus is their unique benefactor.[58]

Thus far the dramatist has offered us a fairly uncomplicated identification between the power of Zeus and the aggressive use of force: Zeus's *kratos* is *bia*. But in the choral ode which begins at 526 matters become more problematical. Hitherto Zeus has been described as a cruel despot; yet suddenly the Okeanids sing of the need for *piety* towards him (526ff), and of his *harmony*:

†τοὕποτε†
τὰν Διὸς ἁρμονίαν θνατῶν παρεξίασι βουλαί. (550f)

Never *[text obscure, but a negative seems certain]* will mortals' plans trespass outside the harmony of Zeus.

But, as the action develops, Zeus will show himself once more to be not merely a stern punisher but a cruel torturer as he tries to extort the secret from Prometheus. Is there an irreconcilable contradiction between the 'despotic' and 'benevolent' conceptions of Zeus? In a famous exposition of the dilemma, Karl Reinhardt denied any such difficulty. According to him, the force and the harmony are two aspects of the same divinity, just as in the 'Hymn to Zeus' at *Ag.* 182 the *charis* of the lord of the universe is *biaios* when it comes upon men.[59] However, there is a grave objection to this supposed analogy between the two plays. In *Agamemnon bia* receives the sanction of the supreme god only when (as in the case of the chastisement of Troy) it is used to further the cause of *dike*. By contrast, in *P.V. bia* is manifestly not a *charis*—it has in fact no relation to justice at all.[60] What then of the invocation of Zeus's 'harmony'? I think we must assume that the chorus is being credited with the kind of insight into and beyond events which they could not have in terms of their 'character', but which it is useful, from the point of view of the dramatist, for them to be able to express. They are relating the stage action not to the law of Zeus as so far exemplified, but to his law as, in time, it will become. In other words the chorus' remark about Zeus's harmony is a prefiguration of the eventual change which will come about in the universe when at last Prometheus and Zeus are reconciled and the temper of the divine regime softens.

The second antistrophe constitutes a transition to the· next episode. The Okeanids are struck by the contrast between the plight of Prometheus as they see it before their eyes and their memory of the happy marriage, conducted under the auspices of *peitho* (πιθών, 560), when Prometheus was wedded to the Okeanid Hesione. In terms of dramatic impact this makes a good foil for the entry of the demented Io, who is suffering the painful consequences of a union contracted under the sign of *bia*. And there may, too, be a prefiguring (as Thomson suggests in his commentary) of that other possible future union of which the threat looms over the action and which is so central to Prometheus' own fate: the marriage of Zeus with one who will bear a son more powerful than its father. But at any rate the passage is an effective bridge between the areas we described earlier as 'cosmic' and 'erotic'.

'Why should I mention Io? Why indeed? I have no notion why.' These wicked words from Housman's legendary *Fragment* must have flitted across the brain of many a critic of *P.V.* in moments of idleness or perplexity. But the Io scene is really no irrelevance. Both Io and Prometheus are victims: she of Zeus's sexual *bia*, he of his political *bia*. The interest of this part of the play stems from the differing attitudes and prospects of the two persecuted individuals whose paths have briefly crossed.

In her distracted and bewildered question at 578ff Io shows that, although she cannot fathom the reason for her sufferings, she knows well enough who their instigator is. As many commentators have observed, Aischylos goes out of his way to lay the blame for Io's troubles on Zeus rather than Hera. In other tellings of the myth (e.g. A. *Supp.* 295ff) the major factor is Hera's jealousy; but in *P.V.*, although that motive is not absent (cf. 592, 600 (?), 703-4, 900), it pales in importance beside the ever-present figure of Zeus.

Prometheus recognizes in the new arrival a fellow victim of *bia* (592). Like the pain of Prometheus, that of Io too needs a μῆχαρ, 'remedy', or φάρμακον, 'healing cure' (606), and she asks if any such healing is in prospect. In answer Prometheus first reveals his identity but then, ever concerned for the well-being of mortals, is reluctant to cause Io more anguish by revealing the future to her. Eventually he consents; but first, at the request of the chorus, Io sets her own fate in context.

Dreams came to her whose purpose was to *peithein* the young maiden to accept Zeus's love:

αἰεὶ γὰρ ὄψεις ἔννυχοι πωλεύμεναι
ἐς παρθενῶνας τοὺς ἐμοὺς παρηγόρουν
λείοισι μύθοις· (645-7)

Constantly night visions would come to me in my room, seducing me with smooth words...

and to offer her the delights of ἵμερος, 'desire', and Κύπρις, 'sex' (649, 650; cf. πόθος, 'longing', at 654). But when immediate compliance did not follow, the divine tone altered: Io was to be driven from her father's house and set a-wandering. If not, Zeus would adopt his familiarly violent approach:

κεὶ μὴ θέλοι, πυρωπὸν ἐκ Διὸς μολεῖν
κεραυνὸν ὃς πᾶν ἐξαϊστώσοι γένος. (667-8)

And if he (sc. my father Inachos) refused (sc. to expel me) then Zeus's fiery thunderbolt would fall and utterly eradicate the race.

Io's father did refuse, but Zeus's *bia* was not to be gainsaid:

ἀλλ᾽ ἐπηνάγκαζέ νιν
Διὸς χαλινὸς πρὸς βίαν πράσσειν τάδε. (671-2)

... but Zeus's bridle compelled him to do this against his will (*pros bian*).

Without delay her shape was changed and the gadfly came to plague her. Once more there is a significant difference from other versions of the myth.[61] In the Danaids' account (A. *Supp.* 307) the gadfly is only sent after the murder of Argos, and is a product of Hera's jealousy; while in *P.V.* the plain inference is that it was Zeus who was responsible for sending it.

So the context of Io's fate is set; and it links her with Prometheus. But in the future their fates will diverge. He will be motionless; she, always wandering. At 707-35, the Titan prophesies the next stage of the mortal's travels and then, turning to the chorus, draws the inference which the play so far has unequivocally substantiated and which unites his own experience with Io's:

> ἆρ' ὑμῖν δοκεῖ
> ὁ τῶν θεῶν τύραννος ἐς τὰ πάνθ' ὁμῶς
> βίαιος εἶναι; (735-7)

Does the ruler of the gods not seem to you to be, in all matters equally, violent?

Next, by a perfectly seamless transition (Io: 'How can I bear it?' Prometheus: 'How would you react to *my* fate, then?'), dramatic interest switches back to Prometheus' own future. He mentions a circumstance which, because of her past, is of concern to Io also—the eventual overthrow of Zeus:

> Πρ.   ἥδοι' ἄν, οἶμαι, τήνδ' ἰδοῦσα συμφοράν.
> Ιω   πῶς δ' οὐκ ἄν, ἥτις ἐκ Διὸς πάσχω κακῶς; (758-9)

> Pr.   You would rejoice, I think, to see that outcome.
> Io   How could it be otherwise, in view of the pain I suffer at
>   Zeus's hands?

Quite naturally, in view of the bond of sympathy which life has created between Prometheus and Io, he reveals to her more about the great secret: it will be as a result of a marriage—how fittingly ironical in the context of his relations with Io—that Zeus will fall. Now the future opens up still further. Is there no means, asks Io, by which that downfall might be avoided (769)? 'Not unless I am released.' 'Who could release you if Zeus were unwilling?' 'One of your descendants.' So at one stroke, and for both characters, it comes to seem that the awful present may end in something better: for Io, there will be a child; for Prometheus, a deliverer.

Two more narratives are spoken by Prometheus, in which he completes his account of Io's wanderings, past and to come. He ends with the event which prefigures, and is the physical prerequisite for, his own release: the union of Io with Zeus. As in the Okeanids' words about Zeus's harmony, we are given a glimpse of a world in which force is not the only determinant of relations between individuals:

ἐνταῦθα δή σε Ζεὺς τίθησ' ἐγκύμονα⁶²
ἐπαφῶν ἀταρβεῖ χειρὶ καὶ θιγὼν μόνον· (848-9)

There Zeus will impregnate you, laying a gentle hand upon you, merely touching.

Among Io's descendants the contrast between erotic *peitho* and *bia* will be graphically illustrated once more: the sons of Aigyptos will use force; so in turn will their brides; but μίαν... παίδων ἵμερος θέλξει, 'desire will charm (*thelgein*) one of the girls' (865). And so the line will be continued until the birth of him who will free Prometheus.

The ode which follows Io's exit is flat as poetry but relevant thematically. The idea 'May I keep out of Zeus's way' grows naturally enough from the Io episode, and has a kind of echo in the theme of Zeus's own unwisdom in marriage—the burden of Prometheus' secret. This is indeed the point with which the last scene opens, as Prometheus launches into a defiant outburst (907-10). He becomes more and more outspoken, and the chorus fears for him (932); but he will not bend. Eventually one last character approaches with the intention of persuading Prometheus to yield up his secret.

Hermes' tone is as curt and rude (cf. 944) as his message: 'Give up your secret, and don't try any double-dealing.' For

Ζεὺς τοῖς τοιούτοις οὐχὶ μαλθακίζεται. (952)

Zeus is not softened by such behaviour.

But if Zeus does not soften, nor does his adversary:

ἁπλῷ λόγῳ τοὺς πάντας ἐχθαίρω θεούς,
ὅσοι παθόντες εὖ κακοῦσί μ' ἐκδίκως. (975-6)

In a word, I hate all the gods who, having received benefit from my hands, repay me with abuse and injustice.

Nevertheless, before the final catastrophe we see one more glimmer of hope:

Πρ.   ὤμοι. Ἑρ. τόδε Ζεὺς τοὖπος οὐκ ἐπίσταται.
Πρ.   ἀλλ' ἐκδιδάσκει πάνθ' ὁ γηράσκων χρόνος. (980-1)

Pr.   Alas!   Herm.   That is a word which Zeus does not know.
Pr.   Ageing time teaches everything.

This is an unambiguous statement to the effect that Zeus might, in time, change; with the implication that Zeus's relations with Prometheus might change too. But, till then, Prometheus will speak in the accents of the typically Sophoklean impasse:

Ερ. τόλμησον, ὦ μάταιε, τόλμησόν ποτε
      πρὸς τὰς παρούσας πημονὰς ὀρθῶς φρονεῖν.
Πρ. ὀχλεῖς μάτην με, κῦμ᾽ ὅπως παρηγορῶν. (999-1001)

Herm. Fool. Make yourself see sense, in view of the anguish you are in.
Pr.   It is pointless to annoy me further: it is as though you were exhorting a wave of the sea.

Peitho has failed:

Ερ. λέγων ἔοικα πολλὰ καὶ μάτην ἐρεῖν.
      τέγγῃ γὰρ οὐδὲν οὐδὲ μαλθάσσῃ λιταῖς
      ἐμαῖς...
      σκέψαι δ᾽, ἐὰν μὴ τοῖς ἐμοῖς πεισθῇς λόγοις... (1007-14)

Herm. Apparently, however much I say, it will be to no effect. You are neither softened nor soothed by my words... Yet consider, if you do not comply with what I say...

and threats follow, including that alluding to the hideous liver-devouring eagle. But even so the future is not wholly bleak: Hermes tells Prometheus not to expect an end to his pain *until*[63] one of the gods[64] is willing of his own accord to go into Hades and Tartaros (1027ff).

The chorus recognizes the gravity of the Titan's situation, and reacts with another thoroughly Sophoklean intervention: *pithou*, 'be persuaded', 'obey' (1039). But, secure in the knowledge of his own immortality (1053), Prometheus calls down the universe upon him. Hermes urges the chorus to disperse so as to avoid being implicated in the disaster which is shortly to overtake the rebel; but, in a gesture unique in extant tragedy, they decline to be persuaded:

      ἄλλο τι φώνει καὶ παραμυθοῦ μ᾽
      ὅ τι καὶ πείσεις· οὐ γὰρ δή που
      τοῦτό γε τλητὸν παρέσυρας ἔπος. (1063-5)

Say something else, exhort me differently, if you would persuade me: for this word which you have dragged in is not to be borne.

After this last defiance of Zeus's power there is no more room for
argument. A mighty cataclysm—however enacted on stage—
apparently takes place; and Prometheus, screaming out the injustice
of his treatment, is engulfed.

There is strong evidence in favour of the view that *P.V.* was
followed by a *Prometheus Luomenos*.[65] Not only do numerous
allusions in *P.V.* point to a future release, but the scholiast on *P.V.*
511 (=fr. 320 M) states explicitly that Prometheus was set free 'in the
next play'. We possess several fragments from *Luomenos*, and among
the information they contain are the facts that: (i) Prometheus was
bound to a rock in the Caucasus where his liver was daily consumed
by Zeus's bird (e.g. fr. 324 M); (ii) he was visited by a chorus of Titans
who, being free, must presumably have made up their quarrel with
Zeus (fr. 322 (a) M; cf. fr. 324);[66] (iii) his attitude—if, as is
reasonable, we go by Cicero's rendering of a part of the play[67]—has
been transformed from bold intransigence to an anguished longing
for death; (iv) release comes eventually when Herakles shoots the
eagle (cf. esp. fr. 332 M). The intriguing problem of whether
Herakles freed Prometheus with Zeus's consent or without it is
unfortunately not one which we can solve in the present state of the
evidence.[68]

If there were two Prometheus plays, instinct prompts us to look for
a third. The telling points recently made by West[69] emphasize the
probability that this was *Prometheus Purphoros*, and that it came
before *P.V.* rather than after *Luomenos*. That is to say, its subject will
have been Prometheus' theft of fire and his bringing of it to mortals.
We thus have the plausible plan for the trilogy of 'Crime-
Punishment-Reconciliation'.[70] As in the case of the Danaid plays, it is
easy to be over-influenced by the perhaps untypical pattern of the
Oresteia. Nevertheless it is surely beyond doubt that the conflict and
stubbornness of *P.V.* ended in concord. (We have specific hints of this
in *P.V.* itself, as well as the more general implication of the dramatic
shift from binding to freeing.) Whether or not Peitho presided over
any union[71] at the end of the trilogy we do not know; but she was
surely there in spirit, healing the wounds inflicted by the various acts
of *bia*—cosmic, erotic, moral—explored in *P.V.*

3.3 *Oresteia* and conclusion

As I suggested in the Introduction, a full account of *peitho* in the *Oresteia* would require more space than is available here. But I offer some brief comments, which may also serve to draw together some of the points made about *Suppliants* and *P.V.*

In *Agamemnon* we are presented with a series of acts of *bia*. To counter this violence there is no healing *peitho*. True, *peitho* is referred to and even enacted from time to time, but it is either the ruinous *peitho* which leads to destruction, or it is deception masquerading as *peitho*. The *locus classicus* for ruinous *peitho* is *Ag.* 385-6, the beginning of the first antistrophe of the first stasimon:

> βιᾶται δ᾽ ἁ τάλαινα Πειθώ,
> προβούλου παῖς ἄφερτος ῎Ατας·

Baneful Peitho, irresistible child of Ruin-who-plans-beforehand, forces him.

The genealogy of Peitho given here bears no relation to the mythological or cult tradition. It is evidently Aischylos' invention, designed to link the evil persuasion at work early in the trilogy with other demonic forces which can speed a man's ruin. But to whom does the generalization about Peitho refer? We saw earlier how Peitho is often associated with the elopement of Helen. Coupling this fact with the obvious applicability of the first strophe to *Paris*, we must conclude that one of the connotations of the phrase βιᾶται δ᾽ ἁ τάλαινα Πειθώ is the abduction of Helen. At the end of the antistrophe the chorus confirms that it had Paris and Helen in mind:

> οἷος καὶ Πάρις ἐλθὼν
> ἐς δόμον τὸν ᾽Ατρειδᾶν
> ᾔσχυνε ξενίαν τράπε-
> ζαν κλοπαῖσι γυναικός. (399-402)

So too did Paris come to the house of the Atreidai, and shame his host's table by stealing away his wife.

But like so much else in this stasimon 385-6 are double-edged. The operation of Peitho here is strongly reminiscent of that of the παρακοπά ('delirium' — literally, 'knocking-sideways') which affects Agamemnon at 223; and both of them are τάλαινα, 'baneful'. As

Goheen has argued,[72] the chorus' words at 385-6 are quite as relevant to Agamemnon as to Paris. In taking the decision to kill Iphigeneia, Agamemnon was under the influence of ruinous *peitho*.[73]

The great example of deception masquerading as *peitho* is of course the scene in which Klytaimestra induces Agamemnon to walk over the fabrics into the palace. About the complex significance of Agamemnon's act there is now a measure of scholarly agreement. Firstly, as Goheen has shown,[74] the colour of the fabrics is that of congealed blood. In encouraging Agamemnon to walk along this path, Klytaimestra is urging him to follow a path which looks to the audience like a trail of blood flowing out of the palace—an ominous action in a trilogy which so often asserts the maxim that violence begets violence, and blood blood. Agamemnon will walk through a stream of blood to a bloody death. Secondly, what the king is doing is trampling, πατῶν (the last word he utters before his death-cry: 957); and this too assimilates his action symbolically to deeds of injustice elsewhere in the trilogy which are described through the same metaphor.[75] Thirdly, to tread on costly fabrics is, as John Jones argued,[76] precisely to destroy one's own material wealth and thus to demonstrate a perhaps risky confidence that it can be renewed. But why does Agamemnon yield? At the beginning of his first speech (810-13) he states that he has exacted a 'just' punishment from Priam; at 919ff he recognizes that the act of trampling is appropriate to a barbarian; at 936 he says that Priam would have done this deed. And yet Agamemnon, Priam's adversary, gives way. It is as if all the parallels between Troy and Argos with which *Agamemnon* has hitherto confronted us have exerted such pressure that the king is forced to conform to the pattern. But that is mere mysticism: surely the real answer lies in the architect of Agamemnon's decision, Klytaimestra? At this point we must look briefly at two famous 'psychological' explanations for Agamemnon's 'change of mind'. The first is that of Fraenkel, in whose opinion Agamemnon yields out of a sense of weariness and because, being (in the word which, perhaps understandably, has become the most notorious in the entire commentary) a 'gentleman', he finds it hard to say no to a lady. Unfortunately there is nothing in the Greek to support either aspect of this interpretation.[77] Nor is there any more to be said for the contrary hypothesis embraced by Denniston/Page, according to which Agamemnon is 'instantly ready to do this scandalous act the moment his personal fears of divine retribution and human censure are, by whatever sophistry, allayed' (note on 931ff). There is not a jot of evidence to suggest that Agamemnon is a hypocrite: his reservations, expressed before, during and after the stichomythia, are never offered to us by Aischylos as anything but genuine.

Are we then forced, with Dawe, to conclude that 'Agamemnon surrenders... only because it was *dramatically necessary* that he should do so'?[78] We can agree with Dawe that the confrontation scene is a splendid piece of theatre: 'in taking advantage of the physical requirements of the action, and elevating the question of the king's progress into the palace into a clash of wills, Aischylos has shown one more sign of the accomplished skill which sets the *Oresteia* so far ahead of his earlier experiments in drama'.[79] But to talk of dramatic necessity in these terms is to risk reducing a play to a mere series of manipulations of the audience's emotions, with the result that drama becomes indistinguishable from melodrama.[80]

There is another and more satisfactory interpretative way out. Looking at the stichomythia during which Agamemnon is induced to yield, we find that what takes place is not *peitho* in the sense of a gradual and rational argument culminating in the persuasion of one party by another. Instead, the pattern is as follows: Klytaimestra leads, Agamemnon responds; but always the initiative is with Klytaimestra, and the answers given by Agamemnon are never the 'best' ones available to him;[81] eventually Klytaimestra says *pithou*, 'obey', 'be persuaded' (943)—and he gives way. We cannot ascribe detailed psychological motivation to Agamemnon's change of mind without importing into the Greek what is not there. But that does not mean that the scene seems to us inexplicable in terms of human behaviour; after all, a situation in which one person outwits another,[82] and induces him to take a self-glorifying stance in spite of his own better judgement, is perfectly comprehensible and feasible to us. It is just that Aischylos has dramatized not the 'mechanics' of *peitho* but its implications in terms of the power of the victor and the helplessness of the victim.

The deceitful *peitho* of Agamemnon by Klytaimestra thus 'makes sense' if interpreted on the purely human level as an act of persuading between two individuals. But the example of a scene from another tragedy may help us to see another dimension to the drama. In *Bakchai* Dionysos, while manipulating Pentheus, suddenly and instantaneously 'persuades' him—here too the relation between powerful victor and powerless victim is more important than the mechanics of persuasion—through the utterance of the monosyllabic interjection ἆ, 'ah!' (810), to go to Kithairon to spy on the maenads. Now this episode is the more relevant because, as was plausibly argued by Dawe,[83] the state in which Pentheus finds himself is one of *ate*, 'ruin', 'ruinous infatuation'. Here, surely, is a further key to the scene before us in *Agamemnon*. Now, as at the time of the sacrifice of Iphigeneia, Agamemnon is a victim of that *peitho* which is the child of *ate*. Now, as then, he is able to reason lucidly—914-30 and 944-9 are just as 'sensible' as 206-17—and yet on each occasion blindness leads him to take a fatal decision. But there is a crucial difference between the two situations. At Aulis Agamemnon was in charge; but at Argos it is Klytaimestra who dominates. At Aulis he persuaded himself; at Argos he is persuaded by another. From the human point of view Klytaimestra simply has the facility of *peitho dolia*, 'tricky persuasion'. But is a more sinister power not already (cf. 1500ff, 1507ff) at work through her?[84] As well as being a human act of persuading, the confrontation between Agamemnon and Klytaimestra is also an exemplification of the divine power of Ate.

In *Choephoroi*, as in *Agamemnon*, the healing power of *peitho* is conspicuous by its absence. There is no remedy or cure, as Elektra says at 418-22. And, in particular,

πάρεστι σαίνειν, τὰ δ' οὔτι θέλγεται· (420)

One may fawn—but these [wrongs] are not charmed away.

Thelgein, the effect produced by *peitho*, has as yet no place. Orestes confirms the fact when he interprets Klytaimestra's dream:

δεῖ τοί νιν, ὡς ἔθρεψεν ἔκπαγλον τέρας,
θανεῖν βιαίως· (548-9)

As she nourished a monstrous beast, she must die by violence (*biaios*).

But the enemy is strong, and open *bia* may not work. So, just as Agamemnon's murderers killed him by *dolos*, they will in their turn fall to *dolos* (556-7). The reciprocity is paralleled in the dramatic structure: just after the mid-point of *Agamemnon* was the deception of husband by wife; just after the mid-point of *Choephoroi* is the deception of mother by son. The chorus, involved in the success or failure of the plot, invokes appropriate deities:

νῦν γὰρ ἀκμάζει Πειθὼ δολίαν
ξυγκαταβῆναι, χθόνιον δ᾽ Ἑρμῆν
καὶ τὸν νύχιον τοῖσδ᾽ ἐφοδεῦσαι
ξιφοδηλήτοισιν ἀγῶσιν. (726-9)

Now is the time for tricky Peitho to join in the contest, and for Hermes, god of earth's depths and of the night, to watch over these struggles with the sword.

Hermes has been with Orestes from the start, indeed from the first word, of the play, and his aid will be invaluable in an intrigue (cf. 812-18); but now there is need of another divinity, whom Aischylos describes in the phrase *Peitho dolia.* It is not only Orestes who requires the aid of deceitful Peitho: the chorus itself attempts and—a moment unique in extant tragedy—manages successfully to persuade (cf. 781) the Nurse to carry a crooked message (773) to Aigisthos, the success of which trick is vital to the fulfilment of Orestes' plan.

The plan works: Aigisthos dies. Klytaimestra recognizes how it has come about:

δόλοις ὀλούμεθ᾽ ὥσπερ οὖν ἐκτείναμεν. (888)

We shall perish by trickery *(doloi),* as we ourselves killed.

And she, too, soon falls. Bloody *bia* follows bloody *bia,* with no end in sight. As Orestes rushes out driven by the Furies, the chorus asks when the power of *ate* will cease (1073-6), and *ate,* we recall (cf. *Ag.* 385-6) is the begetter of destructive *peitho.*

In *Eumenides,* at last, frank and open *peitho* brings about reconciliation and soothes the hurts of the past. The tone is set near the beginning, when Apollo bids Orestes escape from Delphi and be of good courage:

μολὼν δὲ Παλλάδος ποτὶ πτόλιν
ἵζου παλαιὸν ἄγκαθεν λαβὼν βρέτας·
κἀκεῖ δικαστὰς τῶνδε καὶ θελκτηρίους
μύθους ἔχοντες μηχανὰς εὑρήσομεν
ὥστ᾽ ἐς τὸ πᾶν σε τῶνδ᾽ ἀπαλλάξαι πόνων. (79-83)

> Go to the city of Pallas, embrace her ancient image, and sit there as a
> suppliant; and there, with judges and charming *(thelkterious)* words
> for this case, we shall find some means to procure your full deliverance
> from these woes.

The house of Atreus will eventually feel the power of words that charm, the beneficent *peitho* whose home is Athens.

The final resolution in *Eumenides* is not the trial of Orestes but the subsequent argument between Athene and the Furies; and it is through the power of *peitho* that the younger goddess effects the conversion of these potential demons of blight to their new role as bringers of prosperity and fertility and as guardians of justice within the framework of the city. When, cheated of victory at the trial and thus dishonoured, the Furies threaten to bring sterility to leaf and mankind alike (785, 815), Athene responds with *peitho:*

> ἐμοὶ πίθεσθε μὴ βαρυστόνως φέρειν. (794)
>
> Be persuaded by me: do not take this angrily.

The Furies are evidently δυσπαρήγοροι, 'hard to persuade' (cf. 384), for gods as well as mortals since they repeat their curses word for word. This time Athene varies her tactics. As the good and just city, which normally operates by *peitho*, may still call upon *bia* in the last resort, so Athene relies on the thunderbolt of Zeus to protect Athens if necessary:

> κἀγὼ πέποιθα Ζηνί, καὶ τί δεῖ λέγειν;
> καὶ κλῆδας οἶδα δώματος μόνη θεῶν
> ἐν ᾧ κεραυνός ἐστιν ἐσφραγισμένος. (826-8)
>
> And I have trust in Zeus—what more need I say? And I, alone among
> the gods, know the keys of the chamber in which the thunderbolt is
> sealed away.

But, having stated the threat, she immediately turns away from it to *peitho:*

> ἀλλ' οὐδὲν αὐτοῦ δεῖ. σὺ δ' εὐπιθὴς ἐμοὶ
> γλώσσης ματαίας μὴ 'κβάλῃς ἔπη χθονί... (829-30)
>
> But there is no need of it (sc. the thunderbolt): be persuaded by me,
> and do not pointlessly cast threats against the land.

Still the elder goddesses protest: they are not ready to heed *peitho,* and regard their defeat by the younger Olympians as *doloi* (846, 880). This time Athene prefers mellifluous eloquence to menaces:

τοιαῦθ' ἑλέσθαι σοι πάρεστιν ἐξ ἐμοῦ,
εὖ δρῶσαν, εὖ πάσχουσαν, εὖ τιμωμένην
χώρας μετασχεῖν τῆσδε θεοφιλεστάτης. (867-9)

Such gifts you may accept from my hands: doing good, receiving good, to have an honoured place in this god-blessed land.

For the last time the Furies remain adamant; but the dignity in Athene's words shows that the accusations of *dolos* are misplaced. Beginning by linking herself with the 'men who hold the polis' (883), she explicitly invokes the power in which she trusts:

ἀλλ' εἰ μὲν ἁγνόν ἐστί σοι Πειθοῦς σέβας,
γλώσσης ἐμῆς μείλιγμα καὶ θελκτήριον... (885-6)

But if you revere the holy power of Peitho, the delight and charm of my words...

There could be no clearer illustration of the unity of the *peitho* spectrum. The context of this speech is political, yet the vocabulary *(meiligma, thelkterion)* used to qualify the persuasion at work in that context is erotic; at *Ag.* 1439 Klytaimestra calls her husband the *meiligma,* 'darling', of every little Chryseis at Troy; while, as we have seen, *thelk-/thelg-* words are regularly associated with the charms and enchantments of love. Both aspects of *peitho* are relevant to the finale of *Eumenides,* since it celebrates the blessings in store for the polis as a result of the fruitfulness of unions sanctioned by Peitho.

The appeal to justice (cf. 888: 'It would not be *right* for you to refuse a good bargain any longer') and to the 'holy reverence of Peitho' works: θέλξειν μ' ἔοικας, 'it seems that you will charm me' (900). (Just as in the scene where Klytaimestra persuades Agamemnon, there is no detailed psychological motivation for the process of persuading. In both that instance and the present one *peitho* works almost uncannily—in *Agamemnon,* for evil; in *Eumenides,* for good.) Instead of curses, blessings are what the Furies, soon to be the Kindly Ones, are invited to heap upon the land of Attica; and best of those blessings is fruitfulness of earth and of man (907ff). The Furies retain their privilege, the punishment of wrongdoers (cf. esp. 932-7), but it is the *charis* they offer which receives all Aischylos' emphasis and most of his poetry. In gratitude, Athene speaks again of the power which has enabled her to convert the Furies:

> στέργω δ' ὄμματα Πειθοῦς,
> ὅτι μοι γλῶσσαν καὶ στόμ' ἐπωπᾷ
> πρὸς τάσδ' ἀγρίως ἀπανηναμένας.
> ἀλλ' ἐκράτησε Ζεὺς ἀγοραῖος... (970-3)

I love the eyes of Peitho, who guides my tongue and mouth against these who denied so savagely. But victory went to Zeus of the agora...

Zeus is the prime mover, but the more immediately helpful divinity is Peitho. But why the *eyes* of Peitho? Eyes are mentioned several times in the trilogy, but three cases in *Agamemnon* seem to be the most relevant. The first is at line 240, where Iphigeneia strikes her murderers with a look:

> ἔβαλλ' ἕκαστον θυτή-
> ρων ἀπ' ὄμματος βέλει φιλοίκτῳ...

She struck each of her sacrificers with a piteous arrow from her eye...

Here the eyes which shoot forth an arrow are those of a young maiden, to be sure, but this is hardly a situation in which an erotic overtone can convincingly be said to be present. However, such an overtone certainly is present at 742 where, in evoking the arrival of Helen at Troy, the chorus sings of a μαλθακὸν ὀμμάτων βέλος, 'a soft arrow from the eyes'.[85] More dubious is the sense of 416-19, which I give with Fraenkel's translation:

> εὐμόρφων δὲ κολοσσῶν
> ἔχθεται χάρις ἀνδρί,
> ὀμμάτων δ' ἐν ἀχηνίαις
> ἔρρει πᾶσ' Ἀφροδίτα.

The grace of shapely statues is hateful to the husband, and when the eyes are starved, all charm of love is gone.

Critics disagree about whose eyes are in question: the abandoned husband's (as Fraenkel takes it) or the absent wife's (in which case a literal version will be, 'in the absence of *her* eyes'). Maybe the ambiguity is intentional. But in any case what is clear is that a connection is implied between eyes and love—a connection which is frequent in other Greek poetry too.[86] I assume then that at *Eumenides* 970 Athene is thinking of Peitho as a charmer, in all senses.

Where healing Peitho rules, Peitho the child of Ruin has no place; and so the chorus prays that civil strife, presided over by the bloody spirit of Ate (982), may never rage in Athens. Athene duly thanks them for 'finding the way of good speech' (988). A procession forms and, in a mood of solemn festivity, the Furies are escorted from the scene and taken to their new home in Athens.

Although objections can be made to the linking of the Danaid and Prometheus trilogies and the *Oresteia*[87]—particularly, of course, if the Aischylean authorship of *P.V.* is called into question—it is hard to deny that all three groups of plays apparently exhibited a fundamental confidence in the power of persuasion ultimately to solve problems of human (and divine) stubbornness, resentment and conflict. True, *peitho* in Aischylos is not in all circumstances a good—as *Agamemnon* and *Choephoroi* show, it can be demonic and destructive. But in general it constitutes a healing and charming agency whose significance can without absurdity be likened to the reconciling power of love in Shakespearian tragedy.

We have no idea how far the totality of Aischylos' output may have corresponded to this scheme. The *Seven* trilogy clearly did not: at its end there is no healing, only catastrophe. Now *Seven* was put on in 467; the Danaid plays, the *Oresteia* and (probably) the Prometheus plays were all later. Are we justified in saying that Aischylos had 'not yet' worked his way to the artistic vision expressed in his 'last phase'?[88] We know far too little about his whole *oeuvre* to be able to tell. (It is worth recalling that *Persians,* in which the values of the Athenian democracy are affirmed if anything even more clearly than in Athene's praise of *peitho* in *Eumenides,* was put on as early as 472.) But it may very well be the case that the role of *peitho* extends beyond the 'last phase'. For instance, in the *Eleusinians,* probably the last play of a trilogy on the theme later used by Euripides for his *Suppliants,* one thing which distinguished Aischylos' treatment from that of the younger tragedian was precisely a resolution reached by persuasion rather than by force.[89] It has been argued too that *peitho* was an important theme in the lost *Ransoming of Hektor.*[90] But we are by now in the realm of wholesale guesswork, and it is probably wise to let the imagination rest at this point. Suffice it to say that several of Aischylos' dramas display a confidence in the power of *peitho* to heal disputes and soothe anger. It was a confidence not shared by Aischylos' great younger rival in the Athenian theatre.

4

SOPHOKLES

Introduction[1]

Few critics of Greek drama would deny that, of the three major tragedians, it is least difficult to generalize about Sophokles. Aischylos' extant work comprises, in spite of several constant preoccupations, a series of unique and dissimilar items. Euripides, although (or perhaps because) his surviving *oeuvre* is more than twice the size of those of his fellow dramatists, offers a Protean variety of tones, styles and dramatic structures which makes the identification of typically 'Euripidean' characteristics a hazardous business. But with Sophokles—always allowing for the possibility of an optical illusion caused by the circumstance that history may not have left us with a representative sample—one senses more strongly a mood, a use of language, a dramatic technique which are shared, to a greater or lesser extent, by all the seven plays.

Of these three features—mood, language, technique—it is surely the first which contains the quintessence of Sophoklean tragedy. In Aischylos we witness terrible and violent actions, but often they are part of a wider scheme involving a movement from conflict to reconciliation, and always they stand in an intelligible relationship to the will of the gods. In Sophokles the gloom and the violence are still there, but instead of the wider, hopeful scheme there is something more enigmatic, more uncertain, more remote. In the *Oresteia*, for example, the cry τὸ δ' εὖ νικάτω, 'let the good prevail', is, after much suffering, eventually answered, and the good does prevail; but in Sophokles' *Trachiniai* the chorus' question about Zeus's concern for his children (139-40) receives at best an ambiguous answer in the course of the action: Herakles is sceptical about Zeus's fatherly care for him,[2] Hyllos is practically at one (*Tr.* 1264-9) with Gloucester's bitter cry,

> As flies to wanton boys, are we to th' Gods;
> They kill us for their sport.

and even the chorus' coda,[3] while it sets a quiet seal on the drama (κοὐδὲν τούτων ὅ τι μὴ Ζεύς, 'there is none of these things that is not Zeus') is hardly to be regarded as an accepting or harmonious conclusion if we remember the appalling human wreckage to which τούτων, 'these things', points. Again, more than once Aischylos dramatized a world in which, after all the brutality, a healing took place, and a balancing of consequences to deserts; but when Sophokles wrote *Antigone* he created something more terrifying: a universe in which consequences are quite out of proportion to deserts (cf. Eurydike) and in which the ultimate triumph of right and harmony is no more than a vain hope.

Consider, for instance, an expression which lies close to the centre of the Sophoklean tragic mood: ἰοὺ ἰού (untranslatable, like most interjections). It is sometimes an exclamation of surprise or consternation with a purely local reference, as when Neoptolemos cries out on noticing the putrid rags which betray the presence of Philoktetes (*Phil.* 38). But more often it is an exclamation uttered at points of great crisis, coincident with a realization of almost metaphysical dimensions: 'So that is the pattern; that is how the pieces fit together; that is how the world goes.' ἰοὺ ἰού says the messenger in *Ajax*, as he hears the fatal news that the hero is no longer in his tent (*Aj.* 737). ἰοὺ ἰού says Jocasta at the beginning of the final, desperate couplet which she speaks in *O.T.* (1071). ἰοὺ ἰού says Oidipous as the truth bursts upon him (*O.T.* 1182). ἰοὺ ἰού says Herakles, as the name of Nessos tears away the veil which has been obscuring the past (*Tr.* 1143-5). At such moments the energy built up through the use of irony is suddenly released; and the end towards which this released energy is employed by Sophokles is the enforcement of a sense of the *limitations* of human insight and the inadequacy of human action.

But Sophokles was not an ancient Samuel Beckett. Suicides may be rather frequent in Sophokles' plays, but the context in which they occur is neither godless nor meaningless. The gods' will may be hard for mortals to fathom, and it may not match human notions of justice; but the gods are indisputably there,[4] as ever-present, and as inscrutable, as the ἄρκτου στροφάδες κέλευθοι, 'circling paths of the Bear' (*Tr.* 130-1). But it is not the gods who are the principal source of meaning in the tragedies: it is man. In Sophokles' universe man does not passively accept, he demands, affirms, strives. With one or two exceptions (Deianeira; perhaps Philoktetes) the main characters are not warm or lovable; but they do act with a passionate intensity (to which Bernard Knox has given the name 'the heroic temper') which remains vivid in the mind of the spectator even after the persons concerned have been battered, and often brought to death, by calamity. It is this passionate intensity of character which, together with the feeling that there *is* a divine will if only we could descry it, counterbalances the impression of man's limitations and of the world's injustice to produce that tragic outlook, poised somewhere between hope and despair, which we associate with Sophokles.

Generalizations about Sophokles are, then, feasible; but it remains true that each of the dramas is a unique statement. Not the least important respect in which this is true is in regard to *peitho*. In four of the plays—*Ajax, Antigone, Oidipous Tyrannos, Elektra*—we see variations upon a pattern whose nature and implications have been set out by Knox. The pattern centres on a tragic figure of great moral authority (a description which, in spite of his transgressions and angry outbursts, one unhesitatingly applies to Oidipous) who holds fast to his or her own course, and resists every attempt to deflect him or her from that course. One of the modes of approach to the central figure is *peitho*; and in each case it is the failure of *peitho* which is dramatized: Tekmessa fails, Ismene fails, Jocasta fails, Chrysothemis fails. This failure not only serves to isolate the central figure; it is also a good index of the atmosphere of the dramas, an atmosphere marked by stubbornness, intractability, intransigence: Ajax dies rather than make a compromise; Antigone is fiercely devoted to her brother and is killed for it; Oidipous is determined to know the truth at any cost; Elektra is the embodiment of ruthless single-mindedness.

But there are two other plays, *Philoktetes* and *Oidipous at Kolonos* (*O.C.*) (both late, and probably the two latest extant works), in which *peitho* receives a more nuanced and complex examination. Like *Elektra, Philoktetes* and *O.C.* are about the reaching of an 'end' which is in a sense fixed from the outset. The 'end' of *Elektra* is the avenging of Agamemnon by stealth, as the oracle of Apollo has enjoined (32ff);[5] the 'end' of *Philoktetes* is the securing of Philoktetes by the Greeks and his transference to Troy, which has been predicted in certain prophetic utterances revealed in the course of the play; and the 'end' of *O.C.* is the passing-away of Oidipous and the securing of his powerful influence as a hero after death (which matters are again alluded to in prophetic utterances). Now in *Elektra* the focus of interest is not upon an argument about *means*: as has been said, the god's instructions imply from the outset the use of *dolos*, and sure enough *dolos* is the method employed. But in *Philoktetes* and *O.C.*, because there is no such prior preference for a given moral procedure, there is accordingly room for debate about which moral procedure would most suit the circumstances. And in fact the whole of *Philoktetes* and a not inconsiderable part of *O.C.* are involved with the problem of '*How* should we win the hero?' In so far as they constitute Sophokles' only surviving explorations of the rival claims of *peitho*, *bia* and *dolos* in the crucible of a particular crisis, we shall concentrate on these two works.

4.1 *Philoktetes*

One of the most fascinating aspects of *Philoktetes* is the way in which Sophokles explores the various means, both verbal and other, which men can adopt to secure the ends they desire. Odysseus persuades Neoptolemos; Neoptolemos deceives Philoktetes; Philoktetes tries to persuade Neoptolemos; Odysseus threatens the use of force; Neoptolemos, renouncing deception, tries to persuade Philoktetes; Philoktetes succeeds in persuading Neoptolemos; Herakles gives commands.[6] The complex pattern of relationships of which the play is made up is thus very closely connected with changes in the sorts of discourse (persuasion, guile, injunction, threat, silence, and so forth) employed by the different characters. We shall look first at those sorts of discourse, and shall then be in a better position to observe the general importance of *peitho* in *Philoktetes*.

To understand Philoktetes' use of language we must first understand his condition.[7] At 1017-18 he reflects on the time when he was originally abandoned:

> ...με προὐβάλου
> ἄφιλον ἐρῆμον ἄπολιν ἐν ζῶσιν νεκρόν.

> ...you cast me forth friendless, alone, without a city, a corpse amongst the living.

He is an outcast from society. This exclusion has several aspects. First, from the purely geographical point of view he is on a deserted island (1-2, 687-8, etc.). The word ἐρῆμος, 'alone, deserted', recurs frequently (34, 228, 265, 269, 471, 487, 1018, 1070). We learn that Philoktetes lives at the ἐσχατιά (144), a word connoting territory which is at or near the margin of cultivable land.[8] He has no one to care for him, and sees no companion's face (169ff). Numerous details of his everyday life emphasize his extra-societal situation. His home is a rocky cave (e.g. 16, 27, 159-60, 952, 1001-2, 1081). When Odysseus asks about the οἰκοποιός...τροφή, provision for a man's abode, which Philoktetes has at his disposal, he learns that he has merely a bed of leaves and an αὐτόξυλον ...ἔκπωμα, 'cup of mere wood' (32, 35). Jebb's note is good here: 'αὐτόξυλον, "of mere wood", means here, "of wood not artistically treated"; the piece of wood remained as nearly in its original state as was compatible with its serving for a cup.' Philoktetes is living at the boundary between wild and civilized existence.[9] He has πυρεῖα, means of kindling fire — that minimum requirement of human culture (36, 296-7)—but he does not 'gather for food the fruit of holy Earth' like other ἀνέρες ἀλφησταί, ordinary men (709).[10] Nor has he tasted wine these last years, having had to make do instead with whatever the local stagnant pools might offer (714ff).[11] In fact Philoktetes' condition has been in many respects little better than that of an animal. Indeed, as has often been noted,[12] his predicament is repeatedly presented in language normally associated with animals. The word αὔλιον, which is used to describe his living quarters,[13] is applied in the *Homeric Hymn to Hermes* (103, 106) to the byre into which the cattle of Apollo are driven, and in Euripides' *Cyclops* (345, 593) to the monster's den.[14] The food which Philoktetes eats is described in 'animal' terms,[15] and animals have been virtually his only companions (183-5). In short, not only is the disease which attacks him ἄγριος, 'wild' (173, 265-6), he has himself been 'made wild' (ἀπηγριωμένον, 226; ἠγρίωσαι, 1321).

Consider now the sort of discourse used by this character who is, in Vidal-Naquet's phrase, 'un mort social'.[16] It is true that at times during the play, particularly when he is in conversation with Neoptolemos, Philoktetes is capable of speaking in a moving and eloquent way. But there are also very many occasions when his use of language is far from being controlled or articulate. At 9-11 Odysseus recalls the time when the outcast was abandoned:

> ...ἀγρίαις
> κατεῖχ' ἀεὶ πᾶν στρατόπεδον δυσφημίαις,
> βοῶν, στενάζων.

> ...he was for ever disturbing the whole army with his wild cries, shouting and shrieking.

Since then almost the only interlocutor he has had has been Echo—that is, himself (188-90).[17] The sounds which the chorus recognizes as characteristic of Philoktetes are anguished and inarticulate cries (201-9, 213-18). These sounds are his unmistakable trademark (209). We learn that he was 'his own neighbour', with no one nearby to be his κακογείτων, 'neighbour in sorrow', to whom he could pour out his lament, and in whom he could find a response (691ff). The terrifying scene between Philoktetes and Neoptolemos at 730-826 is the dramatic enactment of this lament. Pain reduces Philoktetes to a combination of silence and inarticulate spasms of language:

> Νε. ἕρπ' εἰ θέλεις. τί δή ποθ' ὧδ' ἐξ οὐδενὸς
>   λόγου σιωπᾷς κἀπόπληκτος ὧδ' ἔχῃ;
> Φιλ. ἄ ἄ ἄ ἄ. (730-2)

> Ne. Come on, if you will. Why are you silent for no reason, standing there stupefied?
> [Philoktetes moans]

At 740-50 Philoktetes is reduced to the production of disjointed, almost 'animal' noises. Further series of interjections follow, until he lapses into the temporary silence of sleep. When he reawakens, and then learns how he has been tricked, he has no further use for conversation, and returns to his one-sided dialogue with the wild nature around him (936-40). At 952 he addresses his cave, and a little later (1081ff) does the same again at greater length. At 1146ff he speaks to the beasts he used to hunt; and even at the very end of the play, when the future is 'settled', he says a long farewell to the various natural features of the island (1452ff, 1461, 1464). Though soon to be restored to the world of human society, he retains the mode of discourse which characterized his extra-societal life on Lemnos.

We turn now to Neoptolemos. In the opening scene it is made clear that Philoktetes is to be taken in by a trick: Neoptolemos must work on him, not openly, but surreptitiously:

> τὴν Φιλοκτήτου σε δεῖ
> ψυχὴν ὅπως λόγοισιν ἐκκλέψεις λέγων. (54-5; cf. also 77-8)

You must trap the soul of Philoktetes by the words you speak.

Neoptolemos would rather use *bia* than *dolos* (90-1); or why not try *peitho* (102)? But Odysseus brushes aside both force and persuasion:

> οὐ μὴ πίθηται· πρὸς βίαν δ' οὐκ ἂν λάβοις. (103)

He will not be persuaded; and you could not take him by force.

So the proposed act of deception goes ahead.[18]

And in the event *dolos* turns out to have been a very effective choice. For Philoktetes is ridiculously easy prey to the deceitful use of language. (Nor is this surprising: 'Speech is civilization itself. The word, even the most contradictious word, preserves contact—it is silence which isolates.'[19]) On coming across the chorus Philoktetes asks to hear them speak (225), and when they have done so he responds with rapture to the sound of Greek. (Notice the near-obsession with 'speech-words': φωνήσατε, 'speak' (229), ἀνταμείψασθε, 'answer' (230), φίλτατον φώνημα, 'dearest sound' (234), πρόσφθεγμα, 'address' (235), γέγωνε, 'utter' (238). As Podlecki puts it, 'it is as if he were savouring the synonyms for the speech-act'.[20]) He talks for a while with Neoptolemos, and then fondly believes he can exercise *peitho* over the young man: πείσθητι, 'be persuaded' (485). Neoptolemos pretends to agree. To compound the deceit, the 'false merchant' enters. His story is that Diomedes and Odysseus have sworn to take Philoktetes 'either by persuasion or by force' (593-4)—no suggestion that they will deceive him.[21] Similarly, the rehearsal of Helenos' prophecy presents it as mentioning the *persuasion* of Philoktetes (612). To this Philoktetes' reaction is unequivocal:

> πεισθήσομαι γὰρ ὧδε κἀξ Ἅιδου θανὼν
> πρὸς φῶς ἀνελθεῖν, ὥσπερ οὑκείνου πατήρ. (624-5)

As soon shall I be persuaded, when I have died, to return again to the light from Hades' realm—as his (sc. Odysseus') father did.

'To think', he remarks to Neoptolemos, 'that Odysseus thought he could get round me by *logoi malthakoi*, soft words! I would sooner listen to the serpent that bit me!' (629-32). The 'merchant' has done his job by directing Philoktetes' attention towards a possible assault on his resolve through *peitho*. Thus the actual mode of attack —deception—proceeds unhindered.

Yet the time eventually comes when the pressures upon Neoptolemos—the power of the truth, the claims of one's *physis* ('nature'), the strength of human sympathy—become so great that he switches from the language of *dolos* to that of 'straight' speech. When he does so, he is at first reduced to the same state of fumbling linguistic inadequacy which we found to be a feature of Philoktetes' discourse on occasions:

> Νε.   παπαῖ· τί δῆτ' ἂν δρῷμ' ἐγὼ τοὐνθένδε γε;
> Φιλ.   τί δ' ἔστιν, ὦ παῖ; ποῖ ποτ' ἐξέβης λόγῳ;
> Νε.   οὐκ οἶδ' ὅποι χρὴ τἄπορον τρέπειν ἔπος. (895-7)

> Ne.   Ah! What should I do from this point on?
> Phil.   What is it, my son? Where have your words strayed?
> Ne.   I do not know which way to turn my speech: I am at a loss.

At this stage, of course, Philoktetes is still thinking in terms of 'legitimate' persuasion:

> οὐ δή σε δυσχέρεια τοῦ νοσήματος
> ἔπεισεν ὥστε μή μ' ἄγειν ναύτην ἔτι; (900-1)

> Surely disgust at my wound has not persuaded you to refuse to take me on board?

But no: what has actually happened is that Neoptolemos has (as he admits) perverted language:

> ...κρύπτων θ' ἃ μὴ δεῖ καὶ λέγων αἴσχιστ' ἐπῶν. (909)

> ...hiding what should not be hidden and speaking the basest of words.

Philoktetes realizes that deception has been practised upon him (*apate*-related words at 929, 949, 1136; *dolos* at 948; cf. 1111-12). For the time being discourse between deceived and deceiver stops: while Philoktetes reverts to a 'dialogue' with the landscape, Neoptolemos remains silent (934, 951). As J.-U. Schmidt has perceptively pointed out,[22] Neoptolemos' silence here marks the transition from his role as deceitful liar to that of open truth-teller, his intermediate condition being that of 'nicht mehr und auch noch nicht wieder Reden-Können'. An embarrassed silence is the necessary preliminary to the change from *dolos* to *peitho*.

At 1066-7 Philoktetes is evidently frightened at the prospect of being plunged once more into speechless isolation:

> ὦ σπέρμ᾽ Ἀχιλλέως, οὐδὲ σοῦ φωνῆς ἔτι
> γενήσομαι προσφθεγκτός, ἀλλ᾽ οὕτως ἄπει;

> Offspring of Achilles, shall I not again be spoken to by your voice? Will you just go away like that?

but his mood in subsequent interchanges with the chorus is one of bitter resignation. So it is no surprise that, when Neoptolemos reappears later and offers Philoktetes *logoi*, 'words' (1267), the other's reaction is hostile:

> τοιοῦτος ἦσθα τοῖς λόγοισι χὤτε μου
> τὰ τόξ᾽ ἔκλεπτες, πιστός, ἀτηρὸς λάθρᾳ. (1271-2)

> You were just such a one in your words when you stole my bow— trustworthy, yet secretly treacherous.

This time Neoptolemos uses not *dolos* but *peitho*:

> ἀλλ᾽ ἤθελον μὲν ἄν σε πεισθῆναι λόγοις
> ἐμοῖσιν... (1278-9)

> I wish you had been persuaded by my words...

But it is no use. Even when Philoktetes is receiving the bow back into his hands, he suspects another *dolos* (1288). After Odysseus' final inglorious and unsuccessful intervention, Neoptolemos continues his mature use of *peitho,* as he urges Philoktetes to listen to advice:

> σὺ δ᾽ ἠγρίωσαι, κοὔτε σύμβουλον δέχῃ,
> ἐάν τε νουθετῇ τις εὐνοίᾳ λέγων,
> στυγεῖς, πολέμιον δυσμενῆ θ᾽ ἡγούμενος. (1321-3)

> You have become wild. You do not accept an adviser; when a man does offer you counsel speaking from a well-disposed heart, you hate him, regarding him as a loathed enemy.

Surely now, at last, with mutual trust re-established, *peitho* can work its spell?[23] Indeed it *has* to work its spell, for—so it must seem to the audience—*peitho* is the only way left: after the returning of the mighty bow, Philoktetes cannot be taken by *bia*; and now that he has been made painfully aware of the gap between truth and falsehood, he will not be taken in by *dolos/apate* either.

Philoktetes is placed in an agonizing dilemma:

> οἴμοι, τί δράσω; πῶς ἀπιστήσω λόγοις
> τοῖς τοῦδ', ὃς εὔνους ὢν ἐμοὶ παρήνεσεν; (1350-1)[24]

Alas, what shall I do? How shall I disbelieve the words of this man, who advised me with good intent?

However, he eventually opts for the voyage home. The young man has one last try, but fails again (1373-5). If he cannot persuade Philoktetes in words, then, he concludes (1393ff), 'the easiest course is for me to cease from speech'. And he agrees to take Philoktetes home. It is true that divine intervention countermands this intent but, in so far as the two human agents are concerned, Neoptolemos' attempt to persuade Philoktetes has failed: the use of *dolos* created an atmosphere of mistrust which undermined the operation of *peitho*.

Nevertheless, it is not the case that communication between Neoptolemos and Philoktetes fails completely. For, paradoxically, Philoktetes persuades Neoptolemos, just before the appearance of Herakles. The importance of the fact that, at last, true persuasion has taken place on a basis of mutual sympathy is underlined by Sophokles by means of a technique which he uses often in *Philoktetes*, namely the repetition, usually with significant variations, of a verbal formula or piece of stage action from earlier in the play.[25] Twice during the time when he was deceiving Philoktetes Neoptolemos had said: 'If you like, let us go': ἀλλ' εἰ δοκεῖ, πλέωμεν (526), ἀλλ' εἰ δοκεῖ, χωρῶμεν (645).[26] Now again, at 1402, when Neoptolemos' relationship with Philoktetes is based on truth rather than lies, he uses exactly the same form of words: εἰ δοκεῖ, στείχωμεν, 'If you like, let us go.'[27] Much of *Philoktetes* explores failure in human communication, but there is a strong case for arguing that this relenting by Neoptolemos represents a counterbalancing success, a success which has at least as much emotional impact as the preceding failures.[28]

Next, Odysseus. Although he is present before the audience's eyes for less time than either of the other two principal characters,

Odysseus' influence is felt throughout the play until almost the end. This influence is never stronger than in the first scene, in which he dominates his younger companion. From the outset he is 'working on' Neoptolemos. He flatters him by praising his father Achilles (3-4). After mentioning the abandonment of Philoktetes he adds an extenuating circumstance—he has been told to act thus by 'the commanders' (6). All this is part of his plan to persuade Neoptolemos of the rightness of the scheme to recover the bow. That Odysseus' persuasion is subtle is not surprising, for he is a past master in the art. He knows when words are called for and when they are not (cf. 12, 1047ff); and he has learned by experience that what action cannot achieve, words can:

Οδ. ἐσθλοῦ πατρὸς παῖ, καὐτὸς ὢν νέος ποτὲ
γλῶσσαν μὲν ἀργόν, χεῖρα δ᾽ εἶχον ἐργάτιν·
νῦν δ᾽ εἰς ἔλεγχον ἐξιὼν ὁρῶ βροτοῖς
τὴν γλῶσσαν, οὐχὶ τἄργα, πάνθ᾽ ἡγουμένην. (96-9)

Od. Son of a noble father: when I was young, I too had an idle tongue but an active hand. But now, as I go forth to [apply] the test, I see that for mortals the tongue, not the deed, wins every victory.

Nor is it surprising that Odysseus' persuasion eventually works: for it is persuasion not of one equal by another, but of a novice by an expert. The one explains, the other listens (24-5), and the relationship is decidedly hierarchical—it is as a mere servant or helper (53) that Neoptolemos will act. At 54 the young man asks, 'What are your orders?' (cf. the same phrase at 100). They are, that Philoktetes is to be taken by *dolos*. Neoptolemos is to tell Philoktetes a deceitful story concocted from various elements of truth and falsehood (54ff), and designed to achieve the purpose towards which Odysseus is working:

ἀλλ᾽ αὐτὸ τοῦτο δεῖ σοφισθῆναι, κλοπεὺς
ὅπως γενήσῃ τῶν ἀνικήτων ὅπλων. (77-8)

This very point must be contrived, how you shall succeed in stealing the unconquered weapons.

At first Neoptolemos refuses, but the master arguer re-applies his persuasive skill. He begins as before, with flattery through praise of

Achilles (96). Next he tries to convince Neoptolemos that *dolos* is the only feasible course by asserting, with total confidence, that the other two modes of approach, *peitho* and *bia,* are *not* feasible (103). By 107 Odysseus has carried this point, but Neoptolemos has one crucial argumentative defence left: to use deceit is shameful (108). Odysseus makes no attempt to deny this, for throughout the play he shows himself shrewdly aware of the importance to Achilles' son of the link of *physis,* 'nature', with his father. What Odysseus does is to oppose a different criterion to that of 'fineness/baseness': namely, 'success/ failure'. To take Philoktetes will bring 'gain'—the 'gain' of victory at Troy. When Neoptolemos speaks line 112, it is clear that Odysseus' persuasion has been effective. Had the young man said: 'Gain is not *truly* gain if it is basely won' (as he recognizes at 1246), the outcome would have been different. But, as it is, the interested question, 'How would it profit me...?' shows that the game is over. The moment Odysseus describes the future in a phrase which suggests that Achilles' son can be deceitful and yet still true to the claims of his nobility (σοφός τ'ἂν αὐτὸς κἀγαθὸς κεκλῇ' ἅμα, 'You could be called wise *and* noble at the same time' (119)), he falls into line: 'Very well—I will do it' (120).

In the opening scene Odysseus practises *peitho* and advocates *dolos*—an indication that he is not fussy about means if his desired end is achieved.[29] The rest of the drama corroborates this initial impression. For his use of *dolos* the entire episode involving the 'false merchant' constitutes abundant evidence. *Bia* too is a prominent part of his armoury as moral aggressor. At 103-5 he only rules it out because he thinks it will be ineffective, not because he thinks it is wrong; and, as and when suitable circumstances arise, he has no compunction about using violence.[30] Soon after his intervention at 974, when Neoptolemos was on the point of returning the bow to its rightful owner, Odysseus threatens Philoktetes with violence:

Οδ.   ...ἀλλὰ καὶ σὲ δεῖ
        στείχειν ἅμ' αὐτοῖς, ἢ βίᾳ στελοῦσί σε.

Φιλ.   ἔμ', ὦ κακῶν κάκιστε καὶ τόλμης πέρα,
        οἵδ' ἐκ βίας ἄξουσιν; Οδ. ἢν μὴ ἕρπῃς ἑκών. (982-5)

Od.   ...you too must come with the bow, or these men will bring you
        by force.

Phil. Vicious, brazen scoundrel! Will these men bring me away by force?

Od.   If you do not go willingly.

(That 'willingly' is, of course, illusory; just as, when Odysseus baldly states πειστέον τάδε, 'you must comply in this' (994), there is no contradiction with 103 (οὐ μὴ πίθηται, 'he will not comply/be persuaded'): to force someone to 'be persuaded' is to make a mockery of *peitho*.) At 1003 threats become reality as Odysseus orders his men to restrain Philoktetes from killing himself: they forcibly prevent him from enjoying the last freedom remaining to him, the freedom to choose how and when to die.

At 1047ff Odysseus changes his tactics again, and reverts from violence to language:

πόλλ' ἂν λέγειν ἔχοιμι πρὸς τὰ τοῦδ' ἔπη,
εἴ μοι παρείκοι· νῦν δ' ἑνὸς κρατῶ λόγου.

I would have much to say in reply to his words, if speaking were practicable; but as it is there is just one *logos* (word, argument) of which I am master.

And he succeeds in getting Neoptolemos to accompany him and to leave Philoktetes. However, when Odysseus and Neoptolemos return, no words of Odysseus' have any effect upon his companion, who is intent upon giving back the bow. When Neoptolemos said, 'Justice and expediency make me obey those in authority' (925-6), he was still the subordinate. But by 1225 things are different—he has grasped the true nature of his relationship with Odysseus:

Οδ.   ... ἡ δ' ἁμαρτία τίς ἦν;
Νε.   ἣν σοὶ πιθόμενος τῷ τε σύμπαντι στρατῷ
Οδ.   ἔπραξας ἔργον ποῖον ὧν οὔ σοι πρέπον;
Νε.   ἀπάταισιν αἰσχραῖς ἄνδρα καὶ δόλοις ἑλών.

Od.   ... But what wrong did you commit?
Ne.   I complied with you and the whole army...
Od.   But what did you do that was unworthy of you?
Ne.   I ensnared a man with base deceit and trickery.

Odysseus can no longer hope to *peithein* the other man so, predictably, he tries threats. Neoptolemos is obdurate:

ἀλλ' οὐδέ τοι σῇ χειρὶ πείθομαι τὸ δρᾶν. (1252)

No, not even to your force do I yield obedience.

No 'persuasion', not even that of violence, can shake him now. Odysseus invokes *bia* more directly:

Οδ.   οὔ τἄρα Τρωσίν, ἀλλὰ σοὶ μαχούμεθα.
Νε.   ἔστω τὸ μέλλον. Οδ.   χεῖρα δεξιὰν ὁρᾷς
        κώπης ἐπιψαύουσαν; (1253-5)

Od.   Then we shall fight not the Trojans but you.
Ne.   Let the future take its course.
Od.   Do you see my right hand touching my sword?

But Neoptolemos is equal to the challenge, and Odysseus, subsiding into more vague threats, withdraws.

Further deceit or further persuasion is now impossible; all that is left is force. Odysseus makes one last desperate attempt to use *bia* (1295-8), but his force is met with a greater: the invincible bow. Odysseus' deceit, his persuasion and his force have all been brought to nothing. He leaves the scene for good.

Finally, Herakles. Whatever view one takes about the extent to which the dénouement coheres with the rest of the dramatic action,[31] there can be no doubt that the arrival of the divine hero introduces a new and more authoritative tone to the action. Hitherto we have seen speech and argument as mainly, if not entirely, a fumbling and flawed mode of communication; now, by contrast, we are confronted with the confident language of divine *fiat*. Herakles issues commands (1417, 1421, 1433, 1436, 1440, 1449) and makes definitive pronouncements both about the present (e.g. 1434-5, 1439-40) and about the future (1424, 1427, 1428, 1429, 1438). Podlecki[32] notices that Herakles' words are described three times as *muthoi* (1410, 1417, 1447), and argues that this term, which normally has the very general sense of 'word' or 'story', is here carrying a more precise semantic load, with the meaning '(divine) utterance'. This possibility cannot, I think, be ruled out; and in any case Podlecki has done well to draw our attention to the new sort of discourse which Herakles' pronouncements introduce.

However, from another, related point made by Podlecki one may reasonably wish to dissent. When Philoktetes hears the divine injunction to go to Troy, he answers it with the words οὐκ ἀπιθήσω τοῖς σοῖς μύθοις. (1447)

I shall not disobey your words.

On this Podlecki remarks (p. 245): 'Although Philoktetes has not been persuaded, he will nevertheless not disobey.' This quibble is not to be found in the Greek, *peitho* and *peithomai* being, after all, parts of the same verb.[33] It is quite implausible to deny that Philoktetes goes, at last, willingly to Troy, as is evident if we set the line just quoted into its immediate context:

Φιλ. ὦ φθέγμα ποθεινὸν ἐμοὶ πέμψας,
χρόνιός τε φανείς,
οὐκ ἀπιθήσω τοῖς σοῖς μύθοις.

Phil. Herakles, your voice is welcome to me; at last you have
appeared. I shall not disobey your words.

Mrs Easterling is surely right to argue that in these words, and in the reference to the 'judgement of friends' (1467) which is helping to direct Philoktetes to Troy, 'we should surely see the fulfilment of Helenos' words: Philoktetes is going willingly—and his whole tone in the closing anapaests is one of positive, even joyful, acceptance'.[34] After a chapter of unsuccessful and misguided attempts at using language to get one's own way, *Philoktetes* ends with two successful attempts: the (in the light of the 'known' outcome) startling persuasion of Neoptolemos by Philoktetes, and the climactic, and equally startling, persuasion of Philoktetes by Herakles.

One major issue in *Philoktetes* remains to be discussed: the oracle. Several scholars, among them Bowra and Alt, have argued that the importance of *peitho* in our play is related to the provisions of the oracle of Helenos in the following way. The oracle, it is suggested, enjoined from the first the use of persuasion; and the plan of Odysseus, which did *not* cater for the use of persuasion, thus ended inevitably in failure.[35] So, according to this interpretation, the drama turns on the circumstance that those endeavouring to recover Philoktetes for the Greek army did not comply with the terms of the oracle. As Alt puts it (p. 143), 'Bei aller Verschiedenheit, in der es (sc. das Orakel) erscheint, steht doch fest, dass es für Sophokles auf das ἑκών ['willingly'] ankommt, und da Odysseus dies missachtet, ist sein ganzer Plan von vornherein falsch und zum Scheitern verurteilt.'

The weaknesses in this view of the play have been exposed by a number of critics,[36] and we need here only summarize a few of the most serious objections. Firstly, as Waldock has trenchantly pointed out,[37] nowhere in the play does Sophokles make dramatic capital out of the supposed mis-taking of the oracle.[38] If this was the nub of the plot, one would have expected Sophokles to make the fact rather clearer to his audience than he has actually done. Secondly, it is wrong to treat the prophecy as something 'static', as if it were somehow implicit, in a final and complete form, already from the start of the play. In fact the details of the oracle are allowed by Sophokles to emerge 'in a piecemeal and ambiguous way',[39] so that the audience is never allowed to be quite sure about just what the oracle said. (To give one instance: in the version related by the 'false merchant', not only is the story potentially suspect because of the (to the audience) known duplicity of the narrator, but also the very prophecy he was narrating was uttered to Greeks by a reluctant Trojan—a further potential reason for calling its veracity into question.)[40] Consequently, since the precise terms of the oracle are never established, it is inappropriate to castigate certain of the characters for ignoring those terms. Odysseus and Neoptolemos merely do what most people do when they have inadequate knowledge about the future: they make the best guesses they can on the basis of the information they do have.[41]

However, if the attempt to establish the centrality of *peitho* to *Philoktetes* with reference to what the characters *know* is not successful, there is much more sense in a comparable enterprise with reference to the developing pattern of moral choices made by them. When in the first scene Odysseus rules out any other course than *dolos,* he is not simply rehearsing an abstract syllogism ('*A* and *B* and *C* are the possibilities; but *A* and *B* are in practice unavailable; therefore only *C* remains'), he is also making a moral choice: he is assuming that to deceive a man whom one has already dreadfully wronged is morally acceptable. But, as the whole of the developing relationship between Philoktetes and Neoptolemos—a relationship which culminates in a reconciliation based on trust and achieved through *peitho*—demonstrates, it would have been all along morally preferable to have tried to persuade Philoktetes rather than to have deceived him. And even the gods, who in other Sophoklean plays seem often conspicuously to fail to endorse qualities valued by the human characters, appear in the case of *Philoktetes* to do so: for Philoktetes only goes to Troy when induced to do so by the method which is ethically the most laudable one: *peitho*.

It is chiefly this moral aspect of *peitho* which is explored in *Philoktetes*. Chiefly—but not exclusively: for (in so far as a distinction can be drawn between the two categories) there is a political as well as a moral dimension to the persuasion which is used—at least to that used on Philoktetes. The central figure in the drama is an outcast from society, and as such is inferior to his hunters in status. But, because he has the bow, he is superior in power—hence his adversaries need *dolos*, not *bia* (cf. above, p. 64). The moment when Neoptolemos switches from *dolos* to *peitho* is the moment when he 'grows up' to equality with Philoktetes—hence he no longer needs the mode by which an inferior circumvents a superior, but that by which one equal can try to influence a peer: *peitho*. *Philoktetes* depicts the reintegration of an outcast into the collectivity which rejected him; and the agency of reconciliation is the political mode *par excellence, peitho*.

However, it would be very misleading to suggest that *Philoktetes* ends with as confident an affirmation of the efficacy of *peitho* in the good community as we find in, say, *Eumenides*. Indeed one might make out a case for the opposite view that, taking into account the unflattering light in which the army at Troy is presented, we must regard Philoktetes' reintegration into the army as a thoroughly pessimistic conclusion to the drama.[42] But that too would be an exaggeration. The truth is that the atmosphere at the end of *Philoktetes* is delicately poised between hope and sadness. While it is true that for Neoptolemos to take Philoktetes home would from many points of view set the most satisfactory seal upon the action,[43] it is also true that we want the pair of heroes to win the glory which awaits them at Troy.[44] Thus Philoktetes' ultimate decision to acquiesce in the injunctions of Herakles need not be castigated as a Sophoklean capitulation to 'the demands of the myth'. In going to Troy Neoptolemos and Philoktetes are accepting (as Herakles himself had accepted it before them) a duty to work in and with the wider community in accordance with the divine will.[45] If that community has not so far shown itself to be particularly admirable, at least the persuasion of Neoptolemos by Philoktetes gives grounds for hope that trust and friendship between human beings are possible.

In short, we may say that in *Philoktetes* persuasion is flawed, vulnerable, and sometimes ineffective: being so closely connected with the frailties of mere men, it lacks the magical and quasi-divine quality which it can have in Aischylos; and yet, if grounded in trust, *peitho* can still cause the hardest and bitterest heart to relent.

4.2 *Oidipous at Kolonos*

Critics have sometimes pointed out analogies between *Oidipous at Kolonos* (*O.C.*[46]) and both *King Lear*[47] and *The Tempest*.[48] Hate and love between parents and children, the literal and metaphorical implications of blindness,[49] the mighty wrath of a bowed old man—these are among the great themes shared by *Lear* and *O.C.*; while in the case of *The Tempest* the justness of the comparison derives mainly from the fact that each play is its author's last artistic statement,[50] a forceful yet sublime recapitulation of motifs which had occupied him in his earlier work. It is a measure of the stature of *O.C.* that analogies with these two Shakespearian masterpieces in no way diminish its own power or uniqueness.

Yet that power and uniqueness have not been well served by classical scholars. Less literary criticism, and certainly less good literary criticism, has been written about this play than about any of the other six extant Sophoklean tragedies. True, there have been several helpful essays in interpretation, particularly by English-speaking critics such as Whitman,[51] Linforth,[52] Shields,[53] John Jones,[54] Knox,[55] Easterling[56] and Gellie,[57] but the best comprehensive account of what is at stake in the play remains that given by Jebb in his commentary. At the moment there is in relation to *O.C.* a noticeable absence of the sort of polemical but creative debate which has been generated by, say, *Philoktetes*. Linforth's paper of 1951 represented a considerable advance (in the direction of a correct appraisal of the 'religious' element in the drama), but the ground which he won has been only sporadically re-occupied since. We are in urgent need of a full account of the play, along the lines of Schmidt's book on *Philoktetes*, which will examine together questions of 'meaning' and 'technique',[58] and attempt to locate exactly the areas upon which Sophokles wished to place dramatic emphasis.

In the absence of an agreed and coherent critical direction by which to orient oneself, writing about any particular theme in *O.C.* is especially hazardous, in that it is even more likely than thematic analyses usually are to create the impression that the chosen topic is the key to the drama, what the work is *really* about. Let us, therefore, admit without more ado that the theme of *peitho* does not lie at the heart of *O.C.* At that heart are, rather, such questions as how we evaluate the ambivalent figure of Oidipous (guilty or innocent? stern but just or harsh and vindictive? bringer of pollution or bringer of good fortune?) and what we regard as the significance of his transition from rejected outcast to sought-after and powerful hero; together with those other issues—blindness, anger, parents and chil-dren—which we referred to above in relation to the analogies with *Lear*. However, there can be no doubt that among the subsidiary motifs *peitho* does occupy a prominent place. Sophokles combines it with his main themes in order to sharpen their dramatic edge or to widen their moral and political reference; and in so doing he offers his audience another opportunity to look at a representation of those ways (persuasion, violence, deceit) which men will use to get the better of each other.

A convenient way of approaching our subject will be through some similarities to and contrasts with *Philoktetes*. Both *Philoktetes* and *O.C.* are concerned with the reaching of an end. The end in *Philoktetes* is the securing of the bow and person of Philoktetes; the end in *O.C.* is the securing of the body and goodwill of Oidipous. In each case, that which motivates those who desire to achieve the end is the pronouncement of an oracle, which states that the securing of Philoktetes/Oidipous will bring victory/advantage to those who take possession of him. In each case, again, there arises the question: how is the predicted and desired end to be achieved? And, in each case, Sophokles draws out the moral implications of the various answers to this question by dramatizing attempts to persuade, to deceive, and to use force. Furthermore, both *Philoktetes* and *O.C.* are concerned with the reintegration of a social outcast into the world of the polis, a reintegration which is associated in each case—albeit associated in different ways—with the successful operation of *peitho*: in *Philoktetes peitho* is the means by which Philoktetes is restored to the community, while in *O.C.* it is the mode of behaviour which characterizes the community to which Oidipous chooses to belong.

But there are also relevant differences between *Philoktetes* and *O.C.* Firstly, the question, 'How is Philoktetes to be secured for the Greek side?' is of dramatic relevance from the first to the last scenes of the play; but the question, 'How is the goodwill of Oidipous to be won?' is only a live issue in those episodes which are dominated by Kreon and Polyneikes. Secondly, whereas the relations between *peitho, dolos* and *bia* in *Philoktetes* are so intricate that we were led to adopt the metaphor of a ballet whose choreography it was our business to examine, in *O.C.* by contrast the depiction of the three modes of behaviour is much more straightforward. This is because deception plays only a small part in the action (a fact which, incidentally, is related to a more general feature of the play, namely the relative unimportance of the elsewhere typically Sophoklean concern with the gap between appearance and reality).[59] With the exception of minor references like 230ff, deception in *O.C.* is restricted to Kreon's plan to wheedle himself dishonestly into the favour of Oidipous. The trio is thus to all intents and purposes reduced to a duet, with the *peitho* of Athens and Theseus being opposed to the *bia* of the Theban Kreon. (Matters are, however, somewhat more complicated than this, as we shall see below.) Thirdly, in *O.C.* the political aspect of *peitho* and *bia* is of at least as great importance as the moral aspect; something which could not be said of *Philoktetes.* In fact in discussing *O.C.* we shall find a number of issues raised which take us back to our discussions of, e.g., the *Oresteia* and Aischylos' *Suppliants,* where the significance of persuasion and violence in the democratic Athenian city is highly relevant to the meaning of the drama.

The opening scene builds up a picture of a man who is separated from the place to which he has come: separated physically, for he is blind and everyone else is sighted; and separated socially, for he is an outcast. His only contact with the world comes through the love and nurture given him by Antigone. To the local inhabitants of Kolonos he is an outsider, and he admits that he is a man 'excluded from the polis', *apoptolis* (207; cf. *apolin,* 1357). As such he constitutes a problem for any polis to which he comes: is he to be accepted or not? The problem becomes much more acute when the chorus learns the exile's identity, but after initial consternation (n.b. ἰού, 220) their reaction is unambiguous enough: leave this land, lest you bring trouble upon our city (233-6). Antigone's intercession elicits a more moderate response from the chorus, but Oidipous still appears justified in his bitter reflection that Athens' reputation for protecting the *xenos,* 'stranger', is a sham (258ff). Nevertheless, his speech of self-defence produces a still more cautious reply by the chorus, who agree to leave to their ruler the final decision about this dangerous but possibly powerful (287-8) intruder.

The section of the action introduced by the unexpected arrival of Ismene fulfils an important role in the total dramatic economy, for it describes the real motives and intentions of Kreon and the sons of Oidipous, a description which in the course of the play will offer Oidipous (and the audience) a touchstone upon which to test the words and deeds of Kreon and Polyneikes. For what Ismene says makes it plain that Kreon, Eteokles and Polyneikes are all intent upon the same objective: *kratos,* 'power'.[60] In the past, whereas Antigone and Ismene have taken thought for their father's nurture, Polyneikes and Eteokles have had another priority, namely to get 'rule and a despot's *kratos*' (373). As for the future, the two brothers (416ff) and Kreon (396f), having learnt from an oracle that Oidipous 'will be to the men of that city an object of quest, alive and dead, for the sake of their well-being' (389-90), wish to get *kratos* over him (400, 408; cf. 392, 405)—not in order to give him honourable burial, but in order to use him for their own purposes. (Thus Sophokles prepares the ground for the exploration of means which he conducts later in the play.) Oidipous angrily dismisses any suggestion of a reconciliation, and turns his hopes towards his new polis, Athens (457-60).

With the arrival of Theseus these hopes begin to achieve solidity. In the very first speech which Sophokles gives to Theseus he places him in the same admirable category as that occupied by Odysseus in *Ajax:* he is a man profoundly aware of the limitations of humanity, and of the consequences for moral action entailed by those limitations:

> ...ἐπεὶ
> ἔξοιδ' ἀνὴρ ὢν χὤτι τῆς εἰς αὔριον
> οὐδὲν πλέον μοι σοῦ μέτεστιν ἡμέρας. (566-8)[61]

...for I know that I am a man, and that of tomorrow I have no greater share than you do.

It is quite in accordance with this wise prudence that Theseus will not pass judgement on Oidipous' case until he is in a position to give a sound opinion:

δίδασκ᾽· ἄνευ γνώμης γὰρ οὔ με χρὴ λέγειν. (594)

Tell me; I must not pronounce without due consideration.

And when he has heard Oidipous out—what he has suffered at the hands of Thebes, how he can help Athens, why there might come a time when that help might be needed—Theseus duly does what the chorus had not been willing or able to do: he accepts Oidipous into the polis of Athens:

...χώρᾳ δ᾽ ἔμπολιν κατοικιῶ. (637)[62]

...I will establish him as a citizen in this land.

This polis, like the Argos of Aischylos' *Suppliants,* like the Athens of the *Oresteia,* and indeed like the idealized conception of their own city which the Athenians liked to express (cf. above, p. 55), is a place which stands for reason, law and persuasion against the forces of threat and violence:

Οι. οὐκ οἶσθ᾽ ἀπειλὰς   Θη. οἶδ᾽ ἐγώ σε μή τινα
.   ἐνθένδ᾽ ἀπάξοντ᾽ ἄνδρα πρὸς βίαν ἐμοῦ.
       πολλαὶ δ᾽ ἀπειλαὶ πολλὰ δὴ μάτην ἔπη
       θυμῷ κατηπείλησαν· ἀλλ᾽ ὁ νοῦς ὅταν
       αὐτοῦ γένηται, φροῦδα τἀπειλήματα. (656-60)

Oid. You do not know the threats...
Thes. I know that no man shall remove you from here against (lit. 'in violence against', *pros bian*) my will. Many threats have blustered much in anger; but when good sense (*nous*) masters itself, then threats evaporate.

Thus when Oidipous says that he wishes to stay where he is, since *this* is the spot on which he will reverse the *kratos*-relationship between himself and those who expelled him (644-6), Theseus feels confident that the old man will be safe.

Although it has to be admitted that the Theseus of *O.C.* is one of the flattest characters in the entire corpus of Greek tragedy,[63] the very opposite is true of his city. Within the space of a single stasimon (668-719) Sophokles transforms Athens[64] from an agglomeration of the political virtues to a precisely realized and richly evoked locality, inexhaustibly fertile, blessed by the gods, and heavy with the sights, sounds and tastes of abundant nature.[65] But it remains, as Antigone says at 720-1, for Athens' glorious reputation to be put to the test. For Kreon now comes on to the scene. Surprisingly, in view of what we ' have heard about him, he begins by practising and advocating *peitho*. His first speech is a brilliant combination of subtlety and tact. In order to gain the Athenians' goodwill he flatters them, praising their nobility and their city's strength (728, 733-4). Then he mentions the aim of his visit (already, of course, known to the audience since Ismene came with the news); but quietens any possible anxieties by assuring his hearers that he has come to *persuade* Oidipous to return to Thebes:

> ἀλλ' ἄνδρα τόνδε τηλικόσδ' ἀπεστάλην
> πείσων ἕπεσθαι πρὸς τὸ Καδμείων πέδον... (735-6)

I, an old man, was sent to persuade this man to return with me to the land of Kadmos...

Furthermore, he states that he has been sent on this mission at the behest of the entire city of Thebes:

> ...οὐκ ἐξ ἑνὸς στείλαντος, ἀλλ' ἀστῶν ὕπο
> πάντων κελευσθείς... (737-8)

...not sent out by one, but under orders from all the citizens...

In other words, like Odysseus (*Phil.* 1243, 1257-8, 1294) and Menelaos and Agamemnon (e.g. *Aj.* 1136, 1242-3; cf. 1055), he represents his own conduct as properly democratic, being in accordance not merely with the majority view but with the consensus of the entire citizen body. He even turns directly to Oidipous and employs the same resoundingly democratic appeal:

> πᾶς σε Καδμείων λεὼς
> καλεῖ δικαίως... (741-2)

The whole Kadmeian people rightly calls you...

Kreon is still giving no hint that he will entertain the idea of any other mode of approach but *peitho*:

...σὺ νῦν
πρὸς θεῶν πατρῴων, Οἰδίπους, πεισθεὶς ἐμοὶ
κρύψον, θελήσας ἄστυ καὶ δόμους μολεῖν
τοὺς σοὺς πατρῴους... (755-8)

...in the name of your homeland's gods, Oidipous, be persuaded by me, and hide [your shame], by agreeing to go back to your city and the gods of your fathers...

One last compliment to Athens (758-9) and he is done.

Commenting on Kreon's speech, Linforth[66] rightly points out that Kreon does not know of the old oracle that Oidipous would find rest in a place which now seems likely to turn out to be Kolonos; nor does he know that Oidipous has already been granted sanctuary by Theseus; nor does he know that Oidipous has been told of the machinations in Thebes.

To [Kreon] Oidipous is still the helpless, hopeless wanderer that he has been for years; and though his very use of persuasion indicates that Oidipous may still be supposed to be resentful and stubborn, he is hopeful that he may succeed with soft words. But all that Kreon does not know, Oidipous knows, and the audience knows. Recognizing the skill of Kreon's plea and at the same time its futility, the spectator enjoys the manifest but unobtrusive irony.

That is true; but what is also true is that Kreon is, at best, guilty of *suppressio veri*: he gives no indication of the real motive which is leading him to wish to recover the person of Oidipous. What seemed to be persuasion was in fact deceit; and it is with this point that Oidipous begins his enraged reply.[67]

Oidipous justly accuses Kreon of making skilful but deceitful use of fine-sounding arguments:

ὦ πάντα τολμῶν κἀπὸ παντὸς ἂν φέρων
λόγου δικαίου μηχάνημα ποικίλον... (761-2)[68]

Brazen man! You would draw a cunning stratagem from any righteous argument...

Fair *logos*, which should be used for *peitho*, is being employed as a means to achieve *dolos*. Furthermore, Oidipous rebukes Kreon for trying to drag him back to Thebes by 'speaking harsh things in a softly winning way' (774). Kreon's speech has been dishonest (794), and *peitho* between him and Oidipous is out of the question:

ἐμοὶ μέν ἐσθ' ἥδιστον, εἰ σὺ μήτ' ἐμὲ
πείθειν οἷός τ' εἶ μήτε τούσδε τοὺς πέλας. (802-3)[69]

To me the sweetest thing is if you are able to *peithein* neither me nor
these men here.

Indeed, Oidipous is moved to voice his mistrust of able speakers in
general.[70]

At this point, when *dolos* and *peitho* have both failed, Kreon
changes tack: he threatens violence (814, 817). And he carries out
the threat: Ismene has already been seized (cf. 819), and Antigone is
to be abducted 'against her will, if she refuses to go willingly' (827).
Hearing Antigone's desperate cry, Oidipous calls upon the polis for
assistance; and the polis is indeed concerned, for the use of *bia* brings
into question the very essence of a city which operates by law and
consent:

Χο. πόλις ἐναίρεται, πόλις ἐμά, σθένει. (842)

Cho. My city is being destroyed—my city—by force!

Having used *bia* on the daughters (845, 867) Kreon now proposes to
use it on the blind old father (874). Once again the chorus reacts with
an outraged recognition of the fact that, if force prevails, the *city*
collapses:

τάνδ' ἄρ' οὐκέτι νεμῶ πόλιν. (879)

Then I shall consider this polis to exist no longer.

However, just as an inexorable dramatic logic brought Aischylos'
Argive king back in time, so now Theseus returns to defend the polis.

At once he gives orders for the abductors to be stopped, since he
has no wish to be ridiculed for being 'defeated by *bia*' (903). Then he
turns his attention to Kreon, who is still on the scene. Theseus might
reasonably enough reply to force with force (905-6)—for the
righteous city must have an ultimate sanction if *peitho* fails (as
Athene might have availed herself of the thunderbolt of Zeus, at
Eum. 826-9)—but it is more important that Kreon return the
maidens. However, this does not happen yet, for Theseus has some
home truths (literally) for the aggressor. He lectures Kreon on the
disparity between his conduct and that which is held to be right in
nomos-governed Athens:

⟨σὺ...⟩
ὅστις δίκαι' ἀσκοῦσαν εἰσελθὼν πόλιν
κἄνευ νόμου κραίνουσαν οὐδέν, εἶτ' ἀφεὶς
τὰ τῆσδε τῆς γῆς κύρι' ὧδ' ἐπεσπεσὼν
ἄγεις θ' ἃ χρῄζεις καὶ παρίστασαι βίᾳ.
καί μοι πόλιν κένανδρον ἢ δούλην τινὰ
ἔδοξας εἶναι, κἄμ' ἴσον τῷ μηδενί. (913-18)

> ...you have come to a city which practises *dike* and which does nothing
> without *nomos*; yet, setting aside the land's constituted authority, you
> have broken in, you abduct anything you like, and appropriate it by
> *bia*. You thought my polis was empty of men, or populated by slaves;
> and you thought I was equal to nothing.

Appropriately, Theseus employs persuasion, adducing the argument:
'Thebes would not approve of this sort of violent behaviour, you
know' (919ff). But he ends by suggesting that persuasion will, if
necessary, be backed up with force:

εἶπον μὲν οὖν καὶ πρόσθεν, ἐννέπω δὲ νῦν,
τὰς παῖδας ὡς τάχιστα δεῦρ' ἄγειν τινά,
εἰ μὴ μέτοικος τῆσδε τῆς χώρας θέλεις
εἶναι βίᾳ τε κοὐχ ἑκών· (932-5)

> I said it before, and repeat it now: let the girls be brought here with all
> speed—unless you want to be forced against your will to be a resident
> in this land.

'But Kreon is not finished yet. Deceit and force have both failed,
and now he tries persuasion. Not on Oidipous, but on Theseus...'[71] He
starts with a compliment to Athens, modulates to an implied assertion
of his own rights—these persons whom he has come to fetch are his
kin (942-3)—and then moves on to the offensive by deftly accusing
the Athenians of *bia* (943). At 947-50 he reverts to eulogy,
confessing his incomprehension that the fine city of Athens should
open its arms to a polluted outcast. The most outrageous rhetorical
stroke of all comes at 956-9, where Kreon pleads his age and the
justice of his case—this in front of Oidipous. (Gellie, p. 172, speaks of
'old, slow Kreon' who 'is after all Oidipous' uncle as well as his
brother-in-law'. But Kreon has not been subjected to the debilitating
ravages of exile.) After Oidipous' angry retort, Theseus reaffirms that
he will stand by him: Kreon's *dolos* (1026) has foundered. All that is

left to him is to threaten (1037); but Theseus is unshaken: 'Threaten if you like—but go' (1038).

There follows the chorus' vigorous evocation of the fight with Kreon's men for possession of the daughters of Oidipous. As we have seen, the just city must in the last resort be capable of backing up its persuasion with force: its leader must be 'war-wakeful' (ἐγρεμάχαν, 1054, if the text is sound here) and local contingents and full army alike must be strong in battle (1065-6). But strong they are, and the abductors are vanquished: the victorious hands of Theseus (1102-3) bring Antigone and Ismene back to their father.

The next phase of the action deals with the final, unsuccessful attempt to persuade Oidipous to reject his Athenian future in favour of a return to Thebes. This petitioner is at any rate less bold (1162) and more modest in his demands (cf. 1164-5) than was Kreon; but once Oidipous learns who he is—Polyneikes—he refuses even to hear his voice. However, Antigone intervenes with her own attempt to *peithein* her father; and her persuasion has far greater weight than that of either Kreon or Polyneikes, since it is grounded in love and trust (compare the persuasion of Neoptolemos by Philoktetes). She uses the classic Sophoklean formulae for encouraging the intransigent hero to relent: πιθοῦ μοι, 'comply with my request' (1181); ὕπεικε, 'yield' (1184); εἶκε, 'give way' (1201). Words, she argues, have no compelling force—a man is free to reject what they say:

> οὐ γάρ σε, θάρσει, πρὸς βίαν παρασπάσει
> γνώμης ἃ μή σοι συμφέροντα λέξεται. (1185-6)
>
> Fear not—he will not forcibly (*pros bian*) drag you from your opinion
> by words spoken not for your good.

Yet words do have a kind of magic, and Oidipous would not be the first stubborn heart to be charmed by them:

> εἰσὶ χἀτέροις γοναὶ κακαὶ
> καὶ θυμὸς ὀξύς, ἀλλὰ νουθετούμενοι
> φίλων ἐπῳδαῖς ἐξεπάδονται φύσιν. (1192-4)
>
> Other men too have evil children and a keen wrath, but, in being
> advised, their natures are charmed by the spells of friends.

This is a fine, eloquent and loving speech; and Oidipous is persuaded.

But when Polyneikes does enter and addresses Oidipous, his father, 'like a northern shore beaten by winter storms' (as the chorus sang in the preceding ode at 1240-1), does not utter a word. Antigone acts again as a gently persuasive intermediary, and Polyneikes agrees to put his case. He gives his own version of his mistreatment at the hands of Eteokles, describing what has happened to himself in terms designed to suggest to Oidipous an analogy between the fates of father and son:

> γῆς ἐκ πατρῴας ἐξελήλαμαι φυγάς... (1292)
>
> I have been driven from my fatherland as an exile...

The coming expedition against Thebes will, argues Polyneikes, be a just campaign (cf. πανδίκως; 'in a fully just cause', 1306). Then, as the vehemence of his attempted *peitho* increases, a familiar verbal pattern recurs: 'Relent' (εἰκαθεῖν, 1328), 'Be persuaded and give way' (πιθέσθαι καὶ παρεικαθεῖν, 1334). Interestingly, Sophokles gives Polyneikes almost the same argument which Theseus used earlier in the play.

> ὃς οἶδα καὐτὸς ὡς ἐπαιδεύθην ξένος,
> ὥσπερ σύ...
> ὥστε ξένον γ' ἂν οὐδέν' ὄνθ', ὥσπερ σὺ νῦν,
> ὑπεκτραποίμην μὴ οὐ συνεκσῴζειν... (562-6)
>
> I know that I myself, like you, was brought up as an exile (*xenos*)...
> So I would never turn aside from a stranger (*xenos*), such as you are now, nor refuse my help in saving him...

said Theseus, as he accepted Oidipous' petition.

> ...πτωχοὶ μὲν ἡμεῖς καὶ ξένοι, ξένος δὲ σύ. (1335)
>
> ...I am a beggar and a *xenos*, and you are a *xenos* too.

says Polyneikes, as he tries to get his own petition accepted by Oidipous. Both men's statements may be objectively valid, but Polyneikes' words carry far less weight than Theseus' since there is such a conspicuous discrepancy between the moral authority of the two.

It is this very discrepancy which Oidipous brings out at the beginning of his wrathful reply to the suit. Out of deference to his benefactor Theseus, Oidipous agreed to hear Polyneikes; but

Polyneikes is a villain, and what his father says in response to the attempt to persuade him will not please the son (1348ff). Just as Oidipous exposed the reality behind Kreon's *peitho*, so now he does something similar with Polyneikes. Polyneikes had claimed that both he and his father were beggars, but Oidipous challenges this. 'You were the cause of my exile':

> ... τὸν αὐτὸς αὑτοῦ πατέρα τόνδ᾽ ἀπήλασας
> κἄθηκας ἄπολιν... (1356-7)

> ...Me, your own father, you drove away and made citiless (*apolis*)...

Reacting with if anything even more rage than he had done to Kreon, Oidipous rejects Polyneikes' persuasion. He calls down dire curses upon the mooted expedition of the Seven, and in particular upon both his sons.

This terrible curse sparks off the last major dramatized scene of *peitho* in *O.C.*, that between Polyneikes and Antigone:

> Αντ. Πολύνεικες, ἱκετεύω σε πεισθῆναί τί μοι. (1414)

> Ant. Polyneikes, I beg you to comply with me in one request.

'Turn your back on Argos', she implores him (1416-17); but he too has his honour, and he will not yield (1426). As Kreon was guilty of actually suppressing truth, so Polyneikes intends to suppress it, for he will not disclose to his army Oidipous' doom-laden prophecies (1429-30). Nevertheless, he does show genuine concern for Antigone, and their parting is affecting—particularly if one allows oneself to recall the 'sequel', *Antigone*. In urgent words which are strongly reminiscent of the interchange between Tekmessa and Ajax at *Aj.* 591-5, Antigone makes a final appeal:

> Αντ. μὴ σύ γ᾽, ἀλλ᾽ ἐμοὶ πιθοῦ.
> Πο. μὴ πεῖθ᾽ ἃ μὴ δεῖ. (1441-2)

> Ant. Don't!—listen to me (*pithou*)!
> Pol. Do not urge me (*peithe*) when urging is out of place.

But, though her words are again based on affection, this time they fail to persuade;[72] and Polyneikes leaves the scene to face the fate which, as the audience knows, awaits him.

Three general points about *peitho* in *O.C.* are worth stressing. First, it is a *human* quality, depending for its effectiveness on the moral authority and credibility of the human agents who do the persuading. This anthropocentric aspect of *peitho* may surely be seen as connected with a wider feature of Sophoklean drama, in *O.C.* and elsewhere, namely the weight which human actions bear in the working out of the plot. (The matter is well put by Linforth in the course of an account of the oracles in *O.C.* '... the framework of the play is constructed of the oracles. But the oracles do not fulfil themselves. The moving force which produces the action of the play is not the oracles, but the *knowledge* of the oracles on the part of Oidipous and his kinsmen in Thebes... The oracles supply the warp for the dramatic fabric, but into the warp, and nearly concealing it, are woven the manifold threads of human will and human personality; the pattern of the play is in the woof'.)[73] The success and value of *peitho* in *O.C.* are not a function of any divine or magical power it may have. On the contrary, *peitho* only stands a chance of succeeding when it rests upon feelings of trust and honesty between persuader and hearer, feelings produced by the natures of the characters as human agents. (In this connection one may cite the mysterious coda to *O.C.*: the human *charis* shown by Theseus is reciprocated by Oidipous, and the righteous conduct of the good polis reaps its due reward; but whether *divine* favour smiles on Oidipous is more questionable. It has often been argued[74] that the gods who acquiesced in the hero's destruction in the first Oidipous play raise him up in the second one, but we must beware of imagining that *O.C.* ends in a glorious apotheosis. After all, the voice which summons Oidipous is strange, allusive and enigmatic, and gives no inkling of a majestic or godlike existence for him after his passing.[75])

Secondly, the scenes of *peitho* in *O.C.* play an important part in shaping the audience's attitude towards Oidipous. In view of the fact that Oidipous is physically and morally at the centre of the play, we are as spectators keenly interested in how he reacts to the various attempts to influence his conduct. When he exposes Kreon's *peitho* as fraudulent, we admire his intransigence. When he rebuffs Polyneikes, we are also with him; although here our response is far less clear-cut, in view of Antigone's speech at 1181ff, the savagery of Oidipous' curse, and the sympathy aroused by the parting of Polyneikes and Antigone. If Oidipous' resistance to *peitho* is important in moulding how we see him, his yielding to *peitho* is no less so. That he gives way to Theseus and Antigone (in agreeing to hear Polyneikes) increases rather than diminishes his stature. Without this partial willingness to bend 'one would have far less sense of the greatness... of Oidipous as a tragic figure: we must believe that he remains *open* to persuasion despite his intransigence'.[76]

The third point concerns *peitho* as a political quality. Like Aischylos in *Suppliants* and the *Oresteia*, Sophokles in *O.C.* dramatizes a picture of a city which, while reserving the right to use *bia* for 'positive' ends in an emergency, operates for preference by law, reason and persuasion. Theseus' Athens is a model polis; the principles which it enshrines are wholly admirable. Even at the end of the fifth century, when the bright vision celebrated in Perikles' 'Funeral Speech' had been shattered, Sophokles still affirmed, through the medium of drama, a faith in Athens' ideal self.

5

EURIPIDES

Introduction

Euripides is a dramatist of bewildering variety and puzzling contradictoriness. Far more than Aischylos or Sophokles, he defies reduction to a simple formula.[1] That this is the case may be seen if we notice some of the labels which have been used to characterize him: rationalist, idealist, irrationalist, mystic, misogynist, feminist, and so forth.[2] These positions can be defended from the text, in the sense that it is possible to cite characters uttering views which coincide with the respective labels. But this is an extremely naïve form of dramatic criticism, depending as it does on highly selective quotation. Moreover, the passages selected tend to be ones which are felt to stand out because they are 'out of character' for the speaker, and are hence likely to represent the playwright's own views. However— leaving aside the complex issues involved in deciding what is or is not 'out of character' for a figure on the Greek stage[3] — we must agree with those[4] who have pointed out that there is no earthly reason why Euripides' own views should not be expressed in words uttered *in* character as well as in those apparently uttered out of it. Once this truth is admitted, we have no rule-of-thumb for extracting passages which convey Euripides' 'views'. Euripides wrote whole plays, and his 'views' were conveyed to the audience through those whole plays, not through particular bits of them. His many-sidedness cannot be rendered manageable with scissors and paste.

Reacting against the hazardous enterprise of 'labelling' Euripides, several scholars have turned to a less ambitious area where more solid results may be achieved: the formal and dramatic-structural analysis of specific plays.[5] But the problem of how to cope with Euripides' diversity has not been altogether abandoned. A pragmatic approach was adopted by D.J. Conacher in *Euripidean Drama* (Toronto, 1967). He has sections on 'mythological tragedy', 'political tragedy', 'realistic tragedy', 'romantic tragedy' and 'tragédie manquée'. Sensibly, he does not try to force the plays into a hypothetical development from one sort to another—the early *Hippolytos* and the late *Bakchai* are both 'mythological', the early *Medea* and the late *Orestes* both 'realistic', etc. But, while Conacher respects the many-sidedness of Euripides' output, he is open to the criticism that he compartmentalizes *too* much. He administers a valuable corrective to the labellers, but does not offer us a satisfactory perspective from which we can relate the various dramatic types to one another.

More fruitful is the kind of approach favoured by A. Rivier,[6] who observes that the plays vary in their way of engaging with moral issues. The principal analytical categories which he employs are 'le tragique', 'le romanesque' and 'le pathétique'. The first quality is exemplified, he argues, by what he regards as the five perfect *chefs d'oeuvre* (*Alkestis, Medea, Hippolytos, Iphigeneia at Aulis, Bakchai*), together with *Herakles* which, apart from a lack of compactness in the first five hundred lines, deserves in Rivier's view to be ranked with the great five. Two quotations will help to make clear what it is that Rivier sees as 'tragic' about these six works:

...every tragedy is in a sense religious, since it serves to place man in illuminating contact with that which is beyond him and judges him. (140) A play which excludes the workings of necessity is bound to lack the metaphysical profile characteristic of tragedy. (141)

In other words, 'le tragique' can be present only when human action is set in a wider, constraining metaphysical context. The plays which exhibit 'le romanesque'—*Ion, Iphigeneia in Tauris,* for example—present moral action in a quite different light:

What captivates us [in *I.T.*] is not the characters but what happens to them, the adventures they have. The play is about the game which these three young people are playing with themselves, with chance, with death. (117)

That is, the interest of the drama turns not on human confrontation with a supra-human *necessité* but on the intriguing (in both senses) spectacle of what happens. Lastly there are some works (e.g. *Trojan Women*) which embody 'le pathétique'. Suffering exists here, to be sure; but its metaphysical significance is not explored (contrast *Herakles*): examination of causes is replaced by concentration on the pathetic consequences of evil-doing for its helpless victims.

Rivier's case is argued with far greater care than my summary gives him credit for, but it is still easy enough to pick holes in it. Surely *I.A.* does not rank as a *chef d'oeuvre*? Is not the metaphysical resonance of *Medea* feeble when compared with, say, *Hippolytos* or *Bakchai*? Yet we must not overlook Rivier's insight: that to differentiate between Euripides' plays in terms of the perspective from which moral action is viewed offers us a way of coping with the dramatist's diversity. How this differentiation can work in practice may be seen if we consider a particular contrast drawn by Rivier (p.142), between *Herakles* and *Ion*. The focus of the contrast is the notion of *tyche*. In *Herakles* (esp. 1357) the word connotes 'fate', 'destiny', with its full tragic sense of a devastating and, from the human point of view, irrationally destructive power. In *Ion* it refers to 'chance', 'fortune', 'luck' (1512-15). The semantic distinction parallels a difference in the perspective from which human life is perceived in the two works.[7]

However we regard Rivier's categorization and evaluation of particular plays, his general strategy for dealing with Euripidean variousness is worth borrowing, and a way of doing so is to think of the dramas as occupying positions along a scale. At one end we should want to locate *Bakchai, Hippolytos* and *Herakles*, works in which moral issues are explored in the widest and deepest manner. Next we should place e.g. *Medea*, which shares the seriousness of the other three but lacks their metaphysical scope. A play such as *Suppliants*, with its narrower focus, subjects moral and political action to a less radical (in the etymological sense) scrutiny than do the great three tragedies. (As Zuntz correctly observed: 'the boundless and comfortless universe visualized by Euripides is tragic from end to end. *The slice of it* which he presents in *The Suppliant Women* is not' (my emphasis).)[8] We should put *Suppliants* near the middle of the scale. Finally, at the opposite end to *Bakchai, Hippolytos* and *Herakles* would be, say, *Helen* and *I.T.*, in which fantasy and adventure have replaced anything which we should wish to describe as 'tragedy'. This is not, it must be emphasized, classification for its own sake: it is designed to prevent us from approaching any individual play with inappropriate expectations.

Given that the works of Euripides differ so much in scope and perspective, are we not left with an *oeuvre* as fragmented as ever? To counteract this impression we must highlight features genuinely shared by many or most of the plays. I propose to concentrate on one such feature, both because it is in my view the most important one, and because it relates directly to the theme of this book.

Again and again in Euripides we find issues made *explicit*: matters are debated and argued openly. The reason why it is especially risky with Euripides to choose one speech or one argument from a play and say, 'This is what Euripides believed', is that his works are composed of a series of interlocking arguments. Various characters put cases, trying to persuade each other, and the audience, of the validity of their position. The effect of the play consists of nothing less than the complex impact of all the interlocking persuasions, arguments and cases. An important corollary is that, since the characters are what they can persuade the audience they are, and since the audience makes up its mind about the moral worth of the characters on the basis of their persuasive utterances, it follows that the audience's evaluation of characters may alter if the tone or content of the persuasive utterances changes. Such shifts happen often in Euripides. We shall be looking at one case in *Hekabe*; two others may be mentioned.

In *Andromache* the eponymous character begins in a position of helplessness. As the foreign, imported wife of Neoptolemos she is being persecuted by his Greek-born wife Hermione during his absence. Andromache has fled to the altar of Thetis, whence she delivers a moving, elegiac lament. That the audience's sympathy is with Andromache at this stage is underlined by her stylized debate with Hermione, who alludes to and glories in her fine apparel—any woman in Greek tragedy who takes a vain interest in her appearance is up to no good—and who presents her case in an unpleasant and spiteful way. When Hermione's father Menelaos kidnaps Andromache's baby son in order to force her to leave her refuge at the altar, the moral lines have been pretty clearly drawn. By line 501 the pathos of Andromache's situation increases further: her hands are bound, and she and her son are to be done to death. Subsequently the aged Peleus, Neoptolemos' grandfather, intervenes on Andromache's side, and shows Menelaos up for a blusterer, with the result that Hermione's moral stock falls, by implication, still lower. But with the entry of Hermione's nurse the perspective shifts. It seems that Hermione is now remorseful, frightened of what her husband will say when he returns, and intent on self-destruction. Her abject reappearance confirms this: now it is she who is the powerless victim. Fortunately, just as Peleus had come on to the scene to rescue Andromache, so Orestes now arrives to do the same for Hermione.[9] He further complicates the play's moral landscape by telling Hermione, who had originally been betrothed to him, that he has put in train a plan to kill Neoptolemos, for having stolen his bride. Orestes and Hermione leave together, making way for yet another shift of feeling as Peleus returns. He learns at second hand (through a messenger) and at first hand (as his grandson's corpse is carried on) of Neoptolemos' death. Finally Thetis appears, to locate the action in a wider mythical context. But, though she predicts burial for Neoptolemos, remarriage for Andromache, and a happy, deified, submarine life for Peleus in her own arms, the dénouement cannot remove the impression of a world in which the reaching of sound moral judgements is a precarious and unstable business.[10]

There is an even starker reversal of feeling in *Herakleidai.* In the first part of the play moral issues are displayed in a clear-cut manner. The children of Herakles have come as suppliants to seek the aid of the Athenians, whose noble king Demophon agrees to help them, for all the right reasons (236ff). He also discomfits the unsavoury herald of Eurystheus, who is persecuting the children. As late as the narrative describing the battle between Eurystheus' forces and those championing the cause of the children, Eurystheus cuts a cowardly figure: he refuses to accept Hyllos' challenge to individual combat (813ff). But when Eurystheus has been defeated and is at the mercy of Herakles' mother Alkmene, attitudes alter. The chorus at first refuses to countenance Alkmene's plan to kill the prisoner; and, when he eventually speaks, Eurystheus is far different from what we had been led to expect.

So far we, like the Athenian spectators, have seen him through the eyes of his enemies; we, like them, could not but integrate his actions into the traditional picture of a despicable tyrant. And now here he is himself, and he has a case... It is not as a ruthless addict to violence that Eurystheus has set himself above justice and decency: it was fear that pushed him to reckless violence... [11]

In *Herakleidai* as in *Andromache*, Euripides deliberately puts a moral case as persuasively as he can, then reverses it by looking at the situation through the eyes of the 'guilty' party.

In the theatre these shifts of perspective must have been demanding and puzzling.[12] On the basis of our modest evidence about fifth-century tragedy we may assert that they seem to have been characteristic of Euripides and not characteristic of Aischylos or Sophokles. With good reason, scholars have been inclined to regard *instability* as a major constituent of Euripides' dramatic vision. The point is made strongly by W. Jens: 'Here there is nothing fixed, no ties upon which one might depend. At any moment a sudden change may occur; nothing is permanent. When trouble comes—and it comes without warning—a person is alone. The whole world looks down on the unfortunate.'[13] There is truth in this. As Jens himself notes, Euripides several times draws explicit attention to the lack of a stable relationship between one's expectation of how someone will behave and their actual behaviour. 'There's no art to find the mind's construction in the face' is a sentiment which recurs significantly often;[14] and, lest my argument seem to rest on passage-hunting of the sort that was condemned above, it may be added that Euripides wrote one play, *Helen*, in which the principal theme is the deceptiveness of appearances. Moreover, Euripides also dwells on a more fundamental sort of instability, that to which human fortune is exposed in virtue of the threat posed by violence, whether divine (*Hippolytos, Herakles, Bakchai*) or human (e.g. *Trojan Women, Hekabe*).

But it is not true to say that, in the face of all this, individuals are 'alone'. Even at the end of the three most profoundly bleak tragedies, something is salvaged: Theseus and Hippolytos, Theseus and Herakles, Kadmos and Agaue testify to the strength of *philia* which links one to those allied to oneself by friendship or kinship. This is one tie whose validity is not discredited. Since Greek tragedy examines the tensions latent in moral conduct, it is no surprise that the claims of *philia* are not always free from doubt or conflict[15]—Elektra is drawn in two different directions by *philia*, to avenge her father or to respect her mother. But it remains predominantly true that whoever behaves in accordance with *philia* in Euripidean tragedy is, to that extent, offered for our approbation.

There are other moral positives in Euripides too: the self-sacrifice of Makaria, Menoikeus and the rest; the loyalty and wit of Helen in *Helen*; the behaviour of Admetos towards his *xenoi*. But the presence of such persons does not invalidate the view that Euripides disturbs his audience by the disequilibrium of his plays. In Kitto's words, 'Euripides is "the most tragic of the poets" [an allusion to Aristot. *Poet.* 1453a29] because in his drama this balance, or order, seems the most unattainable.'[16] The notion of unattainable balance, of powerfully conflicting tensions, is important for a full response to Euripides. It is reflected in the deliberate structural dislocations in some of the works; notably *Herakles*, in which the action takes a wholly new direction half-way through when the principal character has been struck—literally out of the blue—with madness. And it is reflected too in the explicitness of the plays, in their construction out of counterstressed arguments which the audience tests and weighs. In this sense Aristophanes was right to have his 'Euripides' espouse *peitho* (cf. above, pp. 43-4). As we hear Alkestis, Admetos and Pheres in *Alkestis*, Helen and Hekabe in *Trojan Women,* or Elektra and Klytaimestra in *Elektra*, it becomes plausible to envisage each character in turn as a defendant, presenting him- or herself, with boundless rhetorical inventiveness and dexterity, in the most suitable light.[17] We have recently been urged[18] to regard Greek tragedy as a drama of significant action; it should not be forgotten that, above all in the hands of Euripides, it was also a drama of the persuasive word.

5.1 *Medea*

In chapters 1 and 2 we underlined the need to refrain from compartmentalizing *peitho* into the political and the magical/erotic. Indeed we have repeatedly come across examples of the indivisibility of *peitho* in this respect, for instance in the reference to Peitho's lovely eyes at the supremely 'political' climax of *Eumenides.* Yet we have also seen how in different contexts different sides of *peitho* are emphasized. The harsh world of Euripidean *Realpolitik* offers further instances of this, since in play after play—*Suppliants, Trojan Women* and (see below, pp. 170-86) *Hekabe* could be cited—*peitho* is deployed in a manner which could no more be described as 'magical' than could the argumentation in the Melian Dialogue. However, to posit a crudely linear historical-evolutionist account of the development from Aischylos to Euripides, according to which the magical/erotic changes to the severely political, does justice neither to the political implications of argument in Aischylos nor to the many-sidedness of *peitho* in Euripides. Thus in *Medea*, although 'political' issues do arise because Medea herself is a person deprived of a polis, the persuasiveness which she exercises has more than a hint of the demonic wiliness which characterizes Klytaimestra in *Agamemnon*; and it draws on magic as well as rhetoric, since Medea has mastery over *pharmaka* in the literal sense as well as over the metaphorical *pharmaka* of the word.[19]

A second point to make about *peitho* in *Medea* relates to Medea's position as a barbarian and a rejected wife. Her inferior position *vis-à-vis* all the men she deals with renders hopeless any use by her of either *bia* or open *peitho*. She is thrown back upon deception. We shall observe how closely *dolos* and *peitho* are intertwined in *Medea*.

Thirdly, we shall notice how Euripides expresses through formalized, even ritualized, patterns on stage (e.g. supplication) the process by which one person gets another to acquiesce.

Lastly—an obvious but crucial point—we shall find examples of what we described earlier as the quintessentially Euripidean characteristic: the depiction of characters who exist in virtue of the cases which they present on their own behalf. The confrontations between Jason and Medea could hardly be bettered as evidence for this.

In the course of the opening speech, delivered by Medea's nurse, two important features of the mythical background are mentioned: the fact that it was *eros* for Jason that brought Medea to Greece (8), and the story of how she demonstrated her devotion to him by inducing the daughters of his usurping enemy Pelias unwittingly to kill their own father (9ff). 'Inducing' is a translation of *peisasa* (derived from *peitho*): from the outset, Medea is presented as mistress of *peitho*. Furthermore, it is relevant that this act of persuasion was, to judge from other mythical accounts,[20] at the same time an act of deceit. Medea tricked the girls into killing Pelias and then boiling his limbs, having convinced them that by so doing they would effect his rejuvenation. Medea's power is *peitho dolia*.

Medea is in exile. Not only is she a fugitive from her Kolchian homeland, but she is now in a Greek city different from the one at which she first arrived. Her condition is dangerously close to that of the tragic figures (Oidipous at Kolonos, Philoktetes, etc.) who are *apoleis,* 'citiless'—particularly as she suffers from the additional handicap of being a woman, and is hence already in a subordinate position. Dishonoured and rejected by Jason in favour of the daughter of King Kreon of Corinth, Medea is behaving in the obdurate manner typical of the Sophoklean 'hero'.

> ὡς δὲ πέτρος ἢ θαλάσσιος
> κλύδων ἀκούει νουθετουμένη φίλων· (28-9)[21]

> She is as immovable as rock or sea-wave when she hears the advice of *philoi.*

The lines may remind us of the unresponsiveness to persuasion of Ajax (*Aj.* 594-5). But Ajax was reduced to that state only after he had tried, and failed in, a desperate move—the *dolos* of attempting to kill the commanders. Medea, too, may 'plan something':

> στυγεῖ δὲ παῖδας οὐδ' ὁρῶσ' εὐφραίνεται.
> δέδοικα δ' αὐτὴν μή τι βουλεύσῃ νέον. (36-7)

> She hates the children and loathes their sight. I fear she may plan some new thing.

That a plan is required sooner rather than later is clear when the children and their tutor come on stage, for the tutor has heard a rumour that Kreon intends to banish mother and children from Corinth. The nurse expresses her fear for the children: Medea is a dangerous woman (90ff).

With the off-stage cry at 96-7, immediately identified as Medea's, the emotional tempo quickens, as is signalled by the metrical shift from iambics to anapaests. Once more the nurse fears the reaction of mother to children, for Medea's nature is ἄγριον, 'wild' (103). In their turn the chorus of local women, although sympathetic to Medea, want to see her face-to-face in order to try to persuade her to relent; but the nurse fears she will be unable to *peithein* her mistress (184). The total effect of the powerful sung scene between the nurse, the off-stage Medea and the chorus (96-213) is to create a sense of Medea's inflexible resistance to persuasion—an impression which is of considerable dramatic importance, as it provides a significant counterweight to the apparent flexibility which Medea's adoption of *peitho dolia* subsequently produces. All the while she is piecing together the various elements of her *dolos,* it is vital that the audience feels the presence of an urgent and passionate purpose which is resolute until it is confronted by the reality of infanticide.

Before making her exit the nurse reflects thus (190ff):

σκαιοὺς δὲ λέγων κοὐδέν τι σοφοὺς
τοὺς πρόσθε βροτοὺς οὐκ ἂν ἁμάρτοις,
οἵτινες ὕμνους ἐπὶ μὲν θαλίαις
ἐπί τ᾽ εἰλαπίναις καὶ παρὰ δείπνοις
ηὕροντο βίου τερπνὰς ἀκοάς·
στυγίους δὲ βροτῶν οὐδεὶς λύπας
ηὕρετο μούσῃ καὶ πολυχόρδοις
ᾠδαῖς παύειν, ἐξ ὧν θάνατοι
δειναί τε τύχαι σφάλλουσι δόμους.
καίτοι τάδε μὲν κέρδος ἀκεῖσθαι
μολπαῖσι βροτούς· ἵνα δ᾽ εὔδειπνοι
δαῖτες, τί μάτην τείνουσι βοήν;
τὸ παρὸν γὰρ ἔχει τέρψιν ἀφ᾽ αὑτοῦ
    δαιτὸς πλήρωμα βροτοῖσιν.

> It would be all right, I think, to consider foolish and not at all wise those men of the past who discovered songs for festivities, banquets and dinner parties, merry music for life; and none has discovered how to stop men's hateful griefs by means of poetry and songs of many notes, the hateful griefs which cause death and misfortunes, ruining families. And yet it is a gain that men heal these by means of songs. But where there are pleasant banquets, why raise vainly the song? For the abundance of the feast already offers a pleasure of its own to men.[22]

The ending is homely and inconsequential, but what precedes it has more serious implications. Song cannot stop grief, says the nurse, yet the attempt to heal grief by song does bring some benefit, some relief. The ambivalence here ascribed to song has been taken to have a bearing on Euripides' attitude to the effect of tragedy as a whole.[23] Whatever of that, it is certainly of relevance to the theme of *peitho* in *Medea*. As depicted in this play, the power of the persuasive word is great, yet it is inadequate to heal the wounds inflicted by broken trust or vicious revenge.

The modulation (214) from anguished cries to consummately skilful argument does not represent a 'change of mood' on the part of Medea, but should rather be seen as a function of the formal shift from sung to spoken language: it is a product of the conventions of tragic utterance rather than a feature of Medea's character.[24] The passion and the resolution are still there, but this time they express themselves in an extended and controlled exercise in *peitho* (214-66). Medea's eventual aim is to induce the chorus 'to be silent' (263) if Medea should devise some 'resource' or 'contrivance' by which to revenge herself on Jason (260-1). The speech immediately achieves its objective; not surprisingly, for it is a masterpiece. She begins by playing for her hearers' goodwill: 'I came out so as to avoid the reproach that I am haughtily keeping myself aloof' (214ff). She also shows herself properly conscious of her position as an alien: 'Certainly, a *xenos* must adapt to the polis' (222). At the heart of the speech is Medea's assertion of what she has in common with those she is persuading—the fact of being a woman.²⁵

> πάντων δ' ὅσ' ἔστ' ἔμψυχα καὶ γνώμην ἔχει,
> γυναῖκές ἐσμεν ἀθλιώτατον φυτόν. (230-1)

> Of all creatures that have breath and judgement, we women are the most wretched.

To regard these lines, and those that follow, as embodying Euripides' own views is quite gratuitous; what matters about them is that they are perfectly judged to win over the female chorus. That is not to say that Medea's opinions are entirely context-bound, however. In particular, line 247 is of significance for an understanding of the drama as a whole:

> ἡμῖν δ' ἀνάγκη πρὸς μίαν ψυχὴν βλέπειν.

> As for us (sc. women)—we are compelled (lit. 'there is an *ananke*, necessity') to keep our eyes fixed on one man.

Medea is a tragedy of *ananke*: not a metaphysical 'necessity', but one implicated in the social circumstances in which Medea finds herself. The 'necessity' which produces disaster here is comprehensible in purely human terms. (That is why, while we recognize the greater depth of *Hippolytos*, *Herakles* and *Bakchai*, we cannot, I believe, avoid finding *Medea* more directly moving.)

If the central part of Medea's speech to the chorus dwells on what she has in common with them, the last section emphasizes how her plight is even sorrier than that of other women. She lacks the three supports which might have mitigated her powerlessness: city, home, friends (253ff). At this rhetorically clinching juncture she makes her request for 'silence', ending with a show-stopping coda:

> ... σιγᾶν. γυνὴ γὰϱ τἄλλα μὲν φόβου πλέα
> κακή τ' ἐς ἀλκὴν καὶ σίδηϱον εἰσοϱᾶν·
> ὅταν δ' ἐς εὐνὴν ἠδικημένη κυϱῆ,
> οὐκ ἔστιν ἄλλη φϱὴν μιαιφονωτέϱα. (263-6)

[I ask you] to keep silent. For in other ways a woman is fearful and
cowardly, when it comes to defending herself and looking upon the
sword; but when she is wronged in the matter of bed, no mind has
thoughts more bloody.

We should not regard Medea as deceiving the chorus at 214-66 (*pace*
Page on 231). The fact that not all her generalizations about women
fit her own case exactly, and the fact that she mentions her lack of a
brother (257) without going into the embarrassing question of what
happened to him,[26] mean only that Medea is doing the best she can as
counsel in her own defence. This is the kind of *peitho* that Euripidean
characters use again and again, though not always so effectively.
Medea does not need to deceive the chorus: they are already
sympathetic to her, and share her powerlessness. It is only with her
superiors in power that Medea must resort to *peitho dolia.*

At about 269 the first 'superior' enters. Kreon recognizes that
Medea is *sophe*, 'clever' (285), and that if he 'is softened' he may
regret it (291). But Medea begins to use her cleverness in the hope of
softening him. As earlier with the chorus, she seeks to disarm her
addressee by taking 'what people think of me' as her point of
departure. 'What people think' is that she is *sophe,* and this has led
them falsely to suspect her.

> ...εἰμὶ δ' οὐϰ ἄγαν σοφή. (305)

...but I am not so clever as all that.

She projects the character of a reasonable and acquiescent person:

> νυμφεύετ', εὖ πϱάσσοιτε· τήνδε δὲ χθόνα
> ἐᾶτέ μ' οἰϰεῖν. ϰαὶ γὰϱ ἠδιϰημένοι
> σιγησόμεσθα, ϰϱεισσόνων νιϰώμενοι. (313-15)

Make your marriage, and good luck to you; but let me remain in this
land. For, though we have been unjustly treated, we shall be silent,
having been defeated by those more powerful.

Kreon resists, but at 324 Medea suddenly puts greater pressure on him by concentrating her *peitho* into the ritual gesture of supplication,[27] thus making explicit her powerlessness in face of his power:

μή, πρός σε γονάτων τῆς τε νεογάμου κόρης.

Do not, I beg you, by your knees, by your newly-wedded daughter.

It is characteristic of the almost exclusively philological bias of Page's commentary that his only remark on this line refers to the unusualness of the double metrical resolution. He notes that one of the other two cases of the phenomenon in *Medea* occurs at 710, where, as at 324, 'the irregular rhythm clearly corresponds to the agitated mood of the speaker'. But *why* is the speaker (Medea both times) 'agitated'? Because, both times, she is initiating her ultimate persuasive resort—the act of supplication.

With unerring accuracy Medea seizes on the potentially weak point at which she can exploit Kreon—his relationship with his child. Kreon admits as much:

Μη. ὦ πατρίς, ὥς σου κάρτα νῦν μνείαν ἔχω.
Κρ. πλὴν γὰρ τέκνων ἔμοιγε φίλτατον πολύ. (328-9)

Med. O my homeland, how I think of you now!
Kr. My country is dear to me, too—dearest of all things, save for my children.

But Kreon is still in control. He threatens to break the deadlock which Medea's supplication has imposed, by using *bia* (335). Medea's response—to ask for just one more day's grace in which to plan for exile and provide for the children—is directed unswervingly at its target:

οἴκτιρε δ' αὐτούς· καὶ σύ τοι παίδων πατὴρ
πέφυκας· εἰκὸς δ' ἐστὶν εὔνοιάν σ' ἔχειν.
τοὐμοῦ γὰρ οὔ μοι φροντίς, εἰ φευξούμεθα,
κείνους δὲ κλαίω συμφορᾷ κεχρημένους. (344-7)

Have pity on them. You yourself are a father of children, so it is reasonable for you to show goodwill. For myself I have no worry about my exile; but, for their subjection to misfortune, I grieve.

Kreon feels *aidos*, the sense of inhibition which ought to make one revere a suppliant (349). To his moral credit, but to his eventual downfall, he agrees to Medea's request.

After a brief, transitional expression of sympathy by the chorus, in which they raise the matter, later to become crucial, of where Medea can seek asylum, Medea herself dominates the stage with a long speech which leaves her purposes no longer in doubt. Her address to and supplication of Kreon was merely a trick (368-70). In the breathing-space thus won, she plans to encompass the deaths of Kreon, Kreon's daughter and Jason (374-5). But how to do it? Two methods, burning[28] the bridal chamber and the stealthy use of the sword, are rejected as involving the risk of capture and hence ignominy: Medea has an Ajax-like consciousness of the threat posed by enemies' laughter to her 'heroic' status.[29] But a third deceitful method, poisoning, is approved:

κράτιστα τὴν εὐθεῖαν, ᾗ πεφύκαμεν
σοφαὶ μάλιστα, φαρμάκοις αὐτοὺς ἑλεῖν. (384-5)

It is best to take the straightest route, the one where our nature is most clever *(sophai)*—to catch them with *pharmaka.*

It is surely a premeditated paradox that a trick is described as 'straight'. Pucci's comment on Medea's alarmingly abnormal form of heroism is illuminating: 'The *arete* of the hero here becomes *sophia*, an improbable heroic virtue... "Straight" is the epithet of truth, justice, and whatever is free from manipulation and trickery. Poisons are not.'[30] The role of a wife should be to receive into the house raw materials brought from outside by her husband, to store them, and, where necessary—preparing food, weaving cloth, etc.—to transform them into useful products. A woman who plots against her husband perverts the wifely role: appropriately she may in myth use either poison (Kreousa in *Ion*; cf. Klytaimestra in *Agamemnon*, likened by Kassandra (1260-1) to one preparing a *pharmakon*) or a 'charmed', lethal robe (Deianeira in *Women of Trachis*; Medea later here; and cf. the robe used to ensnare the returning husband in *Agamemnon*). The 'anti-wife' uses 'anti-produce', and in so doing follows a course that is far from 'straight'.

In imagination Medea has completed the murders (386). She returns to the question which occupied the chorus earlier: what next? No answer presents itself, but, if a refuge does appear, she will put her *dolos* (391) into action. She goes into the enterprise as if into a glorious battle (403):[31] for her, *bia* is out of the question as a mode of action, so her 'heroism' must express itself through other channels.

Like her first great speech, her second ends with a generalization about women:

> πρὸς δὲ καὶ πεφύκαμεν
> γυναῖκες, ἐς μὲν ἐσθλ᾽ ἀμηχανώταται,
> κακῶν δὲ πάντων τέκτονες σοφώταται. (407-9)

Furthermore, I was born a woman, and women are quite resourceless in doing noble things, but are most clever *(sophotatai)* in the contriving of every evil.

As we saw (above, p. 64), the link between women and deceitfulness[32] is well established in Greek myth. This point has a bearing on the debate over whether we accept Page's view of Medea as a 'barbarian sorceress' (xiv of his edition). It is perfectly clear that Medea's use of *dolos* in the situation in which she finds herself does not mark her out as any more 'exceptional' than any of the other (usually Greek, not barbarian) mythical women who resort to similar practices. On the contrary: it is just the means one would expect to be employed. This very expectation is taken up and challenged in the chorus' reflections at 410ff:

> ἄνω ποταμῶν ἱερῶν χωροῦσι παγαί,
> καὶ δίκα καὶ πάντα πάλιν στρέφεται.
> ἀνδράσι μὲν δόλιαι βουλαί, θεῶν δ᾽
> οὐκέτι πίστις ἄραρε·

Waters of holy rivers flow backwards: *dike* and all things are reversed. It is *men's* plans that are deceitful *(doliai)*. Pledges sworn by the gods are no longer firm.

Well aware of the role of the poet in constantly re-forming ancient tradition, Euripides gives his chorus a telling point against the common mythical assumption of women's infidelity: 'If *we* (sc. women) had been granted Apollo's gift of song, we should have sung a rival hymn against *man's* unfaithfulness.' Nor is the opposition man/woman the only one to be severely tested. Medea is non-Greek, yet she deserves sympathy (τάλαινα, 'poor creature', 437; δύστανε, 'poor thing', 442) because she is an exile, without honour, and in a 'husbandless bed' (434ff). In Greece, meanwhile, the *'charis* of oaths' has disappeared, and *aidos* 'has flown away into the sky' (439-40). The chorus has warned that any attempt simplistically to equate 'Greek' with 'good' and 'barbarian' with 'bad' will not do. The effect of the next scene, between Jason the Greek and Medea the barbarian, is to enforce that warning.

The confrontation (or *agon,* as it seems to have become conventional to designate this sort of combination of paired set-speeches and more staccato interchanges)[33] is a perfect instance of Euripidean characters as defendants, presenting their cases so as to achieve the maximum degree of *peitho* with their audience. Medea introduces her defence with a formula that can be paralleled almost exactly from the extant works of the legal speech-writers:

ἐκ τῶν δὲ πρώτων πρῶτον ἄρξομαι λέγειν. (475)

I shall begin my speech with events which happened first.[34]

Themes familiar from the play so far are rehearsed: I betrayed my home, but you betrayed me in return:

προύδωκας ἡμᾶς, καινὰ δ' ἐκτήσω λέχη,
παίδων γεγώτων... (489-90)

You betrayed me, and took a new wife to bed, *although there were children* (sc. from our union)...

The function of marriage was to produce children who would ensure the continuance of the *oikos.* By having children, Medea had fulfilled her role as wife. Jason, who might have pleaded extenuating circumstances if Medea had been childless (490-1),[35] was without even that justification. His behaviour lacks the virtue which some of his moral betters in Euripides possess (Admetos and Herakles in *Alkestis,* Theseus in *Herakles*)—willingness to return *charis* for *charis.* When the powerless Jason supplicated Medea, she accepted him (496-8); now she is the one who must supplicate, but without success.

Jason tries to fight *peitho* with *peitho,* using self-consciously rhetorical language:[36]

δεῖ μ', ὡς ἔοικε, μὴ κακὸν φῦναι λέγειν... (522)

I am obliged, it seems, to be no bad speaker...

τοσαῦτα μέν σοι τῶν ἐμῶν πόνων πέρι
ἔλεξ'· ἅμιλλαν γὰρ σὺ προύθηκας λόγων. (545-6)

Such is my answer to what you said about my exertions; for it was you
who initiated this contest of *logoi.*

But his case is weak. To argue that Kypris, not Medea, was the one
who saved him (527ff) may be subtle but it is also hollow. How about
the argument that Jason *has* reciprocated *charis* for *charis* since he has
given Medea the blessings of Greek culture?

πρῶτον μὲν Ἑλλάδ' ἀντὶ βαρβάρου χθονὸς
γαῖαν κατοικεῖς καὶ δίκην ἐπίστασαι
νόμοις τε χρῆσθαι μὴ πρὸς ἰσχύος χάριν. (536-8)

First, instead of a barbarian land, you dwell in Greece, know *dike,* and
follow *nomoi,* exempt from the gratification of force.

No Greek would have regarded this proposition as self-evidently
absurd; but *in this play* the chorus has already advised of the
flimsiness of the Greek/barbarian distinction,[37] while not long ago
Kreon, Greek ruler of a Greek city, threatened to break by *bia* the
supplication of barbarian Medea (335). Next Jason asserts that,
through being in Greece, Medea has been able to enjoy a reputation
(doxa, 540) for being clever *(sophe,* 539); but the play has already
shown us that *doxa* (cf. 292-3) and *sophia* (285, 303 etc.) can get one
into trouble. As for the argument that by marrying the new princess
he is enhancing the prospects of his children by Medea, this is exposed
by the amazing half-line at 565, which the whole weight of the play
reveals as fraudulent:

σοί τε γὰρ παίδων τί δεῖ;

What need have *you* of children?

Medea's reply retains the self-consciously rhetorical approach to
speaking which has already been noticed.

ἦ πολλὰ πολλοῖς εἰμι διάφορος βροτῶν.
ἐμοὶ γὰρ ὅστις ἄδικος ὢν σοφὸς λέγειν
πέφυκε, πλείστην ζημίαν ὀφλισκάνει·
γλώσσῃ γὰρ αὐχῶν τἄδικ' εὖ περιστελεῖν,
τολμᾷ πανουργεῖν· ἔστι δ' οὐκ ἄγαν σοφός.
ὡς καὶ σὺ μή νυν εἰς ἔμ' εὐσχήμων γένῃ

λέγειν τε δεινός. ἒν γὰϱ ἐκτενεῖ σ' ἔπος·
χϱῆν σ', εἴπεϱ ἦσθα μὴ κακός, πείσαντά με
γαμεῖν γάμον τόνδ', ἀλλὰ μὴ σιγῇ φίλων. (579-87)

In many ways I differ in my opinions from other mortals. For, in my
eyes, whoever is a villain but is clever *(sophos)* at speaking, that man
deserves the greatest punishment. He is confident that he will conceal
his villainy by his speech, so he boldly proceeds with his crimes. But he
is not so clever *(sophos)* as all that. Do not, then, stand before me with
your fair pretence and able speaking; for one word will dispatch you. If
you were honourable, you would have made this marriage with my
consent (lit. *peisanta*, 'having persuaded me'), instead of concealing it
from those close to you.

Her half-line, 'But he is not so clever as all that', is a nice instance of
the verbal ingenuity which Euripides has given to Medea. She made
an almost identical remark to Kreon at 305 ('But I am not so clever as
all that'). The same form of words is used in different contexts, to
different addressees, with different tones—to Kreon, reassuring,
almost wheedling; to Jason, angry and scornful. A similar 'repetition'
occurs at 625 in Medea's shot at the departing Jason, νύμφευε, 'go
and enjoy your marriage', which echoes her νυμφεύετε, 'go and enjoy
the marriage you are making' to Kreon at 313. There the tone was
reassuring (Kreon's reply at 316 makes this certain), but to Jason
Medea's attitude is venomous and bitter. These tonal changes
symbolize the difference between the scenes as a whole. With Kreon
it paid to feign a tactical mildness; Jason, apparently beyond the reach
of mere verbal deception, receives the full torrent of Medea's
resentment.

'The essential relevance of the scene with Aigeus must be its stress
on the value and importance of children.'[38] This is surely right.
Aigeus, king of Athens, is passing through Corinth after a visit to the
Delphic oracle, which he consulted on account of his childlessness
(669-71). With Kreon and Jason the weak spot which Medea probes
is their relationship with their children; with Aigeus, though in his
case the relationship is only hoped for, the same weakness can be
exploited. Placing herself once more in the ritual position of
inferiority Medea supplicates Aigeus (709ff), imploring him to
receive her into his polis:

οὕτως ἔρως σοὶ πρὸς θεῶν τελεσφόρος
γένοιτο παίδων, καὐτὸς ὄλβιος θάνοις.
εὕρημα δ' οὐκ οἶσθ' οἷον ηὕρηκας τόδε·
παύσω δέ σ' ὄντ' ἄπαιδα καὶ παίδων γονὰς
σπεῖραί σε θήσω· τοιάδ' οἶδα φάρμακα. (714-18)

So may your desire, with the gods' aid, become productive of children;
and may you yourself die happy. You do not know what good fortune
you have found here. I shall end your childlessness, give you the power
to beget children. Such are the drugs *(pharmaka)* which I know.

If he offers her a polis of refuge—whose importance the Corinthian
women hailed in the preceding song—she will offer him fulfilment of
his *eros*—whose power the chorus evoked in the same ode. This
promise illustrates Medea's magical-erotic *sophia*: she can create
children. But she can also destroy them. Her *sophia,* like her
peitho—able either to express openly the justice of her case or to
bring about ruin upon those persuaded—is ambivalent.

Aigeus agrees to accept Medea, but she wants him to confirm this
on oath, *Medea* being a play about, among other things, the
consequences of not keeping one's word. Aigeus complies: 'Well, if
you like, I will not refuse you this' (742); his acquiescence recalls
Kreon's. The oath taken, and the third and final stage of her plan
achieved, Medea dismisses Aigeus with total confidence in success:

χαίρων πορεύου· πάντα γὰρ καλῶς ἔχει.
κἀγὼ πόλιν σὴν ὡς τάχιστ' ἀφίξομαι,
πράξασ' ἃ μέλλω καὶ τυχοῦσ' ἃ βούλομαι. (756-8)

Farewell: be on your way. All is now well. I shall come to your city as
soon as possible, having achieved what I intend, and having met the
fortune which I wish to obtain.

The polis of Athens has confirmed its reputation as haven of the
oppressed (cf. the idealizing beginning of the next choral ode); but in
Medea it will receive no ordinary suppliant. For now she lays before
the chorus what she will do before leaving Corinth. Implicit in what
she says is the paradox whereby the language of 'straight' heroism is
applied to a distinctly 'crooked' ruse. She affirms that she will win a
'glorious victory' over her enemies, the word chosen being *kallinikos,*
an epithet of Herakles and a term redolent of Pindar's world of
athletic immortality.[39] Yet it is as mistress of *peitho dolia* that she will

overcome Jason, thanks to *malthakoi logoi,* 'soft words' (776, cf. 316). In order to practise a *dolos* on the princess (783), she will beg that her children be allowed to stay; they will then take the girl a poisoned robe and an equally deadly golden diadem. In accordance with what she perceives as the demands of heroism—to prevent the laughter of her enemies (797), to be harsh to her foes and kind to her friends (809)—she concludes that the murderous plot *must* be followed by the deaths of her own children. She believes she is imprisoned by necessity (814). It is all a consequence of the one occasion when she was not mistress but victim of *peitho*: ἀνδρὸς Ἕλληνος λόγοις πεισθεῖσα, 'persuaded by the words of a Greek man' (801-2).

Metaphorically, the chorus supplicates Medea (853-5), begging her not to kill her children; the children themselves, they imagine, will do the same (863). But so far Medea shows no sign of weakening. When Jason duly arrives, Medea's *peitho dolia* exploits the same self-deprecating tone that deceived Kreon. Another generalization about women—calculated to appeal to Jason, who is himself prone to generalizing about women—is pressed into rhetorical service:

> ἀλλ' ἐσμὲν οἷόν ἐσμεν, οὐκ ἐρῶ κακόν,
> γυναῖκες· οὔκουν χρῆν σ' ὁμοιοῦσθαι κακοῖς,
> οὐδ' ἀντιτείνειν νήπι' ἀντὶ νηπίων. (889-91)

> We are what we are: I won't say an evil—just women. You should not rival us in wickedness, nor return folly for folly.

Medea is in full control, until the tutor brings on her children. As soon as they touch her (899), she is shaken; and it becomes clear that the play may yet develop into a tragedy, in our modern sense. Jason will certainly do nothing which might avert it, for he does not comprehend Medea at all. He sees her as *sophron,* 'sensible', capable of keeping within reasonable limits; in fact she is extreme (cf. 819: 'All *logoi* of compromise (lit. 'in the middle') are superfluous'). She understands Jason well enough, though, and appeases his curiosity with another generalization about her sex:

> γυνὴ δὲ θῆλυ κἀπὶ δακρύοις ἔφυ. (928)

> Women are but females, and prone to tears.

She then moves to the point of her interview with him: 'Ask Kreon that the children be allowed to stay in Corinth.' The next few lines, with their bitter irony at Jason's unconscious expense, reveal the interaction of persuasive wills which Medea's request sets in train and dominates:

Ια. οὐκ οἶδ' ἂν εἰ πείσαιμι, πειρᾶσθαι δὲ χρή.
Μη. σὺ δ' ἀλλὰ σὴν κέλευσον αἰτεῖσθαι πατρὸς
      γυναῖκα παῖδας τήνδε μὴ φεύγειν χθόνα.
Ια. μάλιστα, καὶ πείσειν γε δοξάζω σφ' ἐγώ.
Μη. εἴπερ γυναικῶν ἐστι τῶν ἄλλων μία. (941-5)

Jas. I do not know if I shall *peithein* him; but I must try.
Med. Then tell your wife to beg from her father that the children be reprieved from exile.
Jas. Very well—and I think I shall *peithein* her.
Med. You will if she is like other women.

The last, bitter line is surely meant to reflect Medea's memory of the erotic *peitho* which Jason once exerted over her. Experience has made her less gullible; she can now manipulate *peitho* to her own purposes, and is a shrewd judge of its effect on others. While Jason thinks that he will be able to persuade the princess unaided (962-3), Medea has summed her up more accurately: precious gifts are what will win *her* over:

πείθειν δῶρα καὶ θεοὺς λόγος·
χρυσὸς δὲ κρείσσων μυρίων λόγων βροτοῖς. (964-5)

The saying goes that gifts can move *(peithein)* even gods. For mortals, gold is more powerful than any number of *logoi*.

As the children leave—perhaps, we surmise, for the last time[40]—the chorus is left to reflect. There is no doubt that the *peitho* in Medea's beautiful but dangerous gifts will be irresistible:

πείσει χάρις ἀμβρόσιός τ' αὐγὰ πέπλον
χρυσότευκτόν τε στέφανον περιθέσθαι. (983-4)

The grace *(charis)* and perfumed brilliance of the robe and golden crown will *peithein* her to put them on.

This *peitho* is deceptive, and will lead the girl to *ate*, 'ruin' (987-8).

The children return, in fact for the last time, with their tutor (1002). The success of Medea's *dolos* means that she is now

inextricably caught in the web of necessity which she herself wove:
the children *must* die:

Πα.	τί δαὶ κατηφεῖς ὄμμα καὶ δακρυρροεῖς;
Μη.	πολλή μ' ἀνάγκη, πρέσβυ· ταῦτα γὰρ θεοὶ
	κἀγὼ κακῶς φρονοῦσ' ἐμηχανησάμην. (1012-14)

Tutor.	Why this downcast eye, this crying?
Med.	I *must* cry, old man. The gods and I, in my senselessness,
	contrived this.

Actually the gods have little to do with it: the emphasis throughout
has been on human actions. In the famous farewell to the children
(1021-80), Medea has to face the consequences of those actions.

One of the ideas usually involved when we call something 'tragic' is
wasted potential. In *Medea* it is the mother's bringing up of her
children which is ἄλλως, 'in vain' (1029-30). What their loss will
mean to her can be felt from 1040ff, when the children turn to her and
laugh. Hitherto, laughter has been the reaction with which Medea's
enemies will greet her downfall; now it is something far more
innocent and more painful. Euripides dramatizes a moment like that
when love for Jason once overcame Medea: passion temporarily
overrules 'cleverness'. But this time the moment is short-lived, and
laughter again becomes the scornful weapon with which her enemies
will hurt her (1049-50). Even to admit *malthakoi logoi*, 'soft words',
to her heart she regards as a sign of cowardice (1051-2). As Othello
justifies murder to himself by assuming the role of impartial judge
(e.g. V.ii.88: 'I, that am cruel, am yet merciful'), so Medea distances
herself from the act by representing it as a sacrifice (1054).[41] Once
more she falters, once more she confirms her resolve by arguing that
justice is on her side (1056ff). Finally, she embraces the children and
feels the sweetness of their breath and skin.

Rightly and naturally in view of what they and we have just seen,
the chorus now broods over the sadness of parenthood and the
disappointment and sorrow which it can bring. Then a messenger
enters, to seal the necessity which Medea perceives to be driving her
on. It appears that Kreon's daughter was, as Medea predicted,
instantly susceptible to the *peitho* of the gifts; with what fatal results
for herself and her father, the messenger's narrative makes plain. The
secret power of Medea's *pharmaka* (1126, 1201) has had its ruinous

effect. The chorus sees in this the hand of something more than human, a *daimon* (1231-2). Kreon had jumped to the same conclusion (1208). Given the extraordinary events with which they have been confronted, they could hardly do otherwise. But for the moment the Medea whose behaviour the audience witnesses remains firmly on the human plane.

Twice more she affirms that she *must* kill her children (1240, 1243), and leaves to do so. The chorus hears the offstage cries, and cites the case of Ino, who killed her own children and then committed suicide by throwing herself into the sea. The ending of *Medea* shows that this precedent is unduly pessimistic, for Medea emerges in a position of superiority beyond anything we have seen. Just when the audience is expecting the *ekkuklema* to be rolled out displaying a tableau of the murdered children, Medea appears in a manner reminiscent of a *dea ex machina*, [42] borne upon the chariot of her grandfather Helios.

As the power-relation between Jason and Medea has changed since the action began, the audience's response to their respective 'cases' may need to alter too. Jason's second defence-speech is at 1323-50. He is now *apais*, 'childless', to the sadness of which condition the whole play testifies. What of his protestations against the unfairness of it all?

> τὸν σὸν δ' ἀλάστορ' εἰς ἔμ' ἔσκηψαν θεοί... (1333)

> The gods sent the avenging spirit who should have punished *you* against *me*.

However sympathetic the audience may now be to Jason—and there are analogies with our response to the broken Kreon at the end of *Antigone*—his implied self-exoneration cannot outweigh all the arguments brought against him earlier by Medea. Nor does his characterization of Medea as a monster (1342-3) convince. Her tragedy is that she is *not* outside the human moral game. Its emotional rules still apply to her, in spite of the fact that her dramatic (and literal) superiority make her superficially like Dionysos at the end of *Bakchai*. The difference is that Medea still strongly feels the pull of her relationship with Jason; and this colours her all-too-humanly-intelligible bitterness.

For the end of *Medea is* bitter. Whereas in some Euripidean tragedies (*Hippolytos, Herakles, Bakchai*) human contact enables mortals to salvage something out of the wreckage, here there is no such solace. Jason is prevented from kissing or even touching his children, actions whose emotive impact Medea herself demonstrated earlier.[43] The focus of the drama may have been on interaction between humans rather than between humans and gods, so that the metaphysical precariousness of mortality is not explored; but, within this narrowed scope, Euripides offers a deeply moving picture of the devastation which insensitivity and lack of understanding, vulnerability and resentment, can produce.

Within that framework, the main point to make about *peitho* is its ambivalence. It is an extension and an expression of Medea's *sophia*, that cleverness which enables her to present the justice of her case with unique eloquence, and to work out her plan of horrible revenge with unique flair. Just as *sophia* is a quality of mind that can show itself in other ways than speech, so *peitho*—which, certainly in relation to Medea herself, one might define in *Medea* as the power of influencing others by one's *sophia*—may work through gift, potion, love or words. What matters, of course, is the use to which these means are put. Whether Medea's *sophia* and *peitho* are compatible with the heroic terms in which her actions are often presented in *Medea* is, at the least, an open question. It would seem that, in this play as elsewhere, Euripides was dramatizing a situation in which to act as one must and to act heroically may not be the same thing.

5.2 *Hekabe*

Even while Medea is using *peitho* for purposes which can only be called murderous, she never wholly forfeits our sympathy, because we sense both what she has suffered at the hands of Jason and what anguish is caused her by the prospect of losing her children. Nevertheless, *peitho* in *Medea* is not an agency of healing or delight, and it is undeniably put to morally dubious ends. This aspect of *peitho* is developed in *Hekabe,* but in a way that robs it of all charm and magic. In *Hekabe peitho* is coarsened, almost brutalized, to match the qualities which the stage-figures all too often evince. It is an enormously powerful means, which one has to possess in order to survive.

The tone of the play's moral action is set in the first speech by the ghost of Hekabe's murdered son Polydoros. He had been sent for protection to the Thracian king Polymestor, along with a quantity of gold, which was likewise intended for safe-keeping. Unfortunately, as Medea knew, gold is a strong persuader. Breaking the obligations of *xenia* and abandoning his responsibility as a trustee,[44] Polymestor had killed Polydoros. He did the deed when Troy had fallen, or rather, when Priam had fallen, 'slaughtered at the god-built altar at the bloody hands of Achilles' son' (23-4)—the description conveys not only the cowardice of Polymestor, who waited till he was sure he was on the winning side, but also the sort of conduct perpetrated during the war in whose aftermath *Hekabe* is set. As for the other incident of violence referred to by Polydoros—the sacrifice of Hekabe's daughter Polyxene which the ghost of Achilles has demanded—it may be true to say, with Steidle, that 'the justification of human sacrifice is only called into question in one passing remark by Hekabe at 260ff and is, apart from that, a *donnée* of the drama and hence unproblematical',[45] but the proposed act remains sombre and pitiably wasteful, even if it is not brought about by a motive as squalid as that which, we are told, impelled Polymestor.

There follows a song of foreboding, sung by Hekabe, who has dreamed an alarming dream about Polyxene and Polydoros. The entry of the chorus confirms her fears so far as her daughter is concerned.

> ἐν γὰρ 'Αχαιῶν πλήρει ξυνόδῳ
> λέγεται δόξαι σὴν παῖδ' 'Αχιλεῖ
> σφάγιον θέσθαι· (107-9)

> In the full assembly of the Achaians, it is said, they resolved to sacrifice your daughter to Achilles.

Opinion was divided, but one speaker swayed the crowd:

> σπουδαὶ δὲ λόγων κατατεινομένων
> ἦσαν ἴσαι πως, πρὶν ὁ ποικιλόφρων
> κόπις ἡδυλόγος δημοχαριστὴς
> Λαερτιάδης πείθει στρατιὰν
> μὴ τὸν ἄριστον Δαναῶν πάντων
> δούλων σφαγίων εἴνεκ' ἀπωθεῖν,
> μηδέ τιν' εἰπεῖν παρὰ Φερσεφόνῃ

στάντα φθιμένων
ὡς ἀχάριστοι Δαναοὶ Δαναοῖς
τοῖς οἰχομένοις ὑπὲρ Ἑλλήνων
    Τροίας πεδίων ἀπέβησαν. (130-40)

The zeal of straining arguments was equally balanced, until that
shifting-minded *(poikilophron)*son of Laertes—a sharp one, a
sweet-tongued crowd-pleaser—persuaded *(peithei)* the army not to
rebuff the best of all the Greeks for the sake of sacrificing a slave, nor
to allow any of the dead to stand before Persephone and say that the
Danaans had left Troy's plains without repaying a favour *(charis)* to
those who died for the Greeks.

The sketch of the deviously persuasive Odysseus is very like that
given by the hostile chorus at *Aj.* 148ff; with the difference that in
Hekabe the character of Odysseus as he appears on stage is in accord
with the picture of the tricky orator already given, whereas in *Ajax*
Odysseus' reflective wisdom is in marked contrast with the
impression left by the choral gossiping. On *Hek.* 130ff it is also worth
noting that Odysseus is *poikilophron.* 'Shifting' is rather feeble for
poikilos, which

is used to refer to the sheen of a material or the glittering of a weapon, the
dappled hide of a fawn, or the shining back of a snake mottled with darker
patches. This many-coloured sheen or complex of appearances produces an
effect of iridescence, shimmering, an interplay of reflections which the
Greeks perceived as the ceaseless vibrations of light. In this sense, what is
poikilos, many-coloured, is close to what is *aiolos,* which refers to fast
movement. [46]

Poikilos is used of persons displaying the kind of cunning intelligence
covered by the Greek word *metis,* which is in turn frequently found in
contexts dealing with the contriving of a *dolos.* [47] (A neat example of
the relationship between the semantic areas of *poikilos* and *dolos* is
given by the opening of Sappho's first poem:

ποικιλόθρον' ἀθανάτ' Ἀφρόδιτα,
παῖ Διός δολόπλοκε, λίσσομαί σε·

Immortal Aphrodite of the variegated *(poikilos)* throne, daughter of
Zeus, weaver of *doloi,* I beseech you.) [48]

ὁ ποικιλόφρων ...πείθει, 'the man with the shifting mind persuades',
offers another illustration of the potential interweaving of *peitho* and

dolos.

The chorus urges Hekabe to resort to the only sources of aid which remain to her: supplication of the enemy commander, and invocation of the gods (144ff). Like Medea,[49] she is powerless not simply in virtue of being a woman but because she has no male relative to whom she may turn for redress. Hekabe is *apolis*[50] in a sense hardly less literal than Medea is:

> τίς ἀμύνει μοι; ποία γέννα,
> ποία δὲ πόλις; φροῦδος πρέσβυς,
> φροῦδοι παῖδες. (159-61)

> Who will defend me? What child is left? What city?
> The old man is gone, and the children.

Calling Polyxene out, Hekabe relates to her that the κοινά... γνώμα, 'common opinion' (188-9)—i.e. the view reached in common assembly—is that she should die. Hekabe records the duly democratic nature of the proceedings:

> ἀγγέλλουσ᾽ Ἀργείων δόξαι
> ψήφῳ τᾶς σᾶς περί μοι ψυχᾶς. (195-6)

> They say that the Argives resolved by a vote concerning your life.

As in A. *Supp.* 600ff the terminology (δοκεῖ, 'it is resolved', ψῆφος, 'vote') reflects the usage of the Athenian democratic polis; but the outcome in *Hekabe* is the killing of a young innocent, not the preservation of suppliants—a difference which can scarcely be irrelevant to the way in which Aischylos and Euripides wanted their audiences to evaluate these two deliberative bodies.

Odysseus' opening words (218ff) reinforce the feeling that we have to do with the deliberations, for good or ill, of a democratic polis:

> γύναι, δοκῶ μέν σ᾽ εἰδέναι γνώμην στρατοῦ
> ψῆφόν τε τὴν κρανθεῖσαν· ἀλλ᾽ ὅμως φράσω.
> ἔδοξ᾽ Ἀχαιοῖς παῖδα σὴν Πολυξένην
> σφάξαι...

> Woman, I think you know that the opinion and vote of the army have been ratified,[51] but still I shall tell you. The Argives have resolved to sacrifice your daughter Polyxene...

Relations between the Greeks and Hekabe are not, however, to be regulated by such due and ordered process. 'Do not [bring it about that you must] be dragged away [from Polyxene] by *bia*; do not come to a contest of strength with me; recognize your [lack of] power' (225-7). Hekabe reminds Odysseus of the time when their relation of inferior-superior was reversed. During the war, Hekabe had been in a position to unmask Odysseus as a spy. But Odysseus had used his full persuasive repertoire, including initiating the ritual which placed maximum pressure on the addressee:

> Εκ. ἥψω δὲ γονάτων τῶν ἐμῶν ταπεινὸς ὤν;
> Οδ. ὥστ' ἐνθανεῖν γε σοῖς πέπλοισι χεῖρ' ἐμήν. . .
> Εκ. τί δῆτ' ἔλεξας δοῦλος ὢν ἐμὸς τότε;
> Οδ. πολλῶν λόγων εὑρήμαθ', ὥστε μὴ θανεῖν. (245-50)

> Hek. Did you humbly grasp my knees?
> Od.   So fervently that my hand 'died' upon your robe. . .
> Hek. What did you say then, when you were my slave?
> Od.   Any argument I could muster, to avoid dying.

But now Odysseus has refused to return the *charis*. We recall 131ff where, according to the chorus, Odysseus argued that a *charis* ought to be reciprocated: the inconsistency would suggest that this Odysseus holds the same merely instrumental view of morality as does the Odysseus of *Philoktetes*. By contrast, the Odysseus of *Hekabe* differs sharply from his namesake in *Ajax*, who recognizes (1365) that 'I too shall come to that need'. In *Hekabe* we have mainly to do, not with the tragic equality of all mortals in the face of powers greater than they,[52] but with the painful results to which *inequalities* of power *between mortals* can lead in a world where *tyche*, in the sense of random chance, rules human affairs.

Odysseus' rejection of *charis* is the starting point for Hekabe's mighty attempt to *peithein* him to save Polyxene. In an outburst which may at first sight seem extraneous (perhaps 'an expression of the poet's views') but which actually accords with the bitterly unheroic light in which political behaviour appears in *Hekabe*, Hekabe abuses those speakers who care nothing for the morality of what they are doing provided they achieve their objective of successful public *peitho*:

> ...ἢν τοῖσι πολλοῖς πρὸς χάριν λέγητέ τι. (257)

> ... provided you say something to the taste of the majority.

Yet Hekabe's own method is *peitho,* her own speech self-consciously rhetorical:

> τῷ μὲν δικαίῳ τόνδ' ἁμιλλῶμαι λόγον·
> ἃ δ' ἀντιδοῦναι δεῖ σ' ἀπαιτούσης ἐμοῦ,
> ἄκουσον. (271-3)
>
> That is my argument on the count of equity (*dike*).
> Hear now of your obligation to me to return a favour.

Her appeal culminates in an exact parallel to Odysseus' own earlier behaviour, as she supplicates him (275, 286). One of the arguments she deploys is a bald version of the perception more memorably expressed in the exit-speech of Kassandra in *Agamemnon,* the first words of *Women of Trachis,* or the last words of *Oidipous Tyrannos,* a perception which could stand better than most as a motto for the tragicness of Greek tragedy: 'The powerful should not exercise their power unjustly, nor the fortunate expect their fortune to last for ever. I was fortunate once, but am so no longer: one day took all my success from me' (282-5). She concludes by urging Odysseus to use his *peitho* again upon his fellow-Greeks, in order to effect the reprieve of Polyxene:

> τὸ δ' ἀξίωμα, κἂν κακῶς λέγῃ, τὸ σὸν
> πείσει· λόγος γὰρ ἔκ τ' ἀδοξούντων ἰὼν
> κἀκ τῶν δοκούντων αὐτὸς οὐ ταὐτὸν σθένει. (293-5)
>
> Your authority—even if your arguments are bad—will carry (vb. is *peithein*) your case; for the same *logos* does not have equal weight when it comes from one with standing and from one without.

Odysseus' reply exemplifies what a virtuoso can do with a bad case. His first point is one of Shylockian subtlety: I'll return my favour to *you,* but I am under no obligation to your daughter. *Via* the (surely?) uncontentious generalization that 'too many cities undervalue the noble and eager man', Odysseus slides to the (surely?) equally safe assertion that 'therefore Achilles deserves all honour'. Again, who could disagree with the idea that 'a friend should be honoured when he is dead as well as when he is alive'? The conclusion that Polyxene must die seems inevitable—no reasonable person could reject it. Or rather, no reasonable Greek: for 'you barbarians pay scant respect to *philoi,* and fail to honour your noble dead' (328ff). The implied moral superiority of Greek over non-Greek is emphatically not corroborated by this play, any more than Jason's comparable assertion is in *Medea*; but it enables Odysseus to end on a self-righteous note, a measure of how far his rhetorical expertise has carried him since he began.

Unimpressed, the chorus remarks that to be overwhelmed by *bia* is the slave's lot (332-3). Since there is no independent umpire present, Hekabe can hope for nothing more from her own speaking:

> ὦ θύγατερ, οὑμοὶ μὲν λόγοι πρὸς αἰθέρα
> φροῦδοι μάτην ῥιφέντες ἀμφὶ σοῦ φόνου· (334-5)

> Daughter, my *logoi* about your murder are gone,
> thrown away pointlessly into the air.

But there remains the possibility that the girl herself might *peithein* him, by supplication and by the strength of her moral case:

> πρόσπιπτε δ᾽ οἰκτρῶς τοῦδ᾽ Ὀδυσσέως γόνυ
> καὶ πεῖθ᾽—ἔχεις δὲ πρόφασιν· ἔστι γὰρ τέκνα
> καὶ τῷδε—τὴν σὴν ὥστ᾽ ἐποικτῖραι τύχην. (339-41)

> Fall piteously at the knees of Odysseus here, and
> persuade him (*peithe*)—you have an argument,
> for he too has children—to pity your ill-fortune.

But both Polyxene and Odysseus refuse to play the game of supplication.[53] Odysseus moves his hand and chin out of reach (342-4), so making impossible the physical contact which would have ritually 'locked' him. Polyxene, by contrast, *disdains* to supplicate him, lest she incur the charge of being φιλόψυχος, 'life-loving' (348) —a relative of the word just used by Odysseus (315) in advancing his case, which is thus neatly trumped. Polyxene shows a nobility of disposition which in Euripides seems to flower only in young people. Her final couplet, 'I would be more fortunate dead than living—life without honour would be a great hardship' (377-8) is reminiscent of, say, Sophokles' Ajax (*Aj.* 479-80), Antigone (*Ant.* 96-7) or Elektra (*S. El.* 1320-1), but there is an absence of striving or self-assertiveness (πόνος, 'trouble', 'effort', 378, is revealing) which marks Polyxene off from Sophokles' heroes, hardened in the fire of experience.

Hekabe demands to die with her daughter, saying that there is an *ananke* that this should be so (396). For Odysseus there is no *ananke* but political *ananke*—the relationship of subordination and command between people. He replies: 'I am not aware of having any masters' (397). When two adversaries are so unequal in power the inferior is under strong pressure to *peithesthai*, which is what Odysseus advises Hekabe to do. Her refusal brings stalemate, but Polyxene intervenes for a second time to persuade her mother to relent (πιϑοῦ μοι, 402), since otherwise Odysseus will merely enforce his will by *bia* (406). After a farewell in stichomythia, the two part, Hekabe being left to her misery. She does not, however, collapse completely: the last three lines in the scene are a bitter wish that Helen might be suffering Polyxene's fate—a sign that Hekabe's spirit is not broken, and a prefiguration of her later violent reaction. As Steidle has pertinently observed (p. 46), the cursing of Helen can be done only if Hekabe has raised her body or head from their previous dejection. This visual detail signals, or anyway may be taken as symbolizing, an important distinction between *Hekabe* and *Trojan Women*, the other Euripidean work in which Hekabe has a pivotal role.[54] There, Hekabe's first and last words appropriately refer to her state of (literal) collapse, the visual analogue of her inability to get her way about anything. (The *agon* between her and Helen is indicative: Hekabe has the better of the argument, but Menelaos still takes Helen back to Greece.) In *Hekabe*, Hekabe never ceases trying to put her will into action, and at length succeeds.

In the ode which follows, the chorus-members speculate upon where in Greece their captivity will be. Their images contrast sharply with the unpleasant world of Troy. The women see themselves, not as subservient to Greek men, but as participating in festivals with other, Greek, women, whether on Delos or in Athens. The paradigm offered (compare the 'shield of Achilles' ode in Euripides' otherwise sombre *Elektra*) is not bleak: there is light, celebration and order (Zeus defeats the Titans on the sacred robe of Athene, 472-4). But the report of Talthybios the Greek herald dismantles the brightness. All Hekabe can do in the face of the narrative of Polyxene's sacrifice is toy hopelessly with some thoughts about how it is that people come to be good or bad.[55] She concludes, 'the best you can hope for is to escape disaster from day to day' (627-8).

Soon not even that hope remains. The maid who had gone to the shore for water to wash Polyxene's corpse returns with the news which the audience has known since the prologue. Now truly Hekabe is in that condition of ultimate helplessness—*apais, anandros, apolis*; 'childless, husbandless, citiless' (669)—in which the only ways out are capitulation or desperate resistance. The arrival of Agamemnon precipitates the choice: she chooses resistance.

At once she contemplates adopting the ultimate weapon in the persuader's armoury, supplication. She holds back, fearing the humiliation of rejection, but the pressure of *ananke* (751) overcomes her doubts. She supplicates (752). After a passage of stichomythia in which Agamemnon hears the details of Polydoros' death, Hekabe makes her first great speech of *peitho*. Admitting her own weakness (798; cf. 809-11), she appeals to a higher power, *nomos*:

> ἀλλ' οἱ θεοὶ σθένουσι χὠ κείνων κρατῶν
> νόμος· νόμῳ γὰρ τοὺς θεοὺς ἡγούμεθα
> καὶ ζῶμεν ἄδικα καὶ δίκαι' ὡρισμένοι. (799-801)

> But the gods are strong, and *nomos* which has power over them; for it is by *nomos* that we believe in the gods and live, having defined the boundaries of inequity and equity.

These 'curious and thought-provoking words'[56] are intriguing to historians of fifth-century thought in that they seem to embody a shift between two different sorts of *nomos*, the one a power mightier even than the gods, the other the 'mere' convention which is the sole basis for men's religious beliefs and moral categories.[57] But from the dramatic point of view all we need to observe is that Hekabe is deploying every argument she can in order to support *nomos*, since 'the way things are customarily done' has been doubly flouted by Polymestor, in respect of honouring *xenia* and burying the dead.[58]

When Agamemnon moves to leave—a certain inference from Hekabe's remark at 812—she calls on the divinity who seems to have deserted her:

> τί δῆτα θνητοὶ τἄλλα μὲν μαθήματα
> μοχθοῦμεν ὡς χρὴ πάντα καὶ ματεύομεν,
> Πειθὼ δὲ τὴν τύραννον ἀνθρώποις μόνην
> οὐδέν τι μᾶλλον ἐς τέλος σπουδάζομεν
> μισθοὺς διδόντες μανθάνειν, ἵν' ἦν ποτε
> πείθειν ἅ τις βούλοιτο τυγχάνειν θ' ἅμα;

πῶς οὖν ἔτ' ἄν τις ἐλπίσαι πράξειν καλῶς; (814-20)

Why then do we mortals struggle with and pursue all other objects of learning, as we need to; but as for Peitho, mankind's only ruler, we are not a whit the more eager to acquire her at length by paying for her, so that we might *peithein* in any matter whatever, and get our way too? How, in that case, can we expect to prosper?

But one card remains to be played. Interestingly enough, in view of our investigations into *peitho's* erotic side, it is the *peitho* of Agamemnon's *eros* for Kassandra. The *charis* Hekabe speaks of is no longer the favour of social reciprocity (276) but that of sexual reciprocity (830). When this demeaning argument has been used,[59] there remains only the startling coda:

εἴ μοι γένοιτο φθόγγος ἐν βραχίοσι
καὶ χερσὶ καὶ κόμαισι καὶ ποδῶν βάσει
ἢ Δαιδάλου τέχναισιν ἢ θεῶν τινος,
ὡς πάνθ' ὁμαρτῆ σῶν ἔχοιντο γουνάτων
κλαίοντ', ἐπισκήπτοντα παντοίους λόγους.
ὦ δέσποτ', ὦ μέγιστον Ἕλλησιν φάος,
πιθοῦ, παράσχες χεῖρα τῇ πρεσβύτιδι
τιμωρόν, εἰ καὶ μηδέν ἐστιν, ἀλλ' ὅμως. (836-43)

If only, by the devising of Daidalos or some god, I could have voice in my arms, my hands, my hair, my feet—then, all together, they would cling beseechingly to your knees, urging every type of *logos*. Master, greatest saviour of the Greeks, listen to me *(pithou)*, offer your avenging hand to this old woman, even though she is nothing.

The effect of *peitho* is thus connected with the mythical Daidalos, whose own power extended to the so-called inanimate world; his statues, endowed with the power of movement, set Aristotle speculating: '... suppose *[per impossibile]* that every instrument could obey a person's orders or anticipate his wishes and so fulfil its proper function, like the legendary figures of Daidalos or the tripods of Hephaistos, which the poet says "entered the assembly of the gods of their own motion"...'[60] That *peitho* should have a similarly *automatic* effect might be a consummation devoutly to be wished by Hekabe, but as usual in Greek tragedy *peitho* is perceived in its complex relations with human choices and attitudes, rather than as a sort of unstoppable steamroller.

The completeness with which Hekabe surrenders to the passion for revenge is chilling: 787-845 is the greatest speech in the play. The four lines of chorus which follow are not padding, as they link two ideas which have just been prominent. According to the chorus, *nomoi* have 'defined the *anankai*'by making enemies into friends and friends into enemies (846-9). Heberden's comment is worth recording: 'Here *[nomoi]* perhaps refer to the laws of right and wrong, justice and injustice, which demand the punishment of Polymestor, and thus lead to enmity between those who were friends (Hekabe and Polymestor) and friendship between those who were enemies (Hekabe and Agamemnon).'[61] The 'necessities' thus defined are surely the political necessities which constrain people (as the play so far has amply demonstrated). These, the chorus—perhaps optimistically—suggests, are themselves 'defined' by a higher power.

At any rate, the necessity which constrains Agamemnon is clear from his speech at 850-63: the army. He fears they may say he is 'only doing it for Kassandra', since to the army Polymestor is an ally but Polydoros a foe. Agamemnon bears out Hekabe's generalization that 'no mortal is truly free' (864). In the unpleasant and unstable world of *Hekabe,* the ability to transcend unfreedom[62] is confined to Polyxene, who makes a choice, and to the other characters in so far as they manage—on occasions, and to no very healing or harmonious effect—to get their way.

Hekabe contents herself with asking for Agamemnon's silent acquiescence in her own act of revenge. This must be done by the mode which imposes itself on a desperate inferior in face of an implacable superior:

Αγ.   καὶ πῶς γυναιξὶν ἀρσένων ἔσται κράτος;
Εκ.   δεινὸν τὸ πλῆθος σὺν δόλῳ τε δύσμαχον. (883-4)

Ag.   And how will women get the upper hand over men?
Hek. Numbers make us fearsome opposition, and when we use *dolos* we are hard to combat.

She cites the Danaids and the women of Lemnos, paradigms for the ability of women murderously to circumvent their husbands. But Agamemnon is so weak, or unfree, that there is no need to deceive him. Although he maintains that only the *ananke* of the absence of a favouring wind (900-1) allows him the luxury of granting Hekabe's request, he shows by his acceptance of the formula, 'the vicious must be harmed, the noble must prosper' (903-4; cf. Hekabe at 845)[63] that he has been persuaded.

The theme of women's inferiority in power to men is taken up in the ode at 905ff about the stillness in Troy before the Greeks came; it is only the breadth and painterly skill of passages such as this which make the relentless drive of the dialogue scenes tolerable. After the end of the ode there is no further respite, for the entry of Polymestor heralds the gripping *dolos* episode which takes the work to its conclusion. Hekabe tricks Polymestor into going into the tent[64] by holding out the prospect of more golden treasure to add to what he has already appropriated (n.b. again Medea's maxim). When he has been blinded, and his children killed, by the women, his cries for help bring Agamemnon back. In the play's second *agon*, Agamemnon judges (1129-31) the merits of the two cases argued before him.

As usual, Euripides does his best for his two defendants. Polymestor's speech is not sophisticated, but he does make some apparently cogent points. He admits guilt, but pleads mitigating circumstances: he feared that, if Polydoros had survived, he might have founded a new Troy and attracted more bloodshed to Thrace. More effective than this somewhat speculative argument is the narrative of what the women did to him and his sons; eerie good-humour followed by ghastly violence anticipate the behaviour of the maenads in *Bakchai*. Also reminiscent of *Bakchai* is the hunting imagery *(Hek.* 1171ff), which, as often, is used in relation to an act of *dolos.*[65] Polymestor ends with a reflection like that to which Klytaimestra's deceitfulness leads the chorus in Aischylos' *Choephoroi* and Medea's leads Jason in *Medea*: 'neither sea nor land breeds such a creature (as woman)' (1181-2).

Hekabe, in true professional style, begins by condemning her opponents' use of rhetoric. Another and closely kindred opening for a defence was to profess one's own ignorance of the art of speaking, as Sokrates does in Plato's *Apology*. Here [sc. in *Hek.*] the conventional plea is strengthened by emphasis on the opponent's combination of rhetoric with a bad case. In fact, Polymestor has used very little rhetoric at all... Hekabe herself, like Sokrates, is a much greater master of the art than her opponent.[66]

The self-consciously rhetorical opening to Hekabe's speech is followed by a like transition:

καί μοι τὸ μὲν σὸν ὧδε φροιμίοις ἔχει·
πρὸς τόνδε δ᾽ εἶμι καὶ λόγοις ἀμείψομαι. (1195-6)

Thus far *your* share in my exordium. I shall now turn my attention and reply to *him*.

She proceeds to demolish Polymestor's case brick by brick. Conveniently (but, from a rhetorical point of view, legitimately) ignoring her own pact with Agamemnon, Hekabe argues from probability (*eikos*): 'No amity could subsist between Greek and non-Greek' (1199-1201). Then to specifics: 'You say you feared they might sail again to Thrace and ravage it? Whom do you expect to *peithein* of that?' (1204-5). Lust for gold was the motive—a conclusion which is enforced as Hekabe points out the incompatibility of Polymestor's conduct with any other motive but avarice.

If Polymestor himself were not standing there, physically broken, it would be reasonable to sympathize fully with Hekabe. But he *is* there. Nevertheless, the chorus sees the matter as cut and dried:

φεῦ φεῦ· βροτοῖσιν ὡς τὰ χρηστὰ πράγματα
χρηστῶν ἀφορμὰς ἐνδίδωσ᾽ ἀεὶ λόγων. (1238-9)

Ah! A good cause always supplies you with good arguments.

Agamemnon agrees that Hekabe is in the right, although characteristically he sees his duty to reach a decision as an *ananke* (1241). At any rate, Polymestor loses the case. As one critic has intelligently observed:

It is not so much that Hekabe's argument is stronger than Polymestor's, but that Agamemnon rejects the defeated Polymestor (cf. 1252-3), just as Odysseus had rejected the powerless Hekabe. *It is precisely because he is the victim* that Polymestor's argument can have no force, that Agamemnon can see only that Polymestor is arguing from a self-interested position (1246).[67]

The Sophoklean connection between the power of *peitho* and the moral authority of the persuader is all but (i.e. except for Polyxene) absent from *Hekabe*.

Agamemnon does not confer honour on the defeated party and so ease the bitterness of the verdict—contrast *Eumenides,* where it is the awarding of τιμή, honour, to the defeated Furies which soothes and heals their resentment.[68] Polymestor is squeezed out, so to speak, into the marginal role of a prophet.[69]

His prediction that Hekabe will turn into a dog confirms our sense that circumstances have reduced her to something less than human; the metamorphosis will be merely a logical extension of something already visible to the audience. It also represents an eventual symbolic equalization of fortune between Hekabe and Polymestor: he came on to the scene on all fours after his blinding, she will soon have four legs. There is a kind of *dike* about it. But, as in Euripides' *Elektra*, it is an ugly *dike*. *Hippolytos* and *Bakchai* are also about the re-establishment of an order by a process which looks cruel, but there the order is divine. In *Hekabe,* there is no escape. The focus is narrower. The cruelty and the ugliness are human. No one (except Polyxene) rises above it; particularly not Agamemnon. Although superficially in control at the end, he is confronted, through the words of the powerless Polymestor, by his own ineluctable fate: to be murdered by his wife. As the chorus puts it in the last line, '*ananke* is harsh'.

What, in the unlovely world of this play, is the role of *peitho*? For G.M. Kirkwood[70] its prominence is confined to the second half. In his view there are two Hekabes, one passive and grief-stricken, one a fiend incarnate. The transition from one to the other can be expressed as a change from *nomos* to *peitho*. In the first part of the play, he argues, it is *nomos* that makes the Greeks sacrifice Polyxene (cf. 'it is our *nomos*', 326); and at 799-805 Hekabe appeals to Agamemnon in terms of the high principle of *nomos*. But in the middle of that speech 'suddenly the realization strikes Hekabe that it is useless to depend for success on the strength of pious principles... With great deliberation, Hekabe shifts the ground of her argument: it is only Peitho that has power over men...'[71] The shift to an argument from *peitho* in the encounter with Agamemnon is thus regarded as pivotal from the point of view of Hekabe's character:

The Hekabe who extols Nomos and depends on its power is the crushed but still noble figure of the earlier part of the play; the Hekabe who flings Nomos aside and becomes the embodiment of Peitho, utterly reckless of her own decency, has already embarked on the career of moral degeneration which will culminate in the brutality of her revenge on Polymestor.[72]

As far as concerns the transition from *nomos* to *peitho* within Hekabe's speech to Agamemnon, the preceding interpretation is a thoughtful one. But it cannot be extended to cover the whole play. In the first part of *Hekabe nomos* is far less important, and *peitho* far more important, than Kirkwood allows. One of the many strengths of Steidle's chapter on the play is that he points to parallels between Hekabe's attempted *peitho* of Odysseus and her successful *peitho* of Agamemnon: for instance, in both cases the reluctance of the addressee is physically enacted by a movement away from the addresser (342, 812).[73] This detail of the visual action should remind us of what I have been trying to show all along: that Hekabe is desperate to get her way *throughout*. The explicit appeal to *peitho* signals a change of tactics, not of character.

The moral ambivalence of rhetoric is a theme pursued elsewhere by Euripides: in *Orestes,* for instance, the unsavoury persuasiveness of Talthybios and the ἀθυρόγλωσσος (903, 'fellow who cannot keep his mouth shut') results in the passing of a death sentence on Orestes and Elektra, at an off-stage assembly whose susceptibility to *peitho* is reminiscent of the debate reported in *Hekabe.* In portraying characters who express their unease at the power of political *peitho* Euripides was articulating an attitude which had some currency at Athens. Thoukydides provides ample evidence here: one may recall the passage where his Thebans—themselves of course engaged in a persuasive exercise in opposition to the Plataians—state that 'good deeds do not require long statements; but when evil is done the whole art of oratory is employed as a screen for it'.[74] But it should hardly need re-emphasizing by now that we must beware of inferring that it was 'Euripides' view' that rhetoric was harmful or dangerous. Matters are not so cut and dried. By and large it is true that in *Hekabe* rhetoric appears in a poor light. But in another play with a different focus Euripides evidently felt able to place the moral accent somewhat differently. A brief look at *Suppliants* will demonstrate this.

As in Aischylos' *Suppliants*, the drama concerns the relationship between a ruler and his own polis as well as his attitude towards the hostile polis which he has to confront. The imaginary Athens of Euripides' *Suppliants* is in the (for tragedy) characteristically 'double' condition of being ruled both by the *demos*, 'people', and by Theseus:

δόξαι δὲ χρῄζω καὶ πόλει πάσῃ τόδε.
δόξει δ' ἐμοῦ θέλοντος· ἀλλὰ τοῦ λόγου
προσδοὺς ἔχοιμ' ἂν δῆμον εὐμενέστερον.

καὶ γὰρ κατέστησ᾽ αὐτὸν ἐς μοναρχίαν
ἐλευθερώσας τήνδ᾽ ἰσόψηφον πόλιν. (349-53)

I want this to be approved also by the whole city. And it will be approved, since I wish it ('approve' translates the political word *dokein*, 'to be resolved'). But if I provided some reasons *(logos)* then I would have the *demos* more favourably disposed. For I set the people in sole command when I liberated this city on terms of equal franchise. (Tr. of last sentence borrowed from Collard *ad loc.*)

The doubleness of the political situation envisaged is mirrored in the double function which Theseus perceives *peitho* as fulfilling: it is how things are done in an 'equal' democracy, and it is also the honey-sweet ability of the superior to get compliance from his inferiors. As the Argive king took Danaos before the assembly in Aischylos' *Suppliants*, so Theseus will take Adrastos here. In both cases *peitho* is the aim:

λαβὼν δ᾽ Ἄδραστον δεῖγμα τῶν ἐμῶν λόγων
ἐς πλῆθος ἀστῶν εἶμι· καὶ πείσας τάδε,
λεκτοὺς ἀθροίσας δεῦρ᾽ Ἀθηναίων κόρους
ἥξω· (354-7)

Taking Adrastos as evidence of my *logoi*, I shall go to the assembly of the citizens; and, having persuaded them of this *(peisas)*, I shall collect a chosen group of young Athenians and return.

Similarly, his conduct towards Thebes will be marked in the first instance by *peitho*, and only then, if necessary, by *bia*:

δράσω τάδ᾽· εἶμι καὶ νεκροὺς ἐκλύσομαι
λόγοισι πείθων· εἰ δὲ μή, βίᾳ δορός. (346-7)

I shall do it. I shall go and recover the corpses by persuading *(peithon)* with *logoi*; or, if that fails, by *bia* of arms.

In the altercation with the Theban herald Theseus represents the citizen's free exercise of *peitho* as the hallmark of the democratic polis:

τοὐλεύθερον δ᾽ ἐκεῖνο· Τίς θέλει πόλει
χρηστόν τι βούλευμ᾽ ἐς μέσον φέρειν ἔχων; (438-9)

This is freedom: 'Who has good counsel for the city that he wishes to put "into the middle" (i.e. publish)?'[75]

In short, *peitho* appears in *Suppliants* as morally laudable, and it is associated with other qualities which characterize Theseus' Athenian polis: *nomos, dike,* reason, humanity.[76]

It is clear that the depiction of *peitho* in *Suppliants* differs from that in *Hekabe.* Yet *Suppliants* remains wholly Euripidean: it is a balance of cases, a work constituted by the sum of the arguments which it contains. To describe *Hekabe* as the real world, *Suppliants* as an unattainable ideal, is perhaps to go too far; each work is an independent extrapolation from Athenian life, each is coherent within its own terms. Nevertheless, in order to preserve the ideals implicit in *Suppliants* Euripides had to narrow his dramatic scope very considerably; he had to imagine a world in which people can perform virtuous actions whose value is not undermined either by a feeling of humanity's metaphysical helplessness or by an encircling human viciousness. It may be that the greater power of *Hekabe* as compared with *Suppliants* comes from the fact that it is, in the end, a more truthful and unflinching account of what it was like to be an Athenian towards the end of the fifth century.

POSTSCRIPT

How far the apparent differences between the three dramatists'
depictions of *peitho* are merely a product of *lacunae* in the evidence is
a question which it is hard to answer with assurance. *A fortiori,* any
explanation of these differences in terms of a change in political
climate is bound to remain tentative. The most plausible explanation
would run somewhat as follows: Athenian success in mid-century
generated confidence in the political system which seemed to be
nourishing that success, and this confidence found expression in
certain of Aischylos' works which celebrate the 'democratic' worth of
peitho; however, the reverses suffered by Athens later in the century
shook her faith in herself, and led to the mood reflected in, e.g.,
Hekabe, where political rhetoric is represented as potentially cruel
and demeaning. But it is clear that this explanation fails to account
adequately for all the phenomena. There are, for instance, plays
written in the latter part of the century which retain an *Oresteia*-like
faith in the values of Athenian persuasion—Euripides' *Suppliants,*
and *O.C.* Moreover there are many extant tragedies—*Medea* is an
example—for which an attempt to 'locate' the treatment of *peitho* in a
historically precise setting would be quite unconvincing; the same
goes for efforts similarly to 'locate' the intransigence of the
Sophoklean hero. Nevertheless, it is fair to say that the notion of a loss
of confidence does retain a limited measure of usefulness, if only as a
means of characterizing the contrast between the healing *peitho* of
Aischylos and the brutal rhetoric of some of the Euripidean
war-plays.

Whatever weight we accord to the preceding generalizations, the
main point to emerge from our analyses of particular plays is the
degree of seriousness with which all three dramatists approached
issues of persuasion, deception and violence. On these as on so many
other questions tragedy offered a forum for moral and political
debate at the deepest level. In giving dramatic body to *peitho, dolos*
and *bia* the playwrights were not simply manipulating 'themes' in
some rarefied aesthetic game, but expressing themselves about

profoundly significant human choices. In considering the Greeks' deployment of the three categories we are to a large extent examining an alien world: when Plutarch (*inst. Lac.* 238f) reports of the Spartans that, after a victory, sacrifice of an ox or a cock is made to Ares according to whether it was won by trickery or open force, there is little in our own mental universe to which we can appeal for guidance. Yet as we watch Neoptolemos stand before Philoktetes, or witness the dilemma of a ruler obliged to adjudicate between the claims of a helpless suppliant and a threatening foe, we recognize situations whose moral implications seem by no means foreign to us. To perceive the 'other' in Greek culture is inevitably to become aware of the 'same'.

NOTES

NOTES TO CHAPTER ONE: THE PERSUASIVE WORD IN GREECE

1. J.-P. Vernant, *Les Origines de la pensée grecque*[3] (Paris, 1975) 32.
2. To judge from A. Heubeck, *Schrift* (= *Archaeologia Homerica* III, X) (Göttingen, 1979) 54, recent research has rendered dubious the notion of a class of scribes in Mycenae on the Near Eastern model; but there is no reason to doubt that writing was a skill fundamentally connected with the palaces and palace duties.
3. See J. Chadwick, *The Mycenaean World* (Cambridge, 1976) xiii. On the wider significance of 'alphabetic culture' for Greek thought see Jack Goody and Ian Watt, 'The consequences of literacy', in Goody (ed.), *Literacy in Traditional Societies* (Cambridge, 1968) 27-68; and Goody, *The Domestication of the Savage Mind* (Cambridge, 1977).
4. 'Freedom of speech in antiquity', in *Dictionary of the History of Ideas* (Scribner's, N.Y., 1973) II, 252-63; cf. Momigliano's contribution to S.C. Humphreys, *Anthropology and the Greeks* (London, 1978) 177-93.
5. Cf. P. Wülfing-v. Martitz, 'Grundlagen und Anfänge der Rhetorik in der Antike', *Euphorion* 63 (1969) 207-15, at 208.
6. See F. Solmsen, 'The "gift" of speech in Homer and Hesiod', *TAPhA* 85 (1954) 1-15, repr. in Solmsen, *Kleine Schriften* (Hildesheim, 1968) I, 1-15.
7. M.I. Finley, *The World of Odysseus*[2] (London, 1977) 115.
8. See G.E.R. Lloyd, *Early Greek Science: Thales to Aristotle* (London, 1970) 10ff.
9. On the implications of literacy for criticism of 'traditional' thought see, in addition to works (esp. Goody *Domestication*) cited in n.3 above, O. Murray, *Early Greece* (Brighton, 1980) 91-9, where reservations are expressed about the Goody/Watt hypothesis; G.E.R. Lloyd, *Magic, Reason and Experience: Studies in the Origin and Development of Greek Science* (Cambridge, 1979) 239-40.
10. For a recent consideration of this matter cf. M. Austin and P. Vidal-Naquet, *Economic and Social History of Ancient Greece: an Introduction* (London, 1977) (orig. in French as *Économies et sociétés en Grèce ancienne*, Paris, 1972) 49ff.
11. See J.-P. Vernant (ed.), *Problèmes de la guerre en Grèce ancienne* (Paris, 1968) esp. pp. 28-9 of Vernant's introduction, and the paper on 'La phalange: problèmes et controverses' by M. Detienne, 119-42.

12. See R.J. Bonner and G. Smith, *The Administration of Justice from Homer to Aristotle* (Univ. of Chicago, 1930) I, 67ff.

13. See L. Gernet, 'La notion mythique de la valeur en Grèce', *Journal de psychologie* 41 (1948) 415-62; repr. in *Anthropologie de la Grèce antique* (Paris, 1968) 93-137.

14. Cf. E. Hussey, *The Presocratics* (London, 1972) 14-15.

15. Cf. Momigliano *Freedom* 257.

16. On the difficulty of determining which Ionian cities were democratic before the Persian conquest see J.L. O'Neil, 'Greek democratic constitutions outside Athens' (Cambridge Ph.D. diss., 1974) 221. See also his section on Chios (118-35).

17. Cf. however the reservations about Persian 'tolerance' expressed by P. Tozzi, 'Per la storia della politica religiosa degli Achemenidi', *RSI* 89 (1977) 18-32, esp. 26ff.

18. 3.80.6, tr. de Sélincourt (Penguin, 1954); cf. also the remarks of Athenagoras on *peitho* in a democracy (Thuc. 6.38.4).

19. Numerous definitions of rhetoric repeat or slightly modify this form of words: cf. Josef Martin, *Antike Rhetorik: Technik und Methode* (Munich, 1974) 2-3. The scholarship on rhetoric is, of course, enormous. A useful guide is Jens' article in vol. III of the *Reallexicon der deutschen Literaturgeschichte* (Berlin, 1958-) 432-56.

20. See V. Buchheit, *Untersuchungen zur Theorie des Genos Epideiktikon von Gorgias bis Aristoteles* (Munich, 1960).

21. This view is the one argued in a fine article by Jochen Martin, 'Von Kleisthenes zu Ephialtes. Zur Entstehung der athenischen Demokratie', *Chiron* 4 (1974) 5-42.

22. So Martin *Kl. zu Eph.* 41.

23. See A.H.M. Jones, *Athenian Democracy* (Oxford, 1957) 5; P.J. Rhodes, *The Athenian Boule* (Oxford, 1972) *s.v.* 'Pay' in index.

24. It was famous already in antiquity: see O. Jahn, *Peitho, die Göttin der Überredung* (Greifswald, 1846) 6, nn. 18-19; and cf. the (mainly imperial) echoes listed by Voigt, *RE* XIX. 1 (1937) cols. 194-217 (*s.v.* 'Peitho'), at 204-5.

25. See Jahn *Peitho* 6: 'Denn der Mund ist ja recht eigentlich das Eigenthum der *Peitho*, deshalb hat sie dort ihren Sitz, den sie erst mit dem Lebensodem verlässt.' The connection between *peitho* and lips/mouth is found in contexts which we might describe as 'public' as well as in erotic contexts. A 'public' instance is provided by the *Theogony* passage quoted earlier in this chapter, where words are said to flow like honey from the lips of a king. (See West on *Th.* 83.) On the other hand the following three (late) passages are amatory:

(a) (Aphrodite praising the beauty of Kadmos to Harmonia):
χείλεα σιγήσαιμι· τὸ δὲ στόμα, πορθμὸν Ἐρώτων,
Πειθὼ ναιετάουσα χέει μελιηδέα φωνήν,
καὶ Χάριτες μεθέπουσιν ὅλον δέμας·
('I would not speak of his lips; but Peitho dwells in his mouth, the ferry of the Loves, and pours out honey-sweet speech, and the Graces cherish his whole body.') (Nonn. *D*. 4.139-41; tr. after Rouse, Loeb)

(b) (Dionysos over the corpse of a handsome boy):
οὔ πώ μοι, φίλε κοῦρε, τεὸν στόμα κάλλιπε Πειθώ,
ἀλλὰ σέθεν φθιμένοιο καὶ ἄπνοα χείλεα ναίει.
('Peitho has not yet left your mouth, darling boy, but although you are dead she still abides on those breathless lips.') (Nonn. *D*. 11.280-1; tr. after Rouse)

(c) (From the *Anacreontea*: the poet gives instructions about how to capture his mistress' likeness in a portrait):
...γράφε χεῖλος, οἷα Πειθοῦς,
προκαλούμενον φίλημα...
('...Paint her lips like those of Peitho, inviting a kiss...') (16.24-5 (Teubner, ed. Rose))

26. Radermacher ('ΠΕΙΘΩ und ΔΟΛΟΣ', *JÖAI* 29 (1934) *Heft* 1, 93-6) argues strenuously that we should print Πειθώ τις (capital Π) here. He rightly says there is no objection to the coupling of the indefinite τις with the name of a divinity—his examples of τις Ἀπόλλων (A. *Ag*. 55) and Ἀφροδίτη τις (E. *I.A*. 1264) make the point well. (One of R.'s instances is, though, unsatisfactory: at E. *Alk*. 259ff τις... Ἅιδας are separated by far too many words to support R. 's case; and anyway they may not be part of the same sentence. Furthermore, R. cites A. *Ag*. 288; but there τις Ἥλιος is normal because a comparison is being made (cf. Fraenkel on 288), and in any event—interestingly—ἥλιος (small initial letter) is printed by, e.g., Mazon, Fraenkel and Page.) The orthographical question is perhaps insoluble, but R. sensibly emphasizes that there is no hard and fast break between 'secular' and 'divine' persuasion, and that the Greeks saw divinity in powers which we might see as simply 'abstract'.

27. Cf. M.I. Finley, *Democracy Ancient and Modern* (London, 1973) 17, with ref. to P. Laslett (ed.), *Philosophy, Politics and Society*, 1st series (Oxford, 1956) ch. X, 'The face to face society'.

28. M.I. Finley, 'Athenian demagogues', *P&P* 21 (1962) 3-24, at 13; repr. in Finley, *Studies in Ancient Society* (London, 1974) 1-25, at 13.

29. Cf. Ch. Perelman and L. Olbrechts-Tyteca, *Traité de l'argumentation: la nouvelle rhétorique*[3] (Paris, 1970) 73: 'Le recours à l'argumentation suppose l'établissement d'une communauté des esprits qui, pendant

qu'elle dure, exclut l'usage de la violence.' Speaking of the operation of the Council, the Areopagos and the magistrates under the democracy, Demosthenes recalls that 'not even the most insolent use *bia* (βιάζεσθαι)' to disrupt proceedings (*Against Aristog.* 1.23).

30. Elektra's 'husband' was nobly born (*El.* 37), but nothing comparable is said of the *Orestes* peasant.

31. Mark Hobart, 'Orators and patrons: two types of political leader in Balinese village society', in Maurice Bloch (ed.), *Political Language and Oratory in Traditional Society* (London, 1975) 65-92, at 76-7.

32. Cf. ch. 1 of Finley *Democracy,* esp. 19-20.

33. See J. Gould, '*Hiketeia*', *JHS* 93 (1973) 74-103, at 87ff.

34. Ps.-Xen. *Ath.* 1.6, tr. Bowersock (Loeb).

35. The *locus classicus* is Finley *Demagogues,* esp. 18ff (in reprint).

36. Theseus is willing to have recourse to violence only if persuasion fails:

    δράσω τάδ'· εἶμι καὶ νεκροὺς ἐκλύσομαι
    λόγοισι πείθων· εἰ δὲ μή, βίᾳ δορός. (346-7)

    I shall do it. I shall go and recover the corpses by persuading with words; or, if that fails, by force of arms.

    (For the reading πείθων see Collard's edn (Groningen, 1975) *ad loc.*) G. Grossmann, *Promethie und Orestie* (Heidelberg, 1970), has some excellent remarks on the Athenians' ideal view of themselves: see pp. 111-61, esp. 127-43 ('Das athenische Wesen im Spiegel des Mythos').

37. Thuc. 3.42.2 (tr. Jowett). Compare Hdt. 7.10, where, although the context is autocratic, Artabanos tells Xerxes to his face about the value of debate in the process of reaching decisions.

38. Xen. *Mem.* 1.2.31. It is true that, according to Xenophon, the law was directed specifically against Sokrates (by Kritias, who had a personal score to settle with him); but this does not affect my general point. On the relationship between oratory and democracy, see G. Kennedy, *The Art of Persuasion in Greece* (Princeton, 1963) 29; also the beginning of W. Eisenhut, *Einführung in die antike Rhetorik und ihre Geschichte* (Darmstadt, 1974).

    With the *temporary* ban on teaching the art of words one may compare the *temporary* ban in 440 on comedy (schol. Ar. *Ach.* 67), which may well have been connected with political tensions following the Samian crisis. On the relationship between Athenian freedom of speech and the restrictions which sometimes limited it, cf. recently Lloyd *MRE* 255.

39. Cf. Bonner/Smith *Justice* II, 123.

40. Cf. Bonner/Smith *Justice* I, 325f.

41. Trans. adapted from Bonner/Smith *Justice* I, 221.

42. See further Jochen Martin, 'Zur Entstehung der Sophistik', *Saeculum* 27 (1976) 143-64.
43. Hippias: Pl. *Hp. Ma.* 281a, Philostr. *V.S.* 1.11; Gorgias: e.g. Diod. Sic. 12.53.1ff; Prodikos: Philostr. *V.S.* 1.12.
44. Further east, though, there developed a remarkably similar phenomenon to the sophists, namely the wandering ascetics or 'Parivrājakas'; see R.T. Oliver, *Communication and Culture in Ancient India and China* (Syracuse, N.Y., 1971) 24.
45. Cf. Lloyd *MRE* 89ff.
46. DK A 6; tr. in R.K. Sprague, *The Older Sophists* (Univ. of S. Carolina, 1972) 117-18. The therapeutic power of speech is discussed by Pedro Laín Entralgo in *The Therapy of the Word in Classical Antiquity* (ed. and trans. L.J. Rather and John M. Sharp) (Yale, 1970).
47. See Lloyd *MRE* 97.
48. Cf. G.E.R. Lloyd (ed.), *Hippocratic Writings* (Penguin, 1978) 13, fn.; *MRE* 230-1.
49. Tr. Marchant, Loeb edn. For the importance of obedience in the 'Dorian ethic' see Grossmann *Promethie* 172. Obedience is a characteristic of the Spartan-like 'timocratic' individual in Plato's *Republic* (ἀρχόντων δὲ σφόδρα ὑπήκοος, 549a). The contrast between persuading and obeying is expressed in Greek by πείθειν and πείθεσθαι; for the semantics of these see pp. 48-9.
50. Cf. Momigliano *Freedom* 258.
51. Plu. *Lyk.* 6; cf. Tyrtaios fr. 4 West. See Momigliano *Freedom* 258.
52. L. Radermacher, *Artium Scriptores* (Vienna, 1951) A V 4 ff, B II. The notion that rhetoric was 'invented' at a particular time and place seems to us at first sight odd; yet rhetoric was one of the many techniques which Greeks associated with the name of a 'first finder'—in this case two 'first finders', Korax and Teisias. (In reality the notion of a 'first finder' is not odd. In using the opposition 'before'/'nowadays' to mark the distinction between 'civilized' and 'uncivilized' behaviour, Greek thought was simply expressing in terms of temporal ordering a polarity which is elsewhere expressed by a spatial ordering (Greece/outside Greece). The introduction of one (or two) individual inventor(s) merely has the effect of giving the conceptual distinction greater sharpness.) Rhetoric was said to have been 'found' as a response to the increase in litigation which followed the transition from tyranny to democracy in the 460s in Sicily. Cf. Cic. *Brut.* 46f, with the notes of A.E. Douglas (edn, Oxford, 1966) *ad loc.*; P. Wülfing, 'Rhétorique et démocratie', *LEC* 43 (1975) 107-18.
53. 'Primitive democracy in ancient Mesopotamia', *JNES* 2 (1943) 159-72; 'Early political development in Mesopotamia', *Zeitschr. für Assyr.* 52

(1957) 91-140; *The Treasures of Darkness* (Yale, 1976).

54. Jacobsen in *Before Philosophy: The Intellectual Adventure of Ancient Man,* by H. Frankfort and others (orig. Univ. of Chicago Press, 1946), 140-1 of Pelican edn, 1949; cf. *Treasures* 183ff.

55. E.g. A.L. Oppenheim in I.M. Lapidus (ed.), *Middle Eastern Cities* (Berkeley, 1969) 17; cf. Mogens Trolle Larsen, *The Old Assyrian City-State and its Colonies, Mesopotamia* 4 (Copenhagen, 1976) 161 n.5.

56. Cf. Lloyd *MRE* 242.

57. Inscription of Darius I at Naqsh-i Rustam, a. 58-60, tr. R.G. Kent, *Old Persian*[2] (New Haven, 1953) 138. See R.C. Zaehner, *The Dawn and Twilight of Zoroastrianism* (London, 1961) 157.

58. Cf. R. de Vaux, *Ancient Israel: Its Life and Institutions*[2] (Eng. tr., London, 1965) 99.

59. Cf. John Bright, *A History of Israel*[2] (London, 1972) 245-6.

60. See J. Lindblom, *Prophecy in Ancient Israel* (Oxford, 1962) 203.

61. Lindblom *Prophecy* 108ff.

62. For the efficacious speech of Yahweh, see Lindblom *Prophecy* 114ff.

63. See H.H. Rowley, *Worship in Ancient Israel* (London, 1967) 165ff.

64. See Claus Westermann, *Basic Forms of Prophetic Speech* (Eng. tr., London, 1967) 201.

65. Lindblom *Prophecy* 215.

66. Carthage is rather problematic: 'The reference of some matters and not others to the people rests with the kings in consultation with the elders in case they agree unanimously; but, even if they do not agree (sc. about referring), reference to the people still takes place; and when the kings introduce business before the people, they do not merely let the people sit and listen to the decisions that have been taken by their rulers, but the people have the sovereign decision, and anybody who wishes may speak against the proposals introduced, a right that does not exist under the other constitutions (sc. Sparta and Crete)' (Aristot. *Pol.* 1273a; tr. amended from Loeb version by H. Rackham, London, 1932). It is a moot point whether Carthage was a 'genuine' exception, or an exception which proves the rule (if 'democratic' elements in her constitution are ascribed to Greek influence).

NOTES TO CHAPTER TWO: PEITHO

1. 'Studies in Peitho' (Ph.D. diss., Princeton, 1967). There is also a fairly detailed presentation of factual evidence about *peitho* in H.A. Shapiro, 'Personification of abstract concepts in Greek art and literature to the end of the fifth century B.C.' (Ph.D. diss., Princeton, 1977) 158ff; 257ff.

2. Roscher III.II (1909) cols. 1795-1813; Voigt *Peitho.*

3. Jahn *Peitho.*

4. See A.W. Gomme and F.H. Sandbach, *Menander: A Commentary* (Oxford, 1973), on *Epitrepontes* 555-6 (in their lineation).

5. See H. Usener, *Götternamen* (Bonn, 1896) 364-75; Fraenkel on A. *Ag.* 14; M. Detienne and J.-P. Vernant, *Cunning Intelligence in Greek Culture and Society* (tr. J. Lloyd, Hassocks, 1978) 92 n.1; W. Burkert, *Griechische Religion der archäischen und klassischen Epoche* (Stuttgart, 1977) 286ff, with n.16.

6. Adapted from Shilleto's trans.

7. Jahn *Peitho* 18 translates simply 'die vollendende, ausübende'; but see against this G. Radke *RE* XXII.2 (1954) cols. 1785-6 *s.v.* 'Praxis'. (Radke's view that 'Praxis' is a shortened form of 'Praxithea' is, however, to be regarded as highly dubious.) The clearest passage is E. *Hipp.* 1003-5:

   λέχους γὰρ εἰς τόδ' ἡμέρας ἁγνὸν δέμας.
   οὐκ οἶδα πρᾶξιν τήνδε πλὴν λόγῳ κλύων
   γραφῇ τε λεύσσων.

   To this moment my body is pure of sex. I am ignorant of this act, except for what I have heard in report and seen in pictures.

8. 'A new Greek inscription from Macedonia', *AJA* 37(1933) 602-4.

9. Suda *s.v.* διάγραμμα has this: τὸ μίσθωμα. διέγραφον γὰρ οἱ ἀγορανόμοι, ὅσον ἔδει λαμβάνειν τὴν ἑταίραν ἑκάστην.

10. Cf. R. Häderli, *Die hellenischen Astynomen u. Agoranomen, vornehmlich im alten Athen = Jahrb. für class. Phil., Supplbd* 15 (Leipzig, 1886-7).

11. See J.H. Oliver, *Demokratia, the Gods, and the Free World* (Baltimore, 1960) 116-17.

12. In the course of a scathing review of Robinson's publication, L. Robert (*Opera Minora Selecta* (Amsterdam, 1969) III, 1570-1) argues that *agoranomoi,* in their general role as commercial intermediaries, 'avaient, ce semble, bien des occasions d'invoquer Peitho pour que les affaires s'arrangeassent à l'amiable'. However, Robinson's interpreta-

tion seems to me to give the dedication more point. (Cf. also H. Musurillo, *The Acts of the Christian Martyrs* (Oxford, 1972) 290, for *agoranomoi* with responsibility for a brothel.)

13. For the meagre literary references to 'Peitho' as epithet see Voigt *Peitho* col. 197.

14. *IG* IX.2.236.

15. The evidence is a votive stele published by G.E. Bean and J.M. Cook, 'The Cnidia', *ABSA* 47 (1952) 171-212, at 189-90, with pl. 40(c).

16. *IG* XII.2.73.

17. Cult links between Hermes and Aphrodite are listed by S. Eitrem, *RE* VIII (1913) cols. 738-92 *s.v.* 'Hermes', at cols. 760-1; see further M. Detienne, *Les Maîtres de vérité dans la Grèce archaïque* (Paris, 1967) 66 n. 102. (In commenting on the Aristophanes passage, D. mistakenly writes 'Peitho' instead of 'Pothos', as had Eitrem before him.) For a dedication (at Paros) to 'Peitho and the Charites' cf. W. Peek in *MDAI(A)* 59 (1934) 60.

18. *IG* II.5.1558.1.

19. Tr. Frazer.

20. *IG* I².700, printed and discussed by P. Foucart, 'Inscriptions de l'Acropole', *BCH* 13 (1889) 156-78, at 159-60. Although this inscription does not contain the epithet Pandemos, it was found in significant proximity to two others which do. The three together constitute good evidence for placing the temple at or near their point of discovery, viz. on the south slope of the Akropolis towards the west: see Foucart, *art. cit.* (For another extensive inscription about the cult of Aphrodite Pandemos, see *IG* II/III².659.)

21. Vol. II, 245-6 of his translation and commentary on the *Description of Greece* (London, 1898).

22. 'Aphrodite Pandemos auf attischen Münzen', *SNR* 49 (1970) 5-23.

23. Coins illustrated in C.T. Seltman, *Athens, its History and Coinage before the Persian Invasion* (Cambridge, 1924) pl.XXII, δδ-εε.

24. So Eisele in Roscher III.I (1902) cols. 1506-14 (*s.v.* 'Pandemos (Beiname der Aphrodite in Athen)'), at col. 1511. See Xen. *Smp.* 8.9; Pl. *Smp.* 180d; and other refs. given by Kruse, *RE* XVIII.3 (1949) cols. 507-10 (*s.v.* 'Pandemos'), at col. 509.

25. D. *Prooem.* 54; cf. S. Dow, 'Prytaneis', *Hesperia*, Suppl. I (1937) 1-258, at 8.

26. *IG* III.351.

27. Thasos: *IG* XII.8.360; cf. Voigt *Peitho* cols. 194-5, and J. Pouilloux, *Recherches sur l'histoire et les cultes de Thasos* (Paris, 1954) 333. Sikyon: Paus. 2.7.7. (The myth centres on an act of 'non-erotic'

persuasion.)

28. *Peitho* col. 196.

29. And Peitho in Sikyon—cf. the Paus. ref. in n. 27 above.

30. We may add that at Mylasa in Caria (cf. Am. Hauvette-Besnault and M. Dubois, 'Antiquités de Mylasa', *BCH* 5 (1881) 31-41, at 39-40; Voigt *Peitho* col. 195) the wife of a priest of Peitho was herself priestess of Nemesis; and this is said by Voigt to reflect some nuptial significance in Peitho's cult here. It is impossible to say whether he is right. Nemesis can be a goddess of love as well as an *ultrix* (although the erotic function only becomes prominent in Alexandrian times and later); but we have no idea what her role was at Mylasa.

31. N.b. the affinities with the *peitho* theme as explored by Aischylos; see ch. 3.

32. For Phoroneus as an Argive Prometheus see C.B. Gulick, 'The Attic Prometheus', *HSPh* 10 (1899) 103-14, at 104-5; L. Séchan, *Le Mythe de Prométhée* (Paris, 1951) 9f; also Voigt *Peitho* col. 196, Pepe *Peitho* 62ff, A. Brelich, *Gli eroi greci* (Rome, 1958) 142; 172.

33. As Pepe argues, *Peitho* 72 n.49.

34. O. Höfer, Roscher III.I (1902) col. 1646 (*s.v.* 'Parphasis') characterizes πάρφασις as a 'Personifikation des Zuredens', a definition which would equally well fit πειθώ in many contexts. (For a possible case of the linking of πειθώ and πάρφασις in an erotic context see S. *Tr.* 660-2—where, however, the text is in ruins, and παρφάσει only a plausible guess.)

35. Thus Jahn *Peitho* 11, asserted that, while *charis* signified the woman's influence over the man, *peitho* represented the man's persuasion of the woman. Weizsäcker, *Peitho* col. 1805, expressed the odd view that Peitho is nowhere linked with the Hippolytos saga *because it is the woman, Phaidra, who does the persuading.*

36. Cf. Str. 8(378), and, for Corinth's reputation, Alkiphron letter (iii) 24 (Schepers, Teubner, 1905).

37. For a further possible link between Peitho and prostitution cf. Herod. *Mim.* 7.74.

38. 'Pandora', *Hermes* 49 (1914) 17-38, at 28.

39. For Peitho in Sappho cf. also schol. Hes. *W.D.* 73, who gives the information that Sappho called her 'Αφροδίτης (i.e. 'Αφροδίτας) θυγατέρα.

40. The opposition will be considered further below, but two instances may be mentioned here since they involve oxymoron: Pl. *Sph.* 265d: μετὰ πειθοῦς ἀναγκαίας, and A. *Ag.* 385: βιᾶται δ' ἀ τάλαινα Πειθώ.

41. One instance, a poem by Meleager, may stand for all:

Αἱ τρισσαὶ Χάριτες τρισσὸν στεφάνωμα †σύνευναι†
Ζηνοφίλᾳ τρισσᾶς σύμβολα καλλοσύνας·
ἁ μὲν ἐπὶ χρωτὸς θεμένα πόθον, ἁ δ᾽ ἐπὶ μορφᾶς
ἵμερον, ἁ δὲ λόγοις τὸ γλυκύμυθον ἔπος.
τρισσάκις εὐδαίμων, ἇς καὶ Κύπρις ὤπλισεν εὐνάν
καὶ Πειθὼ μύθους καὶ γλυκὺ κάλλος Ἔρως.

The three Graces [wove?] a threefold crown for Zenophila, a symbol of her threefold beauty. One placed longing upon her skin, one put desire upon her form, one gave sweetness of utterance to her speech. She is thrice blessed: Kypris furnished her bed, Peitho her speaking and Love her sweet beauty.

(Gow and Page, *The Greek Anthology: Hellenistic Epigrams* (Cambridge, 1965) I, 4210ff. For the textual crux in the first line see their commentary *ad loc.*)

42. V. Ehrenberg, 'Eunomia', in *Aspects of the Ancient World* (Oxford, 1946) 70-93, at 77-8.

43. See LSJ *s.v.* φερέπολις.

44. *Eunomia* 78.

45. One of the very few classical instances is in a passage from Xen. *Cyr.* (3.3.8), where the Persian is enjoining stern discipline: 'Thus you must remain in future good soldiers, recognizing that the greatest pleasures and benefits are afforded by obedience (ἡ πειθώ), endurance, and, at times of crisis, exertion and danger.' Here πειθώ is the equivalent of πειθαρχία, 'obedience to authority'. In addition to this passage, there are *Cyr.* 2.3.19 and 3.3.59; after that there is only the historian Herodian (8.7.5), Hierokles (commentary on *Carmen Aureum*, 5.4 - *FPG* I, p. 427), and *P. Oxy.* III, 474, line 37 (2nd cent. A.D.). (At E. *Hyps.* fr. 60.116, πειθώ appears to be used in the passive sense of 'confidence': see Bond's commentary (Oxford, 1963) *ad loc.*)

46. See the explication in the *Thesaurus*: 'in Atheniensium potestate esse, vi ab illis obtinere quod petebant, si verbis s. dicendi facultate et artificio non possent' (*TGL* VI, col 665). Cf. Plu. *quaest. symp.* 745c-d.

47. It is worth noting that this passage provides further confirmation of the absence of a clear division between 'divine' and 'secular' *peitho*. Peitho and the other three abstracts mentioned appear to receive an *ad hoc* deification—they are in a sense only 'metaphorically' divine. And yet they are *powers* who are represented as presiding over the dispute at Andros—and of course the question 'small or capital π?' was as meaningless to Herodotos as to Aischylos. Peitho is *both* a divinity *and* an abstraction.

48. See the comments on ὀπηδεῖ by A.P.D. Mourelatos, *The Route of*

Parmenides (Yale, 1970) 158-60.

49. Dr C.J. Rowe brings to my attention a useful comparative reference, Aristot. *Rh.* 1355a21, where truth and justice are said to be naturally more powerful than their opposites, with regard to engendering conviction in an audience.

For a discussion of some philosophical issues relating to the role of *peitho* in Parmenides' thought (the analysis of which would take us too far afield in the present study), see Mourelatos *Route*, ch. 6, 'Persuasion and fidelity'; also Pepe *Peitho* 226-8.

50. For the problematic invocation δέσποινα, cf. A. Henrichs, 'Despoina Kybele: ein Beitrag zur religiösen Namenkunde', *HŚPh* 80 (1976) 253-86.

51. Note the near-verbatim repetition at Aristainet. *Epist.* 2.1.

52. E. Capps, *Four Plays of Menander*, edn with commentary (Boston, 1910) *ad loc.* (= 338/9 in his lineation).

53. Wilamowitz made a concerted effort to dignify the invocation in *Epitrep.*: 'Habrotonon spricht zuletzt in gehobenem Stile, denn die Peitho ist keine Göttin, bei der eine athenische Hetäre schwören würde; in Lesbos und wo sonst es eine Aphrodite Peitho gab, mochte das anders sein. Der Dichter will, dass Habrotonons Schlusswort in uns nachklingt und wir dem liebenswerten Mädchen, das wir kennen gelernt haben, die erhoffte Freiheit gönnen' (*Menander: Das Schiedsgericht (Epitrepontes)* (Berlin, 1925) 85). But there are no grounds for accepting the geographical distinction implied by W. As we have seen, Peitho was worshipped at Athens as a goddess with erotic and with wider, 'political' significance; and a similar range of functions belonged to her outside Athens too. One would not wish to deny that Peitho was especially important at Athens; but to suggest that the Athenian Peitho was somehow more exalted and un-erotic than her counterparts elsewhere in Greece is not warranted by the evidence.

54. The most valuable, comprehensive and up-to-date secondary source is E. Simon, *EAA* VI, 5-8, *s.v.* 'Peitho'. See also Jahn *Peitho*, Weizsäcker *Peitho*, Voigt *Peitho;* and E. Pottier in Daremberg/Saglio IV.1, 369-71, *s.v.* 'Peitho'. For Peitho in the Helen-Paris story see L.B. Ghali-Kahil, *Les Enlèvements et le retour d'Hélène dans les textes et les documents figurés* (Paris, 1955) *s.v.* 'Peitho' in index.

55. See H. Fuhrmann in *JDAI* 56 (1941) 449-56, with plates 51-4; A. Rumpf, 'Anadyomene', *JDAI* 65-6 (1950-1) 166-74, at 169: E. Simon, *Die Geburt der Aphrodite* (Berlin, 1959) 40f.

56. Ath. 1629; *ARV*[2] II, 1250, 1688; illustration in E. Pfuhl, *Malerei und Zeichnung der Griechen* (Munich, 1923) III, pl. 562. Date about 425:

see J.D. Beazley and B. Ashmole, *Greek Sculpture and Painting to the End of the Hellenistic Period* (Cambridge, 1932) *re* their fig. 108.

57. Cf. Kallimachos' fifth hymn, 13ff, in which the spheres of Aphrodite and Athene are strongly distinguished from each other: in particular, the latter has no unguents or mirrors.

58. B. Schweitzer ('Mythische Hochzeiten', *SHAW*, Phil.-hist. Kl., 1960-1, no. 6) takes this view; C.W. Clairmont ('Bemerkung zum Epinetron des Eretriameisters', *BCH* 86 (1962) 539-42) believes Peitho is holding the mirror.

59. I give here a summary of cases where Peitho appears as a love-goddess *not* specifically connected with 'persuasion' by the context of the story depicted.

   (i) Red-figure Attic pelike from Sicily (fifth century), now in New York. Shows (almost certainly) Mousaios, the singer from Thrace, with his wife and son; four Muses; Aphrodite with Eros and Pothos; Harmonia; and Peitho seated on the right. (*ARV*² II, 1313; cf. G.M.A. Richter in *AJA* 43 (1939) 1-6.)

  (ii) Apulian krater from Ruvo, now in Leningrad. Composition is dominated by Triptolemos on his snake-carriage. Also present are Demeter, two Horai, a satyr, Aphrodite, Eros, and the undemonstrative figure of Peitho. (See L. Stephani, *Die Vasensammlung der kaiserlichen Ermitage* (St Petersburg, 1869) I, 162ff (No. 350); illustrated in A. Baumeister, *Denkmäler des klassischen Altertums* (Munich, 1885-8) III, 1857ff.)

 (iii) Lekythos in Kansas City. Beazley's description is as follows: '... Mother and baby (Kephalos), with Eunomia, Paidia, Peitho, Antheia. On the shoulder, woman (Aphrodite?) and Eros...' (*ARV*² II, 1248).

  (iv) Lekythos by Meidias painter (late fifth century), showing Aphrodite with female attendants. Simon describes the design thus: 'Peitho mette dei rami in un cesto di sacrifici dietro ad Afrodite, presenti Eunomia, Paidia.' (London E 697; *ARV*² II, 1324; Simon *Peitho* 8.)

   (v) Pyxis in New York, late fifth century, manner of Meidias painter. Peitho brings a box of trinkets (?) to Aphrodite. Also present: Hygieia, (Eu)daimonia, Paidia, Eukleia, Aponia. (*ARV*² II, 1328; G.M.A. Richter and M.J. Milne, *Shapes and Names of Athenian Vases* (N.Y., 1935) fig. 145.)

  (vi) Two lekythoi, in private collection in Athens. One of the two has inscriptions securing Peitho, Hygieia, Tyche, Harmonia; also (?) Aphrodite. (Publ. by G. Körte, 'Eichelförmige Lekythos mit

Goldschmuck aus Attika', *Arch. Zeit.* 37 (1879) 93-6, at 95.)

(vii) Aryballos in Athens. Simon: 'Afrodite, Eros, Peitho e Pan assistono ad una lotta tra Peleo e Teti.' (Weizsäcker *Peitho* col. 1803, fig. 4; Simon *Peitho* 8.)

(viii) Small London hydria by Polygnotos. Himeros and Peitho: the former sitting on a rock with (Jahn's suggestion, and the most plausible one I have seen) a spatula, for spreading ointment, in one hand; while Peitho stands to the left with (?) a cup and a receptacle for ointment. (London E 222: *CVA*, Great Britain, B.M. Fascicule VI, 365.5; Jahn *Peitho* 25.)

(ix) Fragment of skyphos in New York. Peitho and Aphrodite (inscriptions) with Eros. Behind Peitho is the top of a sceptre, which could well belong to her. (Metrop. Mus. N.Y. 07. 286. 51; *ARV²* II, 806. See also A. Greifenhagen, *Griechische Eroten* (Berlin, 1957) 43-4 and 77; picture on p. 80, pl. 52.) For the possibility of identifying as Peitho the figure with sceptre on a Würzburg pyxis from Attica (*ARV²* II, 1133) see Greifenhagen *Gr. Erot.* 77, with plates 31-3.

60. 13.186: Ghali-Kahil *Hélène* pl. IV., text 53; *ARV²* I, 458.

61. For the erotic connotations of flowers, see ch. 1 of Greifenhagen *Gr. Erot.*, entitled 'Vielblumige Eroten'. At p. 26 G. writes: 'Blüten und Palmetten in Händen der Eroten sind Zeichen des Lebens und der in ihnen wie in Eros wirksamen zeugenden Urkraft.' G. refers (p. 7) appropriately to Pl. *Smp.* 196a: ἡ κατ' ἄνθη δίαιτα τοῦ θεοῦ (sc. τοῦ Ἔρωτος). But the link between love and flowers is, of course, much older than that. In the *Kypria* the Charites and Horai dress Aphrodite in a garment which has been dipped in the flowers of spring (fr. 4 (Allen) = Ath. 15 (682d-f)); in *Works and Days* the adornment of Pandora, begun by the Charites and Peitho with golden necklaces, is continued by the Horai with spring flowers (73-5); and the scene for one of the frequent *amours* in *Theogony* is ἐν μαλακῷ λειμῶνι καὶ ἄνθεσιν εἰαρινοῖσιν (279). (For a demonstration that 'in the tradition of Greek poetry a description of a flowery meadow occurs frequently in a context of female beauty to be enjoyed', see J.M. Bremer, 'The meadow of love and two passages in Euripides' *Hippolytus*', *Mnemosyne* 28 (1975) 268-80, at 268. See also now O.J. Schrier, 'Love with Doris', *Mnemosyne* 32 (1979) 307-26, at 310.)

Of the many instances in lyric I quote only the most delightful:

φάος δ' ἐπί-
σχει θάλασσαν ἐπ' ἀλμύραν
ἴσως καὶ πολυανθέμοις ἀρούραις·

ἀ δ᾿ ⟨ἐ⟩έρσα κάλα κέχυται τεθά-
λαισι δὲ βρόδα κἄπαλ᾿ ἄν-
θρυσκα καὶ μελίλωτος ἀνθεμώδης·

(Sappho, PLF 96.9-14)

...its [sc. the moon's] light extends over the salt sea alike and the fields of flowers; and the dew is spread abroad in beauty, and rose bloom, and tender chervil and flowery melilot... (tr. D.L. Page *Sappho and Alcaeus* (Oxford, 1955) 88)

The preeminence of the moon's beauty is being used to illustrate the preeminence of a girl's beauty; and the sensuous description of the flowers helps to create a headily erotic atmosphere.

Plants too appear in erotic contexts: see, for instance, the simile at *Od.* 6.162ff, where Odysseus likens Nausikaa to the shoot of a young palm (φοίνικος νέον ἔρνος). A similar idea receives poignant expression when Sophokles' Deianeira compares the life of a young maiden to the sheltered existence of a delicate plant (*Tr.* 144ff). See further E. Langlotz, 'Aphrodite in den Gärten', *SHAW*, Phil.-hist. Kl., 1953-4, no. 2, esp. for the visual arts.

62. 30036; Ghali-Kahil *Hélène* pl. VIII, text 59-61.
63. The vase is discussed by Wilamowitz ('Lesefrüchte', *Hermes* 64 (1929) 458-90, at 485-6). The inscription naming Peitho is clear, as are those indicating Nemesis and Heimarmene; but a fourth has only left us Y.Ε̣ as a clue to her identity. Wilamowitz's comments are a mixture of excellent economy and (on a particular detail) confusion. Referring to the figure accompanying Nemesis, W. says that of her name 'ist nur ein Y sicher, aber das steht so, dass nur ein Buchstabe davor gewesen ist, und da hier kein Wesen, das mit Ευ- anfing, gedacht werden kann, ist Τύχη zuversichtlich zu ergänzen'. Correct. But then W. goes on to muddle Tyche and Nemesis—from the position of the inscriptions it is clear that Nemesis, not Tyche, is the one doing the pointing. But W. is surely right both in his translation of Τύχη—'Erfolg', i.e. a successful outcome to the persuasive enterprise—and (for us more importantly) in his remarks on Nemesis. Ghali-Kahil (*loc.cit.* in n. 62 above) would link her with the Attic 'Nemesis of Rhamnous' cult; but Wilamowitz makes better and simpler sense by seeing in Nemesis 'die strafende Vergeltung der Entführung'. See also L. Petersen (*Zur Geschichte der Personifikation in griechischer Dichtung und bildender Kunst* (Würzburg, 1939) 40-1) for whom Tyche, Nemesis and Heimarmene are 'Erfolg, Strafe und Schicksalsbestimmung'.
64. Three late reliefs further illustrate this latter pattern:

(i) Neo-Attic relief in Naples Museum (6682). Ghali-Kahil *Hélène* pl. XXXIV, text 225; also W. Fuchs in *Ergänzungsheft* XX of *JDAI* (1959) 137-8.

(ii) Metrop. Mus. N.Y. 10.210.27. Relief (no inscription) along lines of Naples relief. See G.M.A. Richter, *Catalogue of Greek Sculptures in the Metropolitan Museum of Art* (Oxford, 1954) pl. CV, no. 144; text 81.

(iii) Relief in Vatican Mus. (Belvedere 58d).

65. H. 525; Ghali-Kahil *Hélène* pl. LXVI, text 90-1.

66. See Petersen *Personifikation* 38.

67. As Petersen (*loc. cit.* in n. 66 above) rightly observes: 'Hinter (dem Menelaos) steht Peitho, nur scheinbar abgewandt (wodurch falsche allegorische Deutungen der Szene entstanden sind): sie blickt über den Henkel des Gefässes auf die ganze Szene und schliesst sie zusammen.' (For the 'allegorical interpretations' see, e.g., Buschor in Furtwängler-Reichhold, *Griechische Vasenmalerei* (Munich, 1932) III, 308-9.)

68. On the Kansas and London lekythoi, (iii) and (iv) in n. 59 above.

69. On N.Y. pyxis, (v) in n. 59 above; and on a hydria in the Hope Collection (E.M.W. Tillyard, *The Hope Vases* (Cambridge, 1923) pl. 15, no. 114; text 63-4).

70. On the onos from Eretria (Pl. 1; n. 56 above), the N.Y. pelike ((i) in n. 59 above), and one of the Athens lekythoi ((vi) in n. 59 above).

71. A. Comotti, *EAA* III, 528 *s.v.* 'Eunomia'.

72. Just this sense of Eunomia is described by Solmsen (with reference to Solon): '... the word [Eunomia] ... denotes not the presence and observation of good laws in the community but rather sound moral conditions, respect for the right of others, moderation, and an orderly and restrained behaviour' (F. Solmsen, *Hesiod and Aeschylus* (Cornell, 1949) 116).

73. See West on *Th.* 902.

74. See A. Andrewes, 'Eunomia', *CQ* 32 (1938) 89-102, at 89.

75. Ehrenberg *Eunomia* 81ff. Furthermore the references to Tyrtaios' poem Εὐνομία show it to have been a political work; cf. Andrewes *Eunomia* 95ff; Ehrenberg *Eunomia* 77ff; R. Hampe, 'Eukleia und Eunomia', *MDAI (R)* 62 (1955) 107-23, at 115ff, esp. 115 n. 47.

76. *Against Aristog.* 1.10-11:

...ὑμᾶς τήμερον ὀρθῶς δεῖ δικάσαι, τὴν τὰ δίκαι᾽ ἀγαπῶσαν Εὐνομίαν περὶ πλείστου ποιησαμένους, ἣ πάσας καὶ πόλεις καὶ χώρας σῴζει...

...You must today make a right decision, and give utmost respect to Eunomia, who loves justice, and who preserves all cities and lands...

77. Like Paidia (on (iii) and (iv) of n. 59 above) who is an apolitical

personification of 'il gioco amoroso'—see C. Gonnelli, *EAA* V, 843 *s.v.* 'Paidia'.

78. See further Roscher in Roscher I.I, 1404-5, Waser in *RE* VI, 1129-31, both *s.v.* 'Eunomia'.
79. *JDAI* 52 (1937) 63 and 71ff, figs. 20-23. Schefold dates the oinochoe to about 400 B.C.
80. *IG* III.1.277.
81. *IG* III.1.277, 623, 624, 733, 738. (Comotti's ref. at *EAA* III, 523 *s.v.* 'Eukleia', is wrong here.)
82. See Frazer's note on the passage (II, p. 124), which gives references not in Jessen's *RE* article, VI, 996-8, *s.v.* 'Eukleia'.
83. Cf. Jahn *Peitho* 26.
84. For Harmonia see Crusius in Roscher I.II, 1830-3, Sittig in *RE* VII, 2379-88, *s.v.* 'Harmonia'.
85. *Hope* 64.
86. Cit. in n. 69 above. For the problem of which figure goes with which inscription, see Voigt *Peitho* col. 215, 2.
87. (vi) in n. 59 above.
88. Körte *Lekythos* 96. Voigt shares this view.
89. Cf. A. Walde-J. Pokorny, *Vergleichendes Wörterbuch der indogermanischen Sprachen* (Berlin-Leipzig, 1926-32) II, 139; C.D. Buck, *A Dictionary of Selected Synonyms in the Principal Indo-European Languages* (Chicago, 1949) 1206; S. Schulz, *Die Wurzel* ΠΕΙΘ-(ΠΙΘ-) *im älteren Griechischen* (Inaugural Dissertation, Freiburg-in-der-Schweiz, 1952) 62-3; Pepe *Peitho* 4; H. Frisk, *Griechisches etymologisches Wörterbuch* (Heidelberg, 1960-72) II, 487-8 *s.v.* πείθομαι; P. Chantraine, *Dictionnaire étymologique de la langue grecque* (Paris, 1968-) III, 868-9, *s.v.* πείθομαι.
90. This way of understanding the relation of the active and the middle fits in, as it happens, with the most likely view of the etymology, viz. that middle preceded active: cf., e.g., Schulz *Wurzel*, Pepe *Peitho*, as cit. in n. 89 above.
91. R. Gusmani, 'I nomi greci in -ώ', *RIL* 96 (1962) 399-412.
92. H. Fränkel, *Dichtung und Philosophie des frühen Griechentums²* (Munich, 1962) 338 n. 15 (= 296 n. 15 in Eng. tr.).
93. Cf. Plato's version, quoted at *R.* 390e: δῶρα θεοὺς πείθει, δῶρ' αἰδοίους βασιλῆας.
94. Cf. R.P. Winnington-Ingram, 'Notes on the *Agamemnon* of Aeschylus', *BICS* 21 (1974) 3-19, at 6-7.
95. Cf. Ap. Rhod. 4.892; L. Kahn, *Hermès passe* (Paris, 1978) 137f.
96. C. Diano, *Saggezza e poetiche degli antichi* (Vicenza, 1968) 249-50; J.

de Romilly, *Magic and Rhetoric in Ancient Greece* (Harvard, 1975), index *s.v.* θέλγειν, θελκτήριον; Kahn *Hermès* 136ff. See also G. Thomson on 185-6 (his lineation) of *Prometheus Bound* (edn, Cambridge, 1932).

97. *Od.* 10.291: ἀλλ᾽ οὐδ᾽ ὣς θέλξαι σε δυνήσεται ('but she will not, even so, be able to bewitch you')—in this case Kirke's enchantment is counteracted by Hermes.

98. See Fraenkel *Ag.*, III, p. 679.

99. W.K.C. Guthrie, *A History of Greek Philosophy*, III: *The Fifth-century Enlightenment* (Cambridge, 1969) 38; see also ch. VIII, 'Rhetoric and philosophy', 176ff.

100. For Aristotle's forerunners see L. Radermacher *Art. Scr.*; for the sophists' interest in language cf. C.J. Classen, 'The study of language amongst Socrates' contemporaries', in Classen (ed.), *Sophistik* (*Wege der Forschung*) (Darmstadt, 1976) 215-47.

101. Guthrie *HGP* 273.

102. For the 'enslaving' power of persuasion according to Gorgias, cf. Pl. *Grg.* 452d ff.

103. Tr. H. Tredennick, *The Last Days of Socrates* (Penguin, 1954).

104. *'Nikokles' or 'The Cyprians'* 6 (slightly amended from Norlin's Loeb tr.) = *Antid.* 254; cf. *Panegyr.* 48. Other *loci* for the connection between language and civilization: S. *Ant.* 354, E. *Supp.* 201ff, Aristot. *Pol.* 1253a10, etc.

105. Cf. *Nikokles* 22, where monarchs can secure the compliance of others by persuasion or force (τοὺς μὲν πεῖσαι, τοὺς δὲ βιάσασθαι); and *To Philip* 16, where Philip needs to possess τὸ πείθειν for his dealings with Greeks and τὸ βιάζεσθαι for his dealings with barbarians.

106. Solon, Kleisthenes (λόγῳ πείσας), Themistokles (ὃ τίς ἂν οἷός τ᾽ ἐγένετο πεῖσαι μὴ πολὺ τῷ λόγῳ διενεγκών;), and Perikles (ῥήτωρ ἄριστος). Of the four together: καὶ τούτων τῶν ἀνδρῶν τῶν τηλικαῦτα διαπραξαμένων οὐδεὶς λόγων ἠμέλησεν...

107. Cf. Grossmann *Promethie* 130.

108. For the ethical significance of human speech see also Aristot. *Pol.* 1253a9-18.

109. Guthrie *HGP* 177, with refs. there.

110. See F.M. Cornford, *Plato's Cosmology* (London, 1937) 361-4; G.R. Morrow, 'Necessity and persuasion in Plato's *Timaeus*', *PhR* 59 (1950) 147-63.

111. See G.R. Morrow, 'Plato's conception of persuasion', *PhR* 62 (1953) 234-50, at 238ff.

112. See p. 54.

113. See pp. 53-4.
114. E 224: *ARV²* II, 1313; good pictures in Pfuhl *Malerei* III, pl. 593, and G. Becatti, *Meidias, un manierista antico* (Florence, 1947) pl. I. See the comments of C. Calame, *Les Choeurs de jeunes filles en Grèce archaïque* (Rome, 1977) I, 329-30, with n. 311.
115. See p. 55.
116. Tr. adapted from Norlin, Loeb edn.
117. The concept of *nomos* is by no means a simple one, of course. Its range—from 'established order or rule, generally agreed to be valid' to 'mere conventional opinion'—is considered by F. Heinimann, *Nomos und Physis* (Basel, 1945) esp. 61-89. See also J. de Romilly, *La Loi dans la pensée grecque* (Paris, 1971) esp. 18ff.
118. Cf. M. Ostwald, *Nomos and the Beginnings of the Athenian Democracy* (Oxford, 1969) 30, whence I borrow the translation.
119. See P. Vidal-Naquet, 'Valeurs religieuses et mythiques de la terre et du sacrifice dans l'*Odyssée*', *Annales (ESC)* 25 (1970) 1278-97, esp. 1285ff. N.b. also the very interesting article by Ch.P. Segal, 'The raw and the cooked in Greek literature: structure, values, metaphor', *CJ* 69 (1973-4) 289-308. Segal has good comments on structural homologies between raw/cooked and, e.g., *peitho/bia*. (On Cyclopes see also G.S. Kirk, *Myth: its Meaning and Functions in Ancient and Other Cultures* (Cambridge, 1970) 162-71.)
120. Cf. p. 54.
121. That language is indeed a uniquely human attribute is still commonly assumed. The assumption has recently been vigorously attacked by S.R.L. Clark in *The Moral Status of Animals* (Oxford, 1977): '...but we remain doubtful that animals could be said to have a language. In part, this doubt is a mere device of philosophy: it is not that we have *discovered* them to lack a language but rather that we define, and redefine, what Language is by discovering what beasts do not have. If they should turn out to have the very thing we have hitherto supposed language to be, we will simply conclude that language is something else again' (p. 96). It is hard to resist the conclusion that Clark is right here. (Compare the similar terminological doubt, recorded by Aristotle at *Ph.* 199a21-3, about whether spiders and ants can be said to produce their edifices by means of *nous* or by some other, non-rational capacity; cf. U. Dierauer, *Tier und Mensch im Denken der Antike* (Amsterdam, 1977) 34 with n. 14.)
122. Tr. Lamb, Loeb edn.
123. Tr. Marchant, Loeb edn. Cf. Aristot. *PA* 660a17-28; Dierauer *Tier* 50f.
124. It will be noted that no mention has been made of the version of

humanity's origins given in *Prometheus Bound*. This is because there is no explicit reference to the role of *language* in the birth of culture. According to Collard (n. on E. *Supp.* 203-4) the 'gift or discovery' of language is 'disguised in the subsidiary skills of number and writing' at *P.V.* 459ff; see Collard's refs. *ad loc.* Alternatively there is Gundert's idea (Dierauer *Tier* 32, n. 4) that κλύοντες οὐκ ἤκουον (*P.V.* 448, 'they gave ear but did not hear'—the subject is the *Urmenschen*) implies that it was only thanks to Prometheus that mankind was able to *understand* speech. There is nothing intrinsically improbable about Gundert's interpretation—Alkmaion (DK fr. 1a) is known to have posited that beasts merely *perceive*, while man *understands*—but on balance I think Dierauer *Tier* (40, n. 5) is right to regard κλύοντες οὐκ ἤκουον as just a reinforcement of βλέποντες ἔβλεπον μάτην. (D. does not in fact rule out Gundert's view, and offers his own only as a possibility.)

125. See Dierauer *Tier* 33, nn. 7,8.

126. A. *Ag.* 1050f, S. *Ant.* 1001f, Ar. *Birds* 199f, A. fr. 728 M, Ion *TrGF* 19 F 33; cf. Hdt. 2.54-7. See Dierauer *Tier* 31.

127. For the contrast in speech between Greeks and barbarians, see C. Bologna, 'Il linguaggio del silenzio', *SSR* 2 (1978) 305-42, esp. 306-7.

128. See pp. 67-90.

129. Cf. Heinimann *Nomos,* index *s.v.* βία, βίαιος.

130. Cf. Heinimann *Nomos* 42.

131. See H.C. Baldry, *The Unity of Mankind in Greek Thought* (Cambridge, 1965) 82-3.

132. See F. Frontisi-Ducroux, *Dédale: mythologie de l'artisan en Grèce ancienne* (Paris, 1975) 188ff; V. Citti, *Tragedia e lotta di classe in Grecia* (Naples, 1978) 176; 180.

133. See pp. 153-70.

134. See p. 181.

135. See p. 88 on A.'s Danaid trilogy.

136. For *Phil.* see pp. 118-32; for *Oresteia,* pp. 105-14.

137. See p. 109.

138. See p. 36.

139. Cf. Kahn *Hermès* 126.

140. On *peitho*'s ambivalence, see Kahn *Hermès* 145.

NOTES TO CHAPTER THREE: AISCHYLOS

1. For the controversy see, e.g., A.F. Garvie, *Aeschylus' 'Supplices': Play and Trilogy* (Cambridge, 1969); Snell on *TrGF* DID C 6.

2. See p. 3.

3. Cf. the remarks of M. Ewans, 'Agamemnon at Aulis: a study in the *Oresteia*', *Ramus* 4 (1975) 17-32, at 18; O. Taplin, *The Stagecraft of Aeschylus* (Oxford, 1977) 18.

4. This goes for most of the subsequent analyses too; although *Philoktetes* lends itself to a rather more schematic approach.

5. I retain Page's brackets (OCT) at the end, but prefer the dative to the—as it seems to me—less elegant accusative αὐτογενῆ φυξανορίαν; which last reading is, however, given also by Friis Johansen in his edition (1970).

6. Perhaps also, as Winnington-Ingram suggests ('The Danaid trilogy of Aeschylus', *JHS* 81 (1961) 141-52, at 150), the Danaids' words already prefigure the later blood-guilt which they will incur through murdering their husbands.

7. For a post-Garvie *mise au point* see S. Ireland, 'The problem of motivation in the *Supplices* of Aeschylus', *RhM* 117 (1974) 14-29.

8. Thus, rightly, Winnington-Ingram *Dan. Tr.* 144: 'The distinction between hatred of a forced marriage and hatred of marriage as such cannot be pressed too far, since, in the dramatic situation, force is the only guise under which marriage presents itself to the Danaids, as an act comparable to war or to the preying of bird on bird.'

   Any suggestions that a fear of *incest* is disturbing the girls should finally have been rendered untenable by Garvie *Supp.* 216. 'Bird eats bird' is not here—though, of course, in another context it could easily be—a metaphor for incest, but rather a metaphor for extreme violence.

9. The *locus classicus* is J.J. Bachofen, *Gesammelte Werke*³ II (*Das Mutterrecht*), ed. K. Meuli (Basel, 1948) 286 n. 1.

10. See K. von Fritz, 'Die Danaidentrilogie des Aeschylus', *Philologus* 91 (1936) 121-36 and 249-69, at 259; repr. in von Fritz, *Antike und moderne Tragödie* (Berlin, 1962) 160-92, at 183.

11. See H.W. Smyth, *Aeschylean Tragedy* (Univ. of Cal., 1924) 58; von Fritz *Danaiden* 183 (in reprint); Garvie *Supp.* 215.

12. Cf. A. *P.V.* 723-4, when Io goes to the land of the *man-hating* Amazons: Ἀμαζόνων στρατὸν ... στυγάνορα.

13. Ireland *Motivation* sets out the points at issue with commendable lucidity, and I am indebted to this article to a considerable extent.

14. That is if we read φίλους. With φιλοῦσ' the sense is, to all dramatic intents and purposes, the same: 'Who would find fault with masters whom one loved?' As Ireland (*Motivation* 19-20) rightly says, the word's function is in either case 'to answer and confirm the ἔχθραν of the previous line, and to achieve this by the sense of sarcasm that is dominant throughout'. In fact Schmidt's φίλους γ' ('who were *dear* to one') is the most idiomatic of all.

15. W. Headlam, 'Upon Aeschylus—I', *CR* 14 (1900) 106-19, at 111-12; R.D. Murray, *The Motif of Io in Aeschylus' 'Suppliants'* (Princeton, 1958) 9.

16. It will be evident that in saying this I am in fundamental disagreement with George Thomson's view of the play. In his discussion in 1971, he set out the essence of his interpretation as follows: 'In the *Suppliants* the daughters of Danaos are being claimed in marriage by their next of kin, the sons of his brother Aigyptos. *The claim is quite proper, because in Attic law* there was nothing to prevent the father from bestowing his presumptive heiress in this way before he died, and on Danaos' death it will become legally binding. If, on the other hand, he should find other husbands for them, the rights of inheritance will pass to their offspring, and so the sons of Aigyptos will have lost their claim. *This then is the issue*' (Thomson, 'The *Suppliants* of Aeschylus', *Eirene* 9 (1971) 25-30, at 25-6; italics mine). Here T. seems to me to make the classic error to which any sociological approach to drama is prone—an error which T. usually avoided in his account of the *Oresteia* in *Aeschylus and Athens*—namely, to boil down dramatic particularity to a residue of social and legal fact, so getting rid of all those things which make the drama unique. For to say, 'The claim is quite proper, because in Attic law...' may be trivially true, but it falsifies the blatantly obvious fact that the conduct of the Aigyptioi is presented to us in this play as highly *improper*; indeed, as odious and offensive. Another result of the process of 'boiling down' is to leave the impression that the socio-legal issue is what the play is essentially 'about'. However, even T. can find only four references to it—hardly a large enough tally to warrant T.'s comparison with the issue of tyranny in *P.V.*, or to rival the importance of *peitho/bia* in *Supp.* (For a more detailed presentation of my disagreement with T., see n. 14 on pp. 198-9 of Buxton *Peitho*.)

17. Cf. W. Nestle, *Menschliche Existenz und politische Erziehung in der Tragödie des Aischylos* (Stuttgart, 1934) 67. At 59-60 he considers the general place of *bia* in Aischylos.

18. See V. Ehrenberg, 'Origins of democracy', *Historia* 1 (1950) 515-48, at 517-24. Ehrenberg, however, underestimates the 'doubleness'—both monarchy *and* democracy are simultaneously present in Argos.
19. The naturalness with which this is said is in itself a hefty blow to the 'incest' theory of the Danaids' motivation.
20. Cf. Vernant in J.-P. Vernant/P. Vidal-Naquet, *Mythe et tragédie en Grèce ancienne* (Paris, 1972) 31ff.
21. Cf. Ewans *Ag. Aul.* 30-1.
22. Ζεὺς μὲν ἀφίκτωρ (1); βαρύς γε μέντοι Ζηνὸς ἱκεσίου κότος (347); μένει τοι Ζηνὸς ἱκταίου κότος (385); φύλαξαι κότον (427).
23. See Murray *Io.*
24. There is doubt about the text of 623.
    > εὐπειθὴς Bothe: εὐπειθεῖς in -θεὶς mut. M; εὐπιθεῖς Blomfield.
    > δημηγόρου δ' ἤκουσεν εὐπειθὴς στροφῆς ('imago ex equis docilibus tracta, genetivo igitur opus est') Friis Johansen.

    Concerning εὐπειθὴς, see Fraenkel on *Ag.* 274 for a demonstration that (i) there is no substance in Blomfield's strictures about the need to write -ι- instead of -ει-; (ii) the meanings 'qui facile persuadet' and 'cui facile persuadetur, qui facile obsequitur' are both attested. Friis Johansen's interpretation is ingenious, but (i) it takes him further than necessary from the MSS; (ii) in a context like this it is surely rather unnatural to take ἀκούω in the sense 'am obedient to'.
25. Reading, with Page, Lachmann's ἐναίμοις for M's ἐν ἄλλοις.
26. Ch. 2, n. 61.
27. For ῥύσιον, see Fraenkel on *Ag.* 535. F. distinguishes between the usual sense ('the thing seized by way of securing a legal claim') and what he sees as a special usage at *Ag.* 535 ('the thing seized', 'plunder'). As far as *Supp.* is concerned, the 'legal' motive is more or less prominent at 728 according as we accept or reject the notion that the Aigyptioi have, as next of kin, a legal claim over their cousins (with a view to marrying them).
28. *Stagecraft* 222ff.
29. *Stagecraft* 228.
30. On the question, 'Did they constitute a supplementary chorus?' cf. Taplin *Stagecraft* 230ff; and see my pp. 85-6.
31. See Garvie *Supp.* 194-5.
32. Cf. n. 30 above.
33. See n. 43 below.
34. 'Progymnasmata', *C&M* 27 (1966) 39-64, at 61-4.
35. Friis Johansen accepts Weil's τέλος for γάμος, but basically he takes the lines in the way I have been recommending.

36. For the association between Peitho, Harmonia and Aphrodite cf. the Derveni papyrus, col. 17. (See R. Merkelbach in *ZPE* 1 (1967) 21-32 at 25ff; W. Burkert, *A&A* 14 (1968) 93-114.)

37. It must surely be the servant-girls who speak 1047-51.

38. A full account of the issues is in Garvie's chapter on 'The Trilogy'.

39. Garvie *Supp.* 164.

40. See Garvie *Supp.* 186-7. Taplin (*Stagecraft* 195ff) looks carefully at the evidence for and against linking *Supp.* with *Danaids* in the same trilogy.

41. Cf. Garvie *Supp.* 226ff.

42. Cf. Grossmann *Promethie* 30-1.

43. Perhaps one last speculation may be indulged. After the *Danaids*, the audience would have watched the satyr-play *Amymone*, about a Danaid who, like her sisters, was threatened with rape (by a satyr), and who (like them?) eventually enjoyed union—in her case, with Poseidon. We know practically nothing about the plot, but the myth has affinities, which Aischylos will have exploited, with the stories of Io and the other Danaids. (Cf. von Fritz *Danaiden* 191-2 (in reprint); Winnington-Ingram *Dan. Tr.* 147; Garvie *Supp.* 233, with n. 2.)

44. E.g. R. Unterberger, *Der gefesselte Prometheus des Aischylos* (Stuttgart, 1968); Grossmann *Promethie*; and now D.J. Conacher, *Aeschylus' 'Prometheus Bound'* (Toronto, 1980), which appeared too late for me to take account of it.

45. M. Griffith, *The Authenticity of 'Prometheus Bound'* (Cambridge, 1977).

46. *Stagecraft* ch. 5.

47. M.L. West, 'The Prometheus trilogy', *JHS* 99 (1979) 130-48.

48. 'Die ἐπιστολαί ... sind Zeus' erste Manifestation', Unterberger *Prom.* 23.

49. See Solmsen *Hes. and A.* 124ff; K. Reinhardt, *Aischylos als Regisseur und Theologe* (Bern, 1949) 29ff.

50. Whether or not we adopt the emendation διέταξε νόμους for MSS διέταξεν ὁμῶς, Zeus's activity as something fair and orderly remains unaffected.

51. Cf. Grossmann *Promethie* 20.

52. P.G. Maxwell-Stuart ('Interpretations of the name Oedipus', *Maia* 27 (1975) 37-43), in discussing Prometheus' punishment (p. 39 n. 13), wishes to deny that the Titan is 'pierced'. While we may agree at once that 'he is *not* crucified in the Christian sense' (M.-S.'s italics), it is impossible to ignore στέρνων διαμπάξ, 'through his chest' (65). Thus Rose, in his commentary on 64-5, has: 'Drive now the pitiless point of a wedge of steel clean through his chest, with all thy force.' For crucifixion and crucifixion-like penalties in the ancient world see M. Hengel, *Crucifixion*

(London, 1977) esp. 11ff.

53. Well discussed by Unterberger *Prom.* 45-6.
54. Cf. Reinhardt *Aisch.* 47.
55. See Solmsen *Hes. and A.* 129 n. 22; Grossmann *Promethie* 95.
56. Cf. B.M.W. Knox, *The Heroic Temper: Studies in Sophoclean Tragedy* (Univ. of Cal., 1964) 45ff.
57. See Thomson's edn *ad loc.* (= 393-6 in his lineation). For medical imagery in *P.V.* see Barbara H. Fowler, 'The imagery of the *Prometheus Bound*', *AJPh* 78 (1957) 173-84, at 174ff.
58. Cf. Reinhardt *Aisch.* 52-3.
59. Cf. Reinhardt *Aisch.* 71.
60. See Grossmann *Promethie* 102ff.
61. Cf. Unterberger *Prom.* 96-7.
62. τίθησ᾽ ἐγκύμονα is Elmsley's conjecture for MSS τίθησιν ἔμφρονα. ἐγκύμονα makes perfect sense, but ἔμφρονα ('in your senses') is not impossible. (It is retained by, e.g., Groeneboom in his 1928 edn of *P.V.*)
63. 'The six occurrences of πρὶν ἄν (sc. in *P.V.*)... may be explained... as proceeding from the unique forward-looking, prophetic atmosphere of this play' (C.J. Herington, *The Author of the 'Prometheus Bound'* (Univ. of Texas, 1970) 73).
64. Apparently Cheiron—cf. Introduction (p. 31) to Thomson *Prom.*; H. Lloyd-Jones, *The Justice of Zeus* (Univ. of Cal., 1971) 97; West *Prom. Tril.* 142.
65. See most recently West *Prom. Tril.*
66. See Séchan *Mythe* 98 n. 16.
67. I am convinced by the arguments of A.D. Fitton-Brown, 'Prometheia', *JHS* 79 (1959) 52-60, who maintains (56-7) that the two extracts quoted by Cicero at *Tusc.* 2.23ff (= fr. 324 M) are Cicero's own translations from the Greek.
68. The only possible clue is *P.V.* 771: Ιω. τίς οὖν ὁ λύσων ἐστὶν ἄκοντος Διός; Io. 'Who then will release you against the will of Zeus?' Fitton-Brown (*Prom.*) argues that this line implies that Prometheus will be released ἄκοντος Διός, 'against the will of Zeus'. But why should *Io*'s words—she is, after all, only a bewildered mortal—be taken as binding on what happens subsequently? Nor do I think there is any justification for Fitton-Brown to say (54 n. 7): 'Schmid's attempt [*Untersuchungen zum Gefesselten Prometheus* (Stuttgart, 1929) 100 n. 2]... to interpret away ἄκοντος Διός as meaning "da (bis jetzt) oder wenn Zeus es nicht will" is in clear defiance of the Greek as written.' On the contrary, a perfectly good free translation of the line would be, 'Who could possibly be the one to free you if Zeus is unwilling to countenance the act?' In the

event Zeus may *not* be unwilling: we do not know yet. (See also Séchan *Mythe* 74, with n. 41.)

69. *Prom. Tril.*

70. West *Prom. Tril.* 131.

71. Cf. the scenario put forward by Grossmann *Promethie* 95: as, in the *Theogony* (886ff), Zeus's marriage to and assimilation of Metis marked a transition to the conditions necessary for a stable and just reign, so in the Prometheus trilogy the dramatist may have symbolized the change in Zeus's reign by the raising of Themis to the status of a consort of the supreme god. (The assumption that Prometheus' mother Themis-Gaia (Ge) appeared in *Luomenos*—an assumption based on the fact that the codex Mediceus includes Ge and Herakles in its list of *dramatis personae* before *P.V.*—has been ingeniously contested by West *Prom. Tril.* 141-2.)

72. 'Aspects of dramatic symbolism: three studies in the *Oresteia*', *AJPh* 76 (1955) 113-37, at 126-32.

73. But we must not jump to the wrong conclusions from this. 'It is particularly to be observed how strongly, with what emphatic words, the poet insists upon the helplessness of the human victim, and the premeditation and violence of the supernatural powers which drive him to sin' (Denniston/Page, n. on 386ff in their edn). This is misleading: the words by which Agamemnon was persuaded (206-17) were his own.

74. *Dram. Symb.* 115ff.

75. See A. Lebeck, *The Oresteia. A Study in Language and Structure* (Washington, 1971) 74ff.

76. *On Aristotle and Greek Tragedy* (London, 1962) 82-90.

77. It is surprising that Dawe, model of sceptical empiricism that he usually is, should regard the 'mental fatigue' approach with favour ('Inconsistency of plot and character in Aeschylus', *PCPhS* 189 (N.S. 9) (1963) 21-62, at 49). The herald's descriptions of the hardships at Troy are surely irrelevant here, as no reference is made to them. (I borrow Dawe's method of arguing.) Or if the hardships *are* relevant, why draw the line at mental fatigue? ('Enter Agamemnon, moist with dew and intermittently scratching.')

78. Dawe *Inconsistency* 50 (italics mine).

79. *Inconsistency* 48-9, n. 2.

80. Cf. P.E. Easterling, 'Presentation of character in Aeschylus', *G&R* 20 (1973) 3-19, at 5.

81. Easterling *Presentation* 12ff.

82. H. Gundert, 'Die Stichomythie zwischen Agamemnon und Klytaimestra', in ΘΕΩΡΙΑ: *Festschrift für W.-H. Schuchhardt* (Baden-Baden, 1960) 69-78, rightly speaks (75) of Klytaimestra beginning 'mit

einer fast sokratischen Wendung'.

83. 'Some reflections on Ate and Hamartia', *HSPh* 72 (1968) 89-123, at 122.

84. Gundert (*Stich.* 77-8) ascribes Agamemnon's *Blindheit* to the influence of the Daimon at work on him through Klytaimestra. This is essentially also the view taken by Lloyd-Jones ('The guilt of Agamemnon', *CQ* 56 (1962) 187-99), who compares *Seven against Thebes,* where Eteokles' decision to fight Polyneikes is taken while he is under the spell of the Erinys.

85. For βέλος used metaphorically of a 'love-provoking glance' see Barrett on E. *Hipp.* 530-4.

86. Cf. West on Hes. *Th.* 910; and esp. E. *Hipp.* 525-6:

Ἔρως Ἔρως, ὃ κατ' ὀμμάτων
στάζεις πόθον,...

Eros, Eros, you who drip down desire over the eyes...

on which Barrett says: 'That sexual desire manifests itself in the eyes is a commonplace of Greek poetry...'—and, he might have added, of human experience. (Cf. also Barrett on *Hipp.* 530-4, with the *Addenda* at pp. 433-4.) See also L. Malten, *Die Sprache des menschlichen Antlitzes im frühen Griechentum* (Berlin, 1961) 24; G. Devereux, 'The self-blinding of Oidipous in Sophokles: *Oidipous Tyrannos*', *JHS* 93 (1973) 36-49, at 42 n. 25; R.P. Winnington-Ingram, *Sophocles: An Interpretation* (Cambridge, 1980) 95 n. 14.

87. Cf., e.g., S. Ireland, 'Dramatic structure in the *Persae* and *Prometheus* of Aeschylus', *G&R* 20 (1973) 162-8, at 162.

88. The phrase is Herington's, cf. 'Aeschylus: the last phase', *Arion* IV, 3 (1965) 387-403, repr. in N. Rudd (ed.), *Essays on Classical Literature* (Cambridge, 1972) 1-17.

89. Plu. *Thes.* 29.4 (= fr. 268 M): συνέπραξε (sc. Theseus) δὲ καὶ Ἀδράστῳ τὴν ἀναίρεσιν τῶν ὑπὸ τῇ Καδμείᾳ πεσόντων, οὐχ ὡς Εὐριπίδης ἐποίησεν ἐν τραγῳδίᾳ, μάχῃ τῶν Θηβαίων κρατήσας, ἀλλὰ πείσας καὶ σπεισάμενος... ('He also helped Adrastos to recover the bodies of those who had been killed before the walls of the Kadmeia at Thebes, and he did this not by defeating the Thebans in battle, as Euripides makes out in *The Suppliants*, but by persuading them to agree to a truce' (based on Scott-Kilvert, Penguin tr., 1960).) Cf. Solmsen *Hes. and A.* 176-7.

90. Cf. Solmsen, *loc. cit.* in previous note.

NOTES TO CHAPTER FOUR: SOPHOKLES

1. In framing these introductory remarks I have drawn on parts of 'Blindness and limits: Sophokles and the logic of myth', *JHS* 100 (1980) 22-37.

2. In the lines

   ὁ τῆς ἀρίστης μητρὸς ὠνομασμένος,
   ὁ τοῦ κατ' ἄστρα Ζηνὸς αὐδηθεὶς γόνος (1105-6)
   the one called son of a most noble mother,
   the one said to be child of Zeus amongst the stars

   there is surely bitterness in κατ' ἄστρα, 'amongst the stars'—cf. Tourneur's *The Atheist's Tragedy*, where D'amville, denying the stars' influence, refers to God as 'him they call the Supreme of the stars' (II. iv. 137).

3. On aesthetic grounds I would rather give 1275-8 to the chorus than to Hyllos—the action is raised at last back to the remote level of the 'wheeling Bear' (129-31), and this is done more impressively and conclusively by the chorus than by an individual closely engaged in the drama. Sophoklean dramatic technique (cf. the choral endings of all the other plays — or, possibly, of all except *O.T.*) might be thought to support this attribution.

4. Cf. R. Lattimore, *The Poetry of Greek Tragedy* (Baltimore, 1958) 102: 'The gods of Sophokles are there, but remote, unattainable as the snows of Olympos...'

5. Sheppard's view (*CR* 41 (1927) 2-9) that Orestes should have asked not how but *whether* to avenge his father's murder is surely a 'sophism' (so Kamerbeek on *El.* 33). As Winnington-Ingram recently put it (*Soph.* 236): 'If Orestes asked about means and not ends, we are given no reason to suppose that the god did not approve the end...'

6. The choreography of this human ballet has been studied by a number of scholars, especially in recent years. An article by A.F. Garvie is directly relevant: 'Deceit, violence and persuasion in the *Philoctetes*', in *Studi classici in onore di Quintino Cataudella* (Catania, 1972) I, 213-26. Valuable too are J.-U. Schmidt, *Sophokles Philoktet: eine Strukturanalyse* (Heidelberg, 1973); and particularly P.E. Easterling, '*Philoctetes* and modern criticism', *ICS* 3 (1978) 27-39.

7. The section on Philoktetes' use of language owes much to P. Vidal-Naquet, 'Le *Philoctète* de Sophocle et l'éphébie', in Vernant/Vidal-Naquet *MT* 159-84; and A.J. Podlecki, 'The power of the word in Sophocles' *Philoctetes*', *GRBS* 7 (1966) 233-50.

216   *Notes to pages 119-120*

8. For ἐσχατιά, see Robert *Op. Min.* II, 820-2; D.M. Lewis, in M.I. Finley (ed.), *Problèmes de la terre en Grèce ancienne* (Paris, 1973) 210-12. For the 'marginality' of Lemnos see Jan Bremmer, 'Heroes, rituals and the Trojan War', *SSR* 2 (1978) 6-38, at 14-15.

9. φλαυρουργοῦ τινος τεχνήματ᾿ ἀνδρός, 'a thing devised by some poor workman' (35-6), makes the same point: the cup has been made but, so to speak, 'only just'.

10. For ἀλφηστής see Jebb *ad loc.*; P. Vidal-Naquet, 'Valeurs religieuses et mythiques de la terre et du sacrifice dans *l'Odyssée*', *Annales (ESC)* 25 (1970) 1278-97, at 1280 n. 3 (= Finley *Terre* 271 n.3).

11. In not drinking wine-mixed-with-water Philoktetes resembles a typical barbarian; cf. F. Graf, 'Milch, Honig und Wein. Zum Verständnis der Libation im griechischen Ritual', in *Perennitas. Studi in onore di Angelo Brelich* (Rome, 1980) 209-21. Some additional material in J.N. Bremmer, 'Marginalia manichaica', *ZPE* 39 (1980) 29-34, at 32-3.

12. E.g. H.C. Avery, 'Heracles, Philoctetes, Neoptolemus', *Hermes* 93 (1965) 279-97, esp. 284-5. A. gives full references to relevant passages in *Phil.*

13. 19, 954, 1087, and the corrupt 1149. Cf. also the semantically related καταυλισθείς (30), αὐλάς (153).

14. The related verb αὐλίζομαι is often used of the habitations of animals (*Od.* 12.265; 14.412; Hdt. 3.110; 9.93.1), and at Eur. *El.* 303-5 it is used of the squalor in which Elektra lives. (See Denniston on *El.* 304. He gives 'am stalled' as the sense of αὐλίζομαι and supports this with parallels.)

15. For βορά (274, 308), see the detailed analysis by Vidal-Naquet, 'Chasse et sacrifice dans *l'Orestie* d'Eschyle', in Vernant/Vidal-Naquet *MT* 133-58, at 148 n. 73. In his review of *MT* (*RPh*, 3ᵉ série, 48 (1974) 122-4) F. Vian disputes the necessary link between βορά and animals, but the passages assembled by Denniston on *El.* 425 corroborate his, Denniston's, conclusion that βορά is 'usually an ugly word, used, *inter alia,* of the food of carnivorous animals and cannibals'. φορβή (43, 162, 707, 711, 1107) had at one time strong associations with animals (cf. LSJ *s.v.* φορβή: '...in Hom. only of horses and asses, *fodder, forage*') but it is uncertain whether this overtone would have been present when Sophokles wrote *Phil.*; Herodotos had already used the word in the general sense of 'food' (1.211.2; 4.121). The most we can say is that Sophokles *may* have been quickening a dead meaning for his particular dramatic purposes.

16. *MT* 169.

17. The occasional involuntary visitor (304ff) has only intensified Philoktetes' sense of loneliness.

18. See Garvie *Deceit* 214ff, who points out that three important stages in the dramatic action correspond to the use of, first, deceit; then, violence; and, finally, persuasion.

19. Thomas Mann, *The Magic Mountain,* ch. 6, tr. Lowe-Porter (=p.715 of the 1960 Fischer edn).

20. Podlecki *Power* 236. A different but related point is made by K. Alt, 'Schicksal und φύσις im Philoktet des Sophokles', *Hermes* 89 (1961) 141-74, at 163 n. 2: 'Auffallend ist bei Sophokles überhaupt *die akustische Empfänglichkeit Philoktets,* die sich durch seine gesteigerte Einsamkeit erklären mag, vgl. 225, 229f, 234, 976, 1295, 1445' (my italics).

21. It is true that at 608 Odysseus is called δόλιος, 'tricky' (if the MSS reading is retained; if we adopt Housman's δόλοις, 'by tricks', my point is in no way affected); but this is, I think one might argue, simply a detail added to make the story more acceptable to Philoktetes.

The fact that the episode with the 'false merchant' diverts Philoktetes' attention towards the ideas of force and persuasion and away from that of deceit has not always been sufficiently appreciated: it is not mentioned in Svein Østerud's article on 'The intermezzo with the false merchant in Sophocles' *Philoctetes* (542-627)', *Classica et mediaevalia F. Blatt septuagenario dedicata, C&M* diss. IX (Copenhagen, 1973) 10-26.

22. Schmidt *Phil.* 176.

23. Cf. Alt *Schicksal* 167: 'erst jetzt, nach der Rückgabe des Bogens, ist mit dem menschlichen Vertrauen die Voraussetzung für das gegeben, was der Schicksalsspruch fordert: ein Entgegenkommen von beiden Seiten'. (We return below to the question of Alt's Bowra-esque view of the oracle.)

24. One of the many networks of correspondences (of both language and action) in this play concerns *aporia,* a word which connotes the helplessness of a person in an acute dilemma. At 757 Philoktetes' anguished cry for pity makes Neoptolemos exclaim, τί δῆτα δράσω; 'What shall I do?' Neoptolemos is again in *aporia* (cf. 898) just before he reveals the truth: τί δῆτ' ἂν δρῷμ' ἐγὼ τοὐνθένδε γε; 'What should I do from this point on?' (895) and ὦ Ζεῦ, τί δράσω; 'Zeus, what shall I do?' (908). After Philoktetes' impassioned speech at 927-62, first the chorus — τί δρῶμεν; 'What are we to do?' (963) — and then Neoptolemos — οἴμοι, τί δράσω; 'Alas, what shall I do?' (969) τί δρῶμεν, ἄνδρες; 'What are we to do, men?' (974) — are in an even more acute dilemma. The situation is resolved by the (for the moment) superior authority of Odysseus, who reduces *Philoktetes* to *aporia* by expressing the intention to abandon him, for the second time, on Lemnos — οἴμοι · τί δράσω

δύσμορος; 'Alas, what shall I do, ill-fated as I am?' (1063). Later, Neoptolemos' kindness (as opposed to Odysseus' callousness) makes Philoktetes ask οἴμοι, τί δράσω; 'Alas, what shall I do?' (1350). And, finally, when Philoktetes has made *his* decision, it is once more Neoptolemos who says, τί δῆτ' ἂν ἡμεῖς δρῷμεν; 'What, then, should we do?' (1393). After the appearance of Herakles there are no more dilemmas (at any rate as far as concerns decisions by the characters):

Φιλ.   οὐκ ἀπιθήσω τοῖς σοῖς μύθοις.
Νε.   κἀγὼ γνώμην ταύτῃ τίθεμαι. (1447-8)
Phil.   I shall not disobey your words.
Ne.   And nor shall I.

25. For variations on the theme of *aporia,* see the preceding footnote. For the repetition of 'significant actions' in general, see O. Taplin, 'Significant actions in Sophocles' *Philoctetes', GRBS* 12 (1971) 25-44.

26. Echoing Philoktetes' own ἀλλ', ὦ τέκνον, χωρῶμεν, 'Well, my boy, let us go' (635).

27. In 526, 645 and 1402 the three verbs which I have translated as 'go' are different in each case, but this is unimportant: far more significant is the repeated pattern. Odysseus' words at 1061 (ἡμεῖς δ' ἴωμεν, 'But, as for us, let us go') are part of the series, which is capped by the chorus' parting χωρῶμεν, 'Let us go', at 1469. (For the significance of entrances and exits in *Phil.* see W. Steidle, *Studien zum antiken Drama* (Munich, 1968) 186f.)

28. The point is developed by Easterling *Phil.* 39.

29. Odysseus has been compared to Mephistopheles (cf. Alt *Schicksal* 147: 'Und nun redet er unverhüllt, fast möchte man es nicht nur sophistisch, sondern mephistophelisch nennen...'), but, at least in respect of his severely 'instrumental' view of moral action, he might with equal justice be likened to Iago. 'The only truth [sc. for Iago] is the one that has instrumental value in a given context' (R.B. Heilman, *Magic in the Web* (Univ. of Kentucky, 1956) 194).

30. Although the phrase 'the *bia* ("force") of x' is in Greek a traditional periphrasis for 'x', it may well be that 'the *bia* of Odysseus' at 314 and 321—both times spoken by men expressing hostility towards Odysseus—is more than just a figure of speech. The same could be true of the identical phrase at 592, in the mouth of the 'false merchant'.

31. For parallels between Herakles and Philoktetes see, e.g., R. von Scheliha, *Der Philoktet des Sophokles* (Amsterdam, 1970) 89.

32. *Power* 245.

33. Cf. Easterling *Phil.* 34.

34. Easterling *Phil.* 34.

35. Cf. C.M. Bowra, *Sophoclean Tragedy* (Oxford, 1944) 265.
36. See esp. Steidle *Studien* 169ff.
37. A.J.A. Waldock, *Sophocles the Dramatist* (Cambridge, 1951) 200 ff.
38. Cf. also Steidle *Studien* 169-70.
39. Easterling *Phil.* 27.
40. It is possible that this latter point would be more at home in an analysis of Euripides; but on reflection I am not convinced that it is without validity.

     On the dubiousness of the version of the prophecy given in the 'false merchant' scene, cf. also Steidle *Studien* 171: 'Zunächst darf bezweifelt werden, dass ausgerechnet in einer Rede, die so viel Trug und Unwahrheit enthält wie die des Emporos [i.e. 'merchant'], ein für die Handlung schlechterdings entscheidendes Motiv zum *erstenmal* zur Sprache gebracht werden kann' (S'ᶜ italics).
41. Cf. D.B. Robinson, 'Topics in Sophocles' *Philoctetes*', *CQ* 19 (1969) 34-56, at 47; Easterling *Phil.* 27.
42. Cf. G.H. Gellie, *Sophocles: A Reading* (Melbourne, 1972) 157-8.
43. Cf. Steidle *Studien* 190.
44. Easterling (*Phil.*) has several useful comments on what the audience *wants* for the characters in the course of the drama.
45. Cf. Steidle *Studien* 192.
46. Inconsistently, I prefer the Latinized form of abbreviation, for reasons of decorum.
47. See M.G. Shields, 'Sight and blindness imagery in the *Oedipus Coloneus*', *Phoenix* 15 (1961) 63-73.
48. See Bowra *Soph. Tr.* 307; K. Reinhardt, *Sophocles* (Eng. tr., Oxford, 1979) 193.
49. For *O.C.* see Shields *Sight*; for *Lear* see R.B. Heilman, *This Great Stage: Image and Structure in 'King Lear'* (Univ. of Washington, 1948) 41-64.
50. This must, of course, in the case of Sophokles remain merely a highly probable inference, the play having been produced by Sophokles' grandson after the death of the author (cf. *Hypoth.* II).
51. C.H. Whitman, *Sophocles: A Study of Heroic Humanism* (Harvard, 1951) 190-218.
52. I.M. Linforth, 'Religion and drama in *Oedipus at Colonus*', *Univ. of Cal. Publications in Classical Philology* 14.4 (1951) 75-191.
53. *Sight.*
54. *Ar.G.T.* 214ff.
55. *HT* 143-62.
56. P.E. Easterling, 'Oedipus and Polynices', *PCPhS* 193 (N.S. 13) (1967) 1-13.
57. *Soph.* 159-83. (In the notes to this chapter G. refers to a valuably wide

spread of secondary literature on *O.C.*)

58. Owing to his son's tragic early death Wilamowitz *père* wrote the *O.C.* chapter in *Die dramatische Technik des Sophokles,* and so we do not have the benefit of what would undoubtedly have been Tycho's shrewd observations on the dramatic technique of *O.C.*

59. Cf. Gellie *Soph.* 159.

60. Cf. Easterling *Oedipus* 4-5, on the phrase θϱόνοι καὶ σκῆπτϱα, 'royal power' (lit. 'thrones and sceptres').

61. Compare the reflective awareness of the instability of human fortune shown by Odysseus at *Aj.* 121-6; also his attitude throughout the final altercation with Agamemnon.

62. Accepting Musgrave's ἔμπολιν, 'citizen', 'one who is within a polis', for MSS ἔμπαλιν, '(?) on the contrary'.

63. This is perhaps inevitable: virtue is the hardest thing in the world to invest with literary life. It can be done, though. Dickens managed it, repeatedly; Hugo's saintly Bishop of Digne in *Les Misérables* comes to mind; so do Manzoni's two contrastingly virtuous men of God, Federigo Boromeo and Fr. Cristoforo.

64. It is hardly necessary to repeat here that, although the ode begins by celebrating Kolonos, it broadens later to embrace Athens and Attica.

65. For one critic, '... the poet's birth-place is idealized and celebrated in the accents of tourist literature' (Gellie *Soph.* 159). The metaphor apparently seems to G. to be a good one, for he repeats it a little later ('If the ode is as narrowly partisan as a travel brochure, that is exactly what it ought to be' — p. 171); but it is in fact as relevant to Sophokles as would be the same comment if passed upon Gaunt's speech 'Methinks I am a prophet new inspired... This royal throne of kings...' from *Richard II.*

66. *Religion* 147.

67. T.G. Rosenmeyer ('The wrath of Oedipus', *Phoenix* 6 (1952) 92-112) does his best for Kreon. 'Kreon', writes R., 'is convinced of the justice of his position. His first speech is proud and yet humane... It is true that Oidipous calls Kreon's speech "the glittering camouflage of a just argument", but Oidipous has his own axe to grind... Within the narrow limits permitted by the religious rules it was the duty of Kreon as a representative of Thebes to recover the person of Oidipous. He tried his best, and Oidipous met him with curses' (from 101-3). But while he is talking to Oidipous Kreon has already had Ismene kidnapped!

68. The two possible ways of construing this are set out by Jebb. I am sure he is right to prefer the way which takes παντὸς with λόγου (tr. 'thou who wouldst borrow a crafty device from any plea of right'; which Jebb glosses: 'as he here uses the λόγος δίκαιος ('righteous argument', 'plea of

right') about duty to friends and fatherland for the purpose of enticing Oidipous back').

69. Cf. also μὴ πείθων ('not persuading'), 797. (The text is doubtful, but that a part of *peithein* stood in it is very probable. We are not sure *who* is unable to persuade, Kreon or Oidipous; but, whoever the subject was, the dramatic result is the same: intransigence.)

70. For Sophoklean characters who express mistrust in those who are glib with words see U. Parlavantza-Friedrich, *Täuschungsszenen in den Tragödien des Sophokles* (Berlin, 1969) 69, with n. 79.

71. Knox *HT* 157.

72. Winnington-Ingram (*Soph.* 274) stresses Antigone's *failure* as a persuader, yet allows too the dramatic impact of her gentleness: 'She fails to prevent terrible events, but by her love and pity mitigates the gross evil of them.'

73. *Religion* 88 (italics his).

74. E.g. by A. Lesky, *Greek Tragedy²* (Eng. tr., London, 1967) 129.

75. For a healthily sceptical view of the importance of 'divine justice' at the end of *O.C.* see Linforth *Religion* 180-4.

76. Mrs Easterling, in a private communication.

NOTES TO CHAPTER FIVE: EURIPIDES

1. 'Euripides lässt sich nicht auf eine Formel verpflichten' (P. Friedländer, 'Die griechische Tragödie und das Tragische', *Die Antike* 2 (1926) 79-112, at 86); '...scheitert jeder Versuch, diesen Dichter mit allgemeiner Kennzeichnung zu erfassen' (A. Lesky, *Gesch. der gr. Lit.*[2] (Bern, 1963) 441). These two remarks are cited by H. Rohdich, *Die euripideische Tragödie: Untersuchungen zu ihrer Tragik* (Heidelberg, 1968) 14, who gives a useful sketch (pp. 13-16) of trends in Euripidean scholarship in the twentieth century.

2. Rationalist: A.W. Verrall, *Euripides the Rationalist* (Cambridge, 1895); W. Nestle, *Euripides der Dichter der griechischen Aufklärung* (Stuttgart, 1901). Idealist: R.B. Appleton, 'Euripides the idealist', *CR* 32 (1918) 89-92, also book with same title, London, 1927. Irrationalist: E.R. Dodds, 'Euripides the irrationalist', *CR* 43 (1929) 97-104. Mystic: H. Reich, 'Euripides, der Mystiker', in *Festschrift zu C.F. Lehmann-Haupts sechzigstem Geburtstage* (Vienna, 1921) 89-93. Misogynist/feminist: see W. Schmid/O. Stählin, *Gesch. der gr. Lit.*[7] (Munich, 1940) I, 3, 321f (esp. 321 n. 6).

3. See xxii ff in the introduction to A.M. Dale's edn of *Alkestis*.

4. Cf. A. Rivier, *Essai sur le tragique d'Euripide*[2] (Lausanne, 1975) 8, quoting H. Weil and E. Rohde.

5. E.g. F. Solmsen, 'Zur Gestaltung des Intriguenmotivs in den Tragödien des Sophokles und Euripides', *Philologus* 87 (1932) 1-17, repr. in *Wege der Forschung* vol. on Eurip., ed. E.-R. Schwinge (Darmstadt, 1968) 326-44; W. Ludwig, 'Sapheneia. Ein Beitrag zur Formkunst im Spätwerk des Euripides' (Diss. Tübingen, 1954); H. Strohm, *Euripides: Interpretationen zur dramatischen Form (Zetemata* 15) (Munich, 1957); A. Spira, *Untersuchungen zum Deus ex machina bei Sophokles und Euripides* (Kallmünz, 1960); plus other works cited by Rohdich *Eur. Tr.* at 14, n. 9. Also E.-R. Schwinge, *Die Verwendung der Stichomythie in den Dramen des Euripides* (Heidelberg, 1968).

6. *Essai.*

7. It might be profitable to risk a tentative Shakespearian analogy. In *Romeo and Juliet, Othello* and *Lear*, 'fate' conspires against good intentions: *if only* Friar Lawrence's letter had reached Romeo in time; *if only* Desdemona had not dropped the handkerchief; *if only* Edmund had thought earlier about the order he gave for Cordelia's murder. Yet in *The Tempest* (I.ii.178) it is 'by accident most strange' that 'bountiful Fortune'

brings Prospero's former enemies to him, so that wrong may be righted and Ferdinand united with Miranda. Different presentations of the notion of chance correspond to different dramatic perspectives.

8. G. Zuntz, *The Political Plays of Euripides* (Manchester, 1955) 24.

9. For the parallel between the situations of Andromache and Hermione, see Steidle *Studien* 123.

10. Cf. A.P. Burnett, *Catastrophe Survived* (Oxford, 1971) 131: '[In *Andromache*] human morals and human actions seem ... to have a sickening fluidity, and this effect, gradually invading the mind of the spectator, is plainly central to the dramatist's concerns.'

11. Zuntz *Pol. Pl. Eur.* 35.

12. For the 'theatrical' aspect of Euripidean shifts see W. G. Arnott, 'Euripides and the unexpected', *G&R* 20 (1973) 49-64.

13. W. Jens at Schwinge *WdF. Eur.* 26.

14. See *Med.* 516ff, *Hipp.* 925ff, *El.* 367ff; also *Her.* 655ff. Relevant is F. Will, 'The concept of χαρακτήρ in Euripides', *Glotta* 39 (1960/61) 233-8.

15. The perilousness even of *philia* is stressed by H.P. Stahl, 'On "extra-dramatic" communication of characters in Euripides', *YCS* 25 (1977) 159-76, at 176.

16. H.D.F. Kitto, *Form and Meaning in Drama* (London, 1956) 238.

17. The remarks by A.M. Dale, Introduction to edn of *Alk.*, xxvii-xxix, could not possibly be bettered.

18. Particularly in the writings of O. Taplin.

19. Gorgias (*Enc.* 14) worked out a full analogy between the effect of a *pharmakon* on the body and that of *logos* on the soul.

20. E.g. Diod. Sic. 4.51-2, where the Peliades are represented as victims of *apate*; Apollod. 1.9.27 (other refs. in Frazer's note, Loeb edn *ad loc.*). See also C. Uhsadel-Gülke, *Knochen und Kessel* (Meisenheim-am-Glan, 1972) 38-9.

21. The 'Sophoklean' characteristics of Medea's heroism have recently been analysed by B.M.W. Knox, 'The *Medea* of Euripides', *YCS* 25 (1977) 193-225.

22. Tr. very slightly adapted from P. Pucci, *The Violence of Pity in Euripides' 'Medea'* (Cornell, 1980) 24-5. (He discusses the passage at 25ff.)

23. See most recently Pucci *Violence* 28, with n. 11.

24. Cf. J. Gould, 'Dramatic character and "human intelligibility" in Greek tragedy', *PCPhS* 204 (1978) 43-67, at 50-1.

25. One of the strengths of Rohdich's chapter on *Med.* (in *Eur. Tr.*) is his insistence on the respects in which Euripides offers Medea as *representative* of womankind.

26. Medea was said to have killed and dismembered Apsyrtos, scattering the pieces to delay her Kolchian pursuers, including Aietes (father of Medea and Apsyrtos).

27. See Gould *Hiketeia* 85-6.

28. A word on the mythical association between 'deceitful women' and fire. When Andromache is accused by Hermione of turning Neoptolemos against her by 'drugs', Andromache's reaction (*Andr.* 269ff) is: 'Some god fixed antidotes for mortals against poisonous creatures; but against something worse than a viper (*echidna*) or than fire no one has yet devised a remedy: I mean a bad woman.' We remember from Hesiod's *Works and Days* that the first woman, dangerous and deceitful Pandora (a δόλον αἰπὺν ἀμήχανον, 'a steep trick which cannot be got out of', 83) was devised ἀντὶ πυρός, 'as an equivalent for fire', 57. And we remember Hesiod's remark later in the same poem (702ff): 'A man can acquire nothing of greater benefit to him than a good wife, and nothing worse than a bad one, one who lays ambushes for dinner (!), a woman who, however strong her husband, *scorches* him without a torch, and consigns him to premature old age.' The notion of a woman *burning up* man's vitality is found elsewhere in Greek (and Latin) poetry; see West on *W.D.* 705. The connection with *gluttony* (cf. 'one who lays ambushes for dinner') is evident: woman is perceived as burning up the resources gathered and brought to her by man. (One of Semonides' gallery of women was 'moulded out of earth, a stunted creature... The only work she understands is eating...' (21ff); another, made from an ass, 'munches in the back room all night and all day, and... munches by the hearth' (46-7); tr. Lloyd-Jones, *Females of the Species* (London, 1975).) For the gluttony of women see esp. West on *W.D.* 373-4; also J.-P. Vernant, *Myth and Society in Ancient Greece* (tr. J. Lloyd, Brighton, 1980) 178f.

29. In addition to Knox *Medea*, see Pucci *Violence* 94, with n. 6.

30. Pucci *Violence* 94.

31. νῦν ἀγὼν εὐψυχίας reminds one of A. *Pers.* 405, νῦν ὑπὲρ πάντων ἀγών, the battle-cry of the Greeks before Salamis.

32. See Solmsen at 332 in Schwinge *WdF. Eur.*

33. For tragedy, see J. Duchemin, *L' 'Aγών dans la tragédie grecque*[2] (Paris, 1968); more generally, see W.J. Froleyks, 'Der ἀγὼν λόγων in der antiken Literatur' (Diss. Bonn, 1973).

34. Cf. And. *De Myst.* 8: κράτιστον οὖν μοι εἶναι δοκεῖ ἐξ ἀρχῆς ὑμᾶς διδάσκειν πάντα τὰ γενόμενα... Lys. 1.5: ἐγὼ τοίνυν ἐξ ἀρχῆς ὑμῖν ἅπαντα ἐπιδείξω τὰ ἐμαυτοῦ πράγματα... Isaios 7.4: ποιήσομαι δ' ὡς ἂν κἀγὼ δύνωμαι διὰ βραχυτάτων τοὺς λόγους, ἐξ ἀρχῆς ὡς ἔχει τὰ γενόμενα διδάσκων ὑμᾶς.

35. See P.E. Easterling, 'The infanticide in Euripides' *Medea*', *YCS* 25 (1977) 177-91, at 184.
36. Cf. Collard, pp. 134-5 of E. *Supp.* commentary, for some sensible remarks on Euripides' influence by, but not slavish adherence to, rhetorical techniques.
37. Cf. Easterling *Infanticide* 191.
38. Easterling *Infanticide* 185. See also D. Ebener, 'Zum Motiv des Kindermordes in der *Medeia*', *RhM* 104 (1961) 213-24, at 215; E. Schlesinger, 'Zu Euripides' Medea', *Hermes* 94 (1966) 26-53, at 48-9.
39. For repeated refs. in Pindar see LSJ *s.v.*
40. Page, in his note on 894, is absolutely right to draw attention to the series of departures and arrivals by the children in the latter part of the play: 'we know that at any moment now they will be leaving the stage for the last time: each time they leave we think "*this is the last time; we shall not see them alive again*": and our suspense is renewed with each return to the stage'.
41. Page *ad loc.* is surely wrong to deny this.
42. See N.E. Collinge, 'Medea *ex machina*', *CPh* 57 (1962) 170-2.
43. Cf. H. Diller, 'Θυμὸς δὲ κρείσσων τῶν ἐμῶν βουλευμάτων', *Hermes* 94 (1966) 267-75, at 270.
44. Cf. Steidle *Studien* 44, with nn. 3,4.
45. Steidle *Studien* 44 n. 2. But it is worth recording a point urged on me by Michael Ewans: the winds do *not* alter immediately after the sacrifice (cf. 900), but only at the very end of the play (cf. 1289-90).
46. Detienne/Vernant *CI* 18.
47. Detienne/Vernant *CI*, index *s.v. dolos.*
48. Note also a revealing MS variant in the first word: for *poikilothron*, some MSS have *poikilophron* ('of the variegated, i.e. shifting, *mind*'). This reading is inferior, as it anticipates and so weakens *doloploke*, 'weaver of *doloi*'; but the two variants show the proximity of the literal and metaphorical senses of *poikilos.* (Cf. also the fable of the fox and the leopard, one *poikilos* in body, one in mind—Aesop, *Fab.* 12.1, Teubner edn.) For *poikilos* as 'shifty' see Collard on E. *Supp.* 187-8a.
49. For parallels see W. Zürcher, *Die Darstellung des Menschen im Drama des Euripides* (Basel, 1947) 73; Steidle *Studien* 50.
50. Conacher *Eur. Dr.* 160.
51. For κραίνω, 'ratify', see A. *Supp.* 608, 622; cf. 624.
52. Exceptions like 282ff do not invalidate the general point.
53. The notion of supplication as a game with rules is explored in J. Gould's fundamental article *Hiketeia.*
54. Again I am indebted to Steidle's discussion here.

55. The thoughts are not 'irrelevant': see D.J. Conacher, 'Some questions of probability and relevance in Euripidean drama', *Maia* 24 (1972) 199-207, at 204.
56. Guthrie *HGP* 23.
57. This 'conscious ambiguity' is discussed by Heinimann *Nomos* 121-2.
58. See Conacher *Eur. Dr.* 161.
59. Hekabe's manoeuvre has been seen as a turning from *nomos* to (implicitly) *physis*, 'nature'—whence the sexual argument about Kassandra is supposedly drawn. I find this interpretation sophistical in the pejorative sense, *pace* C. del Grande, 'Euripide, nomos e physis', *Dioniso* 36 (1962) 46-9, at 49.
60. Aristot. *Pol.* 1253b (tr. adapted from J.E.C. Welldon). The reminiscence, not verbatim, is of *Il.* 18.373ff. For Daidalos' statues see Frontisi-Ducroux *Dédale*, esp. 95ff.
61. Commentary on *Hek.* by C.B. Heberden (Oxford, 1901) on 846-9.
62. For slavery and freedom in *Hek.* see Steidle *Studien* 49-50, with n. 36; S.G. Daitz, 'Concepts of freedom and slavery in Euripides' *Hecuba*', *Hermes* 99 (1971) 217-26.
63. 'Ag. accepts H.'s justice'—M. Tierney (edn with notes, Dublin, 1946, repr. Bristol Classical Press, 1979), on 903-4.
64. The scene is discussed by Schwinge *Stich.* 144ff.
65. See Detienne/Vernant *CI passim*.
66. Tierney *Hec.*, on 1187f.
67. C.A.E. Luschnig, 'Euripides' *Hecabe*. The time is out of joint', *CJ* 71 (1975-6) 227-34, at 233. (Italics in the quotation are mine.)
68. One may usefully compare J. du Boulay's comments on the settling of disputes in a modern Greek village, where the establishment of the truth of the rival claims is less important than the preservation of the honour of the contending parties (*Portrait of a Greek Mountain Village* (Oxford, 1974) 179).
69. This neatly illustrates the mythical association perceived by Greeks between blindness and prophecy; cf. Buxton *Blindness* 27ff.
70. 'Hecuba and Nomos', *TAPhA* 78 (1947) 61-8.
71. *HN* 66.
72. *HN* 67.
73. *Studien* 49.
74. 3.67, tr. Warner. The subject of persuasion in Thoukydides would merit a book as long as the present one. There are many valuable insights in the first of John H. Finley's *Three Essays on Thucydides* (Harvard, 1967).
75. See Collard *ad loc.* for refs. to the actual proclamation in the assembly which Euripides is echoing.

76. It will already be clear that I am generally out of sympathy with those who see *Supp.* as shot through with satirical undertones, and in sympathy with those who take, e.g., Adrastos' Funeral Speech seriously. In the former camp are J.W. Fitton, 'The *Suppliant Women* and the *Herakleidai* of Euripides', *Hermes* 89 (1961) 430-61; Wesley D. Smith, 'Expressive form in Euripides' *Suppliants*', *HSPh* 71 (1966) 151-70; R.B. Gamble, 'Euripides' *Suppliant Women:* decision and ambivalence', *Hermes* 98 (1970) 385-405. In the latter are G. Zuntz, *Pol. Pl. Eur.*, esp. 3-25; C. Collard, 'The funeral oration in Euripides' *Supplices*', *BICS* 19 (1972) 39-53, and *id.* in his edn of *Supp.*

BIBLIOGRAPHY

Listed here, by author's name and abbreviated title, are those works (excluding standard editions and commentaries) which are referred to more than once in this book. Works referred to once only in the book are cited in full at that point, and do not appear below.

Alt *Schicksal:* K. Alt, 'Schicksal und φύσις im Philoktet des Sophokles', *Hermes* 89(1961) 141-74.

Andrewes *Eunomia:* A. Andrewes, 'Eunomia', *CQ* 32 (1938) 89-102.

Bonner/Smith *Justice:* R.J. Bonner and G. Smith, *The Administration of Justice from Homer to Aristotle,* Univ. of Chicago, 1930.

Bowra *Soph. Tr.:* C.M. Bowra, *Sophoclean Tragedy,* Oxford, 1944.

Buxton *Blindness:* R.G.A. Buxton, 'Blindness and limits: Sophokles and the logic of myth', *JHS* 100 (1980) 22-37.

Buxton *Peitho:* R.G.A. Buxton, *'Peitho:* its place in Greek culture and its exploration in some plays of Aeschylus and Sophocles', Cambridge Ph. D. diss., 1977.

Conacher *Eur. Dr.:* D.J. Conacher, *Euripidean Drama,* Toronto, 1967.

Dawe *Inconsistency:* R.D. Dawe, 'Inconsistency of plot and character in Aeschylus', *PCPhS* 189 (N.S.9) (1963) 21-62.

Detienne/Vernant *CI:* M. Detienne and J.-P. Vernant, *Cunning Intelligence in Greek Culture and Society,* tr. J. Lloyd, Hassocks, 1978.

Dierauer *Tier:* U. Dierauer, *Tier und Mensch im Denken der Antike,* Amsterdam, 1977.

Easterling *Infanticide:* P.E. Easterling, 'The infanticide in Euripides' *Medea', YCS* 25 (1977) 177-91.

Easterling *Oedipus:* P.E. Easterling, 'Oedipus and Polynices', *PCPhS* 193 (N.S. 13) (1967) 1-13.

Easterling *Phil.:* P.E. Easterling, *'Philoctetes* and modern criticism', *ICS* 3 (1978) 27-39.

Easterling *Presentation:* P.E. Easterling, 'Presentation of character in Aeschylus', *G&R* 20 (1973) 3-19.

Ehrenberg *Eunomia:* V. Ehrenberg, 'Eunomia', in Ehrenberg, *Aspects of the Ancient World* (Oxford, 1946) 70-93.

Ewans *Ag. Aul.:* M. Ewans, 'Agamemnon at Aulis: a study in the *Oresteia', Ramus* 4 (1975) 17-32.

Finley *Demagogues:* M.I. Finley, 'Athenian demagogues', *P&P* 21 (1962) 3-24; repr. in Finley, *Studies in Ancient Society* (London, 1974) 1-25.

Finley *Democracy:* M.I. Finley, *Democracy Ancient and Modern,* London, 1973.

Finley *Terre:* M.I. Finley (ed.), *Problèmes de la terre en Grèce ancienne,* Paris, 1973.

Fitton-Brown *Prom.:* A.D. Fitton-Brown, 'Prometheia', *JHS* 79 (1959) 52-60.

Frazer *Pausanias:* J.G. Frazer, *Pausanias's 'Description of Greece',* translation and commentary, London, 1898.

von Fritz *Danaiden:* K. von Fritz, 'Die Danaidentrilogie des Aeschylus', *Philologus* 91 (1936) 121-36 and 249-69; repr. in von Fritz, *Antike und moderne Tragödie* (Berlin, 1962) 160-92.

Frontisi-Ducroux *Dédale:* F. Frontisi-Ducroux, *Dédale: mythologie de l'artisan en Grèce ancienne,* Paris, 1975.

Garvie *Deceit:* A.F. Garvie, 'Deceit, violence and persuasion in the *Philoctetes',* in *Studi in onore di Quintino Cataudella* (Catania, 1972) I, 213-26.

Garvie *Supp:* A.F. Garvie, *Aeschylus' 'Supplices': Play and Trilogy,* Cambridge, 1969.

Gellie *Soph.:* G.H. Gellie, *Sophocles: A Reading,* Melbourne, 1972.

Ghali-Kahil *Hélène:* L.B. Ghali-Kahil, *Les Enlèvements et le retour d' Hélène dans les textes et les documents figurés,* Paris, 1955.

Goheen *Dram. Symb.:* R.F. Goheen, 'Aspects of dramatic symbolism: three studies in the *Oresteia', AJPh* 76 (1955) 113-37.

Goody *Domestication:* J. Goody, *The Domestication of the Savage Mind,* Cambridge, 1977.

Gould *Hiketeia:* J. Gould, '*Hiketeia', JHS* 93 (1973) 74-103.

Greifenhagen *Gr. Erot.:* A. Greifenhagen, *Griechische Eroten,* Berlin, 1957.

Grossmann *Promethie:* G. Grossmann, *Promethie und Orestie,* Heidelberg, 1970.

Gundert *Stich.:* H. Gundert, 'Die Stichomythie zwischen Agamemnon und Klytaimestra', in ΘΕΩΡΙΑ: *Festschrift für W.-H. Schuchhardt* (Baden-Baden, 1960) 69-78.

Guthrie *HGP:* W.K.C. Guthrie, *A History of Greek Philosophy,* III: *The Fifth-century Enlightenment,* Cambridge, 1969.

Heinimann *Nomos:* F. Heinimann, *Nomos und Physis,* Basel, 1945.

Ireland, *Motivation:* S. Ireland, 'The problem of motivation in the *Supplices* of Aeschylus', *RhM* 117 (1974) 14-29.

Jacobsen *Treasures:* Thorkild Jacobsen, *The Treasures of Darkness,* Yale, 1976.

Jahn *Peitho:* O. Jahn, *Peitho, die Göttin der Überredung,* Greifswald, 1846.

Jones *Ar. G.T.:* John Jones, *On Aristotle and Greek Tragedy,* London, 1962.

Kahn *Hermès:* L. Kahn, *Hermès passe,* Paris, 1978.

Kirkwood *HN:* G.M. Kirkwood, 'Hecuba and Nomos', *TAPhA* 78 (1947) 61-8.

Knox *HT:* B.M.W. Knox, *The Heroic Temper: Studies in Sophoclean Tragedy,* Univ. of Cal., 1964.

Knox *Medea:* B.M.W. Knox, 'The *Medea* of Euripides', *YCS* 25 (1977) 193-225.

Körte *Lekythos:* G. Körte, 'Eichelförmige Lekythos mit Goldschmuck aus Attika', *Arch. Zeit.* 37 (1879) 93-6.

Lindblom *Prophecy:* J. Lindblom, *Prophecy in Ancient Israel,* Oxford, 1962.

Linforth *Religion:* I.M. Linforth, 'Religion and drama in *Oedipus at Colonus', Univ. of Cal. Publications in Classical Philology* 14.4 (1951) 75-191.

Lloyd *MRE:* G.E.R. Lloyd, *Magic, Reason and Experience: Studies in the Origin and Development of Greek Science,* Cambridge, 1979.

Martin *Kl. zu Eph.:* Jochen Martin, 'Von Kleisthenes zu Ephialtes. Zur Entstehung der athenischen Demokratie', *Chiron* 4 (1974) 5-42.

Momigliano *Freedom:* A. Momigliano, 'Freedom of speech in antiquity', in *Dictionary of the History of Ideas* (Scribner's, N.Y., 1973) II, 252-63.

Mourelatos *Route:* A.P.D. Mourelatos, *The Route of Parmenides,* Yale, 1970.

Murray *Io:* R.D. Murray, *The Motif of Io in Aeschylus' 'Suppliants',* Princeton, 1958.

Pepe *Peitho:* George M. Pepe, 'Studies in Peitho', Ph. D. diss., Princeton, 1967.

Petersen *Personifikation:* L. Petersen, *Zur Geschichte der Personifikation in griechischer Dichtung und bildender Kunst,* Würzburg, 1939.

Pfuhl *Malerei:* E. Pfuhl, *Malerei und Zeichnung der Griechen,* Munich, 1923.

Podlecki *Power:* A. J. Podlecki, 'The power of the word in Sophocles' *Philoctetes', GRBS* 7 (1966) 233-50.

Pucci *Violence:* P. Pucci, *The Violence of Pity in Euripides' 'Medea',* Cornell, 1980.

Radermacher *Art. Scr.:* L. Radermacher, *Artium Scriptores,* Vienna, 1951.

Reinhardt *Aisch.:* K. Reinhardt, *Aischylos als Regisseur und Theologe,* Bern, 1949.

Rivier *Essai:* A. Rivier, *Essai sur le tragique d' Euripide²,* Lausanne, 1975.

Robert *Op. Min.:* L. Robert, *Opera Minora Selecta,* Amsterdam, 1969.

Rohdich *Eur. Tr.:* H. Rohdich, *Die euripideische Tragödie: Untersuchungen zu ihrer Tragik,* Heidelberg, 1968.

Schmidt *Phil.:* J.-U. Schmidt, *Sophokles Philoktet: eine Strukturanalyse,* Heidelberg, 1973.

Schulz *Wurzel:* S. Schulz, *Die Wurzel* ΠΕΙΘ-(ΠΙΘ-) *im älteren Griechischen,* Inaugural Dissertation, Freiburg-in-der-Schweiz, 1952.

Schwinge *Stich.:* E.-R. Schwinge, *Die Verwendung der Stichomythie in den Dramen des Euripides,* Heidelberg, 1968.

Schwinge *WdF. Eur.:* E.-R. Schwinge (ed.), *Wege der Forschung* vol. on Euripides, Darmstadt, 1968.

Séchan *Mythe:* L. Séchan, *Le Mythe de Prométhée,* Paris, 1951.

Shields *Sight:* M.G. Shields, 'Sight and blindness imagery in the *Oedipus Coloneus', Phoenix* 15 (1961) 63-73.

Simon *Peitho:* E. Simon in *EAA* VI, 5-8, *s.v.* 'Peitho'.

Solmsen *Hes. and A.:* F. Solmsen, *Hesiod and Aeschylus,* Cornell, 1949.

Steidle *Studien:* W. Steidle, *Studien zum antiken Drama,* Munich, 1968.

Taplin *Stagecraft:* O. Taplin, *The Stagecraft of Aeschylus,* Oxford, 1977.

Thomson *Prom.:* G. Thomson, edn of *Prometheus Bound,* Cambridge, 1932.

Tierney *Hec.:* M. Tierney, edn of *Hecuba,* Dublin, 1946; repr. Bristol Class. Press, 1979.

Tillyard *Hope:* E.M.W. Tillyard, *The Hope Vases,* Cambridge, 1923.

Unterberger *Prom.:* R. Unterberger, *Der gefesselte Prometheus des Aischylos,* Stuttgart, 1968.

Vernant/Vidal-Naquet *MT:* J.-P. Vernant and P. Vidal-Naquet, *Mythe et tragédie en Grèce ancienne,* Paris, 1972.

Voigt *Peitho:* F. Voigt in *RE* XIX.1 (1937) cols. 194-217, *s.v.* 'Peitho'.

Weizsäcker *Peitho:* P. Weizsäcker in Roscher III.II (1909) cols. 1795-1813, *s.v.* 'Peitho'.

West *Prom. Tril.:* M.L. West, 'The Prometheus trilogy', *JHS* 99 (1979) 130-48.

Winnington-Ingram *Dan. Tr.:* R.P. Winnington-Ingram, 'The Danaid trilogy of Aeschylus', *JHS* 81 (1961) 141-52.

Winnington-Ingram *Soph.:* R.P. Winnington-Ingram, *Sophocles: an Interpretation,* Cambridge, 1980.

Zuntz *Pol. Pl. Eur.:* G. Zuntz, *The Political Plays of Euripides,* Manchester, 1955.

INDEXES

1. GENERAL INDEX

2. INDEX OF PASSAGES QUOTED OR REFERRED TO